'Grounded in both the relevant literature and ~~....~~ ~~........, ....~~ textbook provides students and early stage entrepreneurs with both a theoretical and practical foundation for tackling the many challenges they are likely to confront in establishing and growing a new venture.'

*Winthrop Professor John Watson,*
*The University of Western Australia, Australia*

'An insightful resource book for would-be entrepreneurs.'

*Professor Pooran Wynarczyk,*
*Newcastle University, UK*

'The move away from the heroic concept of the entrepreneur to one that explores the realities of starting up a business is welcome. The book encourages the reader to reflect on the key lessons provided from each chapter in a way that clearly sets out learning objectives supported by case material and sample discussion questions. *Resourcing the Start-up Business* is a refreshing addition to the postgraduate entrepreneurship catalogue.'

*Professor Clare Brindley,*
*Nottingham Business School,*
*Nottingham Trent University, UK*

'An insightful and well-timed publication that goes beyond simply guiding the reader through the resources needed to develop and support entrepreneurs, focusing instead on embedding dynamic learning capabilities through effective experiential learning, and stimulating these nascent entrepreneurs to go on to develop growth-oriented businesses that make a real contribution to economic development. An essential read that offers a link between an entrepreneur's dynamic learning capability when establishing a new venture and the likelihood that that business will grow.'

*David Taylor,*
*Principal Lecturer in Entrepreneurship,*
*Manchester Metropolitan University, UK*

# Resourcing the Start-up Business

Starting a business successfully requires numerous skills and resources. The alarming rate of failure associated with new ventures suggests that potential entrepreneurs would welcome expert advice at the most vital stage in the life of any business: the decision to start-up and the first 12 months of operation.

The expert author team focus on those resources, skills, capabilities and learning processes required by any entrepreneur engaged in starting a new business. Specifically, this text aims to:

- introduce and explain those resources (including finance) that are essential to successful business creation
- identify the key skills and capabilities that are required by entrepreneurs
- highlight the ways in which new resources are combined with the entrepreneur's existing resource base to develop the business effectively
- explore the way entrepreneurs learn in the process of developing their business.

Drawing on the most up-to-date and relevant research, this concise textbook provides students and academics of entrepreneurship with a practical guide to acquiring the appropriate resources in order to start a new firm.

**Oswald Jones** is Professor of Entrepreneurship at the University of Liverpool, UK.

**Allan Macpherson** is Associate Professor of Management at the University of Wisconsin-La Crosse, US, and Professor of Organisational Behaviour at De Montfort University, UK.

**Dilani Jayawarna** is Senior Lecturer at the University of Liverpool, UK.

# ROUTLEDGE-ISBE MASTERS IN ENTREPRENEURSHIP

*Edited by Colette Henry and Susan Marlow*

The **Routledge-ISBE Masters in Entrepreneurship** series offers postgraduate students specialist but accessible textbooks on a range of entrepreneurship topics. Collectively, these texts form a significant resource base for those studying entrepreneurship, whether as part of an entrepreneurship-related programme of study, or as a new, non-cognate area for students in disciplines such as science and engineering, helping them to gain an in-depth understanding of contemporary entrepreneurial concepts.

The volumes in this series are authored by leading specialists in their field, and although they are discrete texts in their treatment of individual topics, all are united by a common structure and pedagogical approach. Key features of each volume include:

- A critical approach to combining theory with practice, which educates its reader rather than solely teaching a set of skills
- Clear learning objectives for each chapter
- The use of figures, tables and boxes to highlight key ideas, concepts and skills
- An annotated bibliography, guiding students in their further reading
- Discussion questions for each chapter to aid learning and put key concepts into practice

## Entrepreneurship
A global perspective
*Stephen Roper*

## Female entrepreneurship
*Maura McAdam*

## Resourcing the Start-up Business
Creating dynamic entrepreneurial learning capabilities
*Oswald Jones, Allan Macpherson and Dilani Jayawarna*

# Resourcing the Start-up Business

Creating dynamic entrepreneurial learning capabilities

**Oswald Jones,
Allan Macpherson and
Dilani Jayawarna**

Routledge
Taylor & Francis Group

LONDON AND NEW YORK

First published 2014
by Routledge
2 Park Square, Milton Park, Abingdon, Oxon OX14 4RN

and by Routledge
711 Third Avenue, New York, NY 10017

*Routledge is an imprint of the Taylor & Francis Group, an informa business*

*British Library Cataloguing in Publication Data*
A catalogue record for this book is available from the British Library

*Library of Congress Cataloging in Publication Data*
Jones, Oswald.
Resourcing the start-up business: creating dynamic entrepreneurial learning capabilities/Oswald Jones, Allan Macpherson and Dilani Jayawarna.
pages cm. – (Routledge-ISBE masters in entrepreneurship)
Includes bibliographical references and index.
1. New business enterprises – Management. 2. Small business – Management. 3. Business planning. 4. Entrepreneurship. I. Macpherson, Allan. II. Jayawarna, Dilani. III. Title.
HD62.5.J6585 2013
658.1′1 – dc23
2013008151

ISBN: 978-0-415-62447-3 (hbk)
ISBN: 978-0-415-62448-0 (pbk)
ISBN: 978-0-203-10456-9 (ebk)

Typeset in Perpetua and Bell Gothic
by Florence Production Ltd, Stoodleigh, Devon, UK

Printed and bound in the United States of America by
Edwards Brothers Malloy

# Contents

*List of figures and tables*                                              xiii
*Series editors' foreword*                                                 xvi
*Case examples*                                                          xviii

1  Introduction: dynamic entrepreneurial learning capabilities             1

   1.1   Introduction                                                       1

   1.2   Learning objectives                                                2

   1.3   Growing importance of entrepreneurship                            2

   1.4   A practice-based approach to entrepreneurial learning             6

   1.5   Summary and key learning points                                  10

   1.6   Discussion questions                                             12

2  The changing nature of entrepreneurial theory                         13

   2.1   Introduction                                                     13

   2.2   Learning objectives                                             14

   2.3   Individuals and opportunities                                    15

   2.4   New venture creation processes                                  18

   2.5   The entrepreneurial process                                     21

   2.6   The process of opportunity creation                             23

   2.7   Summary and key learning points                                 28

   2.8   Discussion questions                                            30

   2.9   Further reading                                                 30

3   Learning to be an entrepreneur                                          31

    3.1   Introduction                                                       31

    3.2   Learning objectives                                               32

    3.3   Models of entrepreneurial learning                               33

    3.4   Universities and graduate incubation                            41

    3.5   Role of active learning and simulation                           44

    3.6   Clubs and societies                                              47

    3.7   Summary and key learning points                                 49

    3.8   Discussion questions                                             50

4   Knowledge, skills and capabilities                                      51

    4.1   Introduction                                                      51

    4.2   Learning objectives                                              52

    4.3   Skills and knowledge: resources at start-up                     52

    4.4   Developing the opportunity                                       53

    4.5   Managing early stage growth: applying knowledge,
          skills and capabilities                                          55

    4.6   Managing others and cultural entrepreneurship                   65

    4.7   Summary and key learning points                                 68

    4.8   Discussion questions                                            69

    4.9   Further reading                                                 69

5   Networks, social capital and entrepreneurial resources                 70

    5.1   Introduction                                                      70

    5.2   Learning objectives                                              71

    5.3   Social networks                                                 71

    5.4   Social capital                                                  75

    5.5   Entrepreneurial social capital                                  80

| | | |
|---|---|---:|
| 5.6 | Social capital and resourcing new ventures | 82 |
| 5.7 | Summary and key learning points | 85 |
| 5.8 | Discussion questions | 86 |

| **6** | **Resourcing start-up businesses** | **87** |
|---|---|---:|
| 6.1 | Introduction | 87 |
| 6.2 | Learning objectives | 88 |
| 6.3 | Resource-based view of the firm | 88 |
| 6.4 | Types of resources | 89 |
| 6.5 | Human capital and entrepreneurship | 92 |
| 6.6 | Accumulation of human capital over the life course | 96 |
| 6.7 | Effects of human capital on entrepreneurial success | 99 |
| 6.8 | Summary and key learning points | 101 |
| 6.9 | Discussion questions | 102 |
| 6.10 | Further reading | 103 |

| **7** | **Enhancing tangible resources** | **104** |
|---|---|---:|
| 7.1 | Introduction | 104 |
| 7.2 | Learning objectives | 105 |
| 7.3 | Tangible resources | 105 |
| 7.4 | Why is it difficult to finance entrepreneurial ventures? A theoretical explanation | 106 |
| 7.5 | Different financial sources for new entrepreneurs | 107 |
| 7.6 | Finance and business lifecycle | 114 |
| 7.7 | Variation in financing strategies for different entrepreneurs | 115 |
| 7.8 | Is there a funding gap for entrepreneurs? | 118 |
| 7.9 | Summary and key learning points | 120 |
| 7.10 | Discussion questions | 121 |

**8  Bootstrapping the start-up business**  **122**

8.1   Introduction  122

8.2   Learning objectives  123

8.3   Defining the concept and theoretical perspectives  123

8.4   Different types of bootstrapping methods for the entrepreneur  125

8.5   Variations in the use of bootstrapping  127

8.6   Bootstrapping as a growth strategy  132

8.7   Bootstrapping in social ventures  137

8.8   Summary and key learning points  138

8.9   Discussion questions  139

8.10 Further reading  140

**9  Dynamic capabilities in entrepreneurial ventures**  **141**

9.1   Introduction  141

9.2   Learning objectives  142

9.3   From resources to dynamic capabilities  142

9.4   Routines that support change  145

9.5   Dynamic capabilities in new ventures  147

9.6   Dynamic capabilities and learning processes  149

9.7   Bootstrapping and bricolage: entrepreneurs acting resourcefully  152

9.8   Summary and key learning points  156

9.9   Discussion questions  157

9.10  Further reading  157

**10  Growing new businesses**  **158**

10.1  Introduction  158

10.2  Learning objectives  159

10.3  Stages of growth and linear growth trajectories  159

10.4   Critical reflections on stage models                     163

10.5   Making sense of crisis in context                        165

10.6   Managing growth dynamically                              167

10.7   Managing growth through resilience                       170

10.8   Summary and key learning points                          174

10.9   Discussion questions                                     174

10.10 Further reading                                           175

11   New businesses and economic development                    176

11.1   Introduction                                             176

11.2   Learning objectives                                      177

11.3   Policy initiatives 1970–2011                             177

11.4   Initiatives to promote entrepreneurship                  179

11.5   The GEM studies                                          183

11.6   Factors influencing new firm formation                   188

11.7   The economic contribution of new businesses              192

11.8   Do new businesses create new jobs?                       194

11.9   Summary and key learning points                          197

11.10 Discussion questions                                      200

11.11 Further reading                                           200

11.12 Appendices                                                200

12   Conclusions: creating dynamic learning businesses          202

12.1   Introduction                                             202

12.2   Learning objectives                                      203

12.3   Theory, practice and learning                            203

12.4   Resources, bootstrapping and bricolage                   205

12.5   Conclusions                                              207

# CONTENTS

12.6   Key learning points                                            208

12.7   Discussion questions                                           209

*Notes*                                                               210
*References*                                                          212
*Index*                                                               245

# Figures and tables

## FIGURES

| | | |
|---|---|---|
| 2.1 | Shane's causal model | 17 |
| 2.2 | Gartner's model of organizational emergence | 19 |
| 2.3 | Entrepreneurial bricolage | 26 |
| 2.4 | Effectual entrepreneurship | 27 |
| 3.1 | Kolb's learning cycle | 35 |
| 3.2 | Extending Kolb's experiential learning cycle | 37 |
| 3.3 | Combining entrepreneurial cognition and practice | 39 |
| 3.4 | Entrepreneurial learning model | 41 |
| 4.1 | Opportunity recognition | 53 |
| 4.2 | Effectuation | 55 |
| 4.3 | Cultural entrepreneurship | 68 |
| 5.1 | Networks, social capital and resources | 71 |
| 5.2 | Dyadic relationship | 72 |
| 5.3 | Open and closed networks | 73 |
| 5.4 | Bridging and bonding ties | 77 |
| 5.5 | Social capital and network evolution | 79 |
| 5.6 | From equivocal to unequivocal reality | 80 |
| 5.7 | Network brokers | 84 |
| 5.8 | Social skills and new venture performance | 85 |
| 6.1 | Resources for the entrepreneur: tangible and intangible resources | 90 |
| 6.2 | Resource needs: from entrepreneur to new venture | 91 |
| 6.3 | Accumulation of human capital over the life course of the entrepreneur | 98 |
| 7.1 | Change in financing strategies along the venture lifecycle | 115 |
| 7.2 | Debt and equity finance: type of venture | 118 |
| 8.1 | Bootstrapping: a theoretical explanation | 124 |
| 8.2 | Bootstrapping techniques | 126 |
| 8.3 | Bootstrapping and business lifecycle | 131 |

8.4  Non-monetary forms of resourcing in social enterprises          138
9.1  From resources to rents                                          143
9.2  Dynamic capabilities in start-up businesses                      155
10.1  Growth in contexts                                              166
10.2  Dealing with crises during growth                               169
10.3  Resilience capacity                                             172
11.1  OECD determinants of entrepreneurship                           181
11.2  The entrepreneurial process                                     183
11.3  Entrepreneurship and economic growth                            184
11.4  Economic groups and entrepreneurship                            189
11.5  U-shaped entrepreneurship curve                                 193
11.6  Levels of entrepreneurship                                      198
11.7  Theory of planned behaviour                                     199

## TABLES

1.1  Developing new routines                                            6
1.2  Routines and entrepreneurial practices                            8
2.1  Start-up activities                                               21
3.1  Entrepreneurial learning tasks                                    38
4.1  Generic competencies                                              58
4.2  Innovation and management: potential tensions                     61
5.1  Types of network ties                                             74
5.2  Bonding and bridging social capital                               79
7.1  Debt and equity finance: advantages and disadvantages            110
8.1  Bootstrapping: internal, social and quasi-market modes of
     resource acquisition                                             127
9.1  Dynamic capabilities in new firms                                146
9.2  Learning modes and activities                                    150
10.1  Greiner's growth phases and their crises                        161
10.2  Growth stage models and processes                               162
11.1  Variations in total entrepreneurial activity (TEA)              185
11.2  Average TEA for three levels of economic activity               188
11.3  Ease of doing business                                          189
11.4  Ease of starting a business                                     190
11.5  Ease of starting a business based on stage of economic
      development                                                     191
11.6  Firm stock by size-band                                         195
11.7  Employment by size-band                                         196

## Chapter 11 appendices

Appendix A    Innovation-driven economies                        200
Appendix B    Efficiency-driven economies                        201
Appendix C    Factor-driven economies                            201

# Series editors' foreword

## RESOURCING THE START-UP BUSINESS: CREATING DYNAMIC ENTREPRENEURIAL LEARNING CAPABILITIES

As editors of this series, our aim is to encourage discussion and engagement with a diverse range of issues critical to contemporary understanding of the entrepreneurial process. To meet this objective, and to offer an informed, multi-contextual perspective of entrepreneurship, we are delighted to welcome the third book within this series – *Resourcing the Start-up Business: creating dynamic entrepreneurial learning capabilities*. In this text, Oswald Jones, Allan Macpherson and Dilani Jayawarna offer valuable insights into the complexities of resource acquisition for establishing new ventures. In keeping with the ethos of the series, the book draws on current themes and empirical work presented in extant literatures while assuming no prior knowledge on the part of the student. In this regard however, given the focus on the postgraduate student cohort, there is a sophisticated tone and delivery that is explanatory but challenging in a fashion not always evident in more descriptive texts.

The authors perfectly capture this balance with their emphasis on and exploration of one of the most critical periods associated with an entrepreneurial venture – the actual decision to start a business and its first year of operation. While this is acknowledged as an important period within the new venture creation process, it is, surprisingly, not sufficiently covered in extant texts, often being overshadowed by the increasing focus on business growth. Mindful that entrepreneurship is a learning journey, the authors thus concentrate on dynamic entrepreneurial learning and its importance to the long-term success of a business. Having illustrated the growing importance of entrepreneurship in their opening chapter, the authors cover key theories relating to the new venture creation process, including opportunity recognition, models of entrepreneurial learning, knowledge and skills acquisition, networks and entrepreneurial capital. With regard to the latter, attention is paid to both tangible and intangible sources of capital, with the acknowledgment that the actual sourcing of such capital will change depending on the type of business being developed, the sector in which it is being established and the type of entrepreneur leading the venture. *Bootstrapping* and *bricolage* strategies – so typical of and critical to the small business start-up – are highlighted throughout the text in both a practical and theoretical context. The book concludes with a review of the factors influencing new firm formation, followed by a useful conclusions chapter that brings together the key learning points of the text.

The overarching aim of the Masters in Entrepreneurship series is to provide a comprehensive overview of the main perspectives on entrepreneurship. The series explores the main approaches to entrepreneurship, as well as the various contexts in which it occurs. The rationale for the series is that we simply cannot understand entrepreneurship sufficiently, nor engage effectively in related contemporary debates, without an understanding of the key theories and concepts that underpin the field. As such, future texts within this series will seek to explore the multi-faceted nature of entrepreneurship as an evolving but truly global phenomenon.

Colette Henry and Susan Marlow, February 2013

# Case examples

We the authors have worked together on the study of entrepreneurship and the management of small firms for more than 12 years. During that time we have published articles on a wide range of topics related to the problems associated with starting and managing smaller firms. Throughout this book, we use a small number of core case examples to illustrate key points related to dynamic entrepreneurial learning. All 10 cases provide important insights into how entrepreneurs overcome the practical problems of establishing new businesses and dealing with decisions about the growth of those businesses.

## ACTIVE PROFILE

Anna Heyes is a graduate of the University of Liverpool. She established *Active Profile* in 2004 and has since won many awards including young entrepreneur of the Year and North West Women in Business 2008 and 2010. Initially, Anna wrote a business plan based on providing companies with business development assistance through networking. Anna's business plan won a prize of £1,000 in a competition at the University of Liverpool Management School. After winning the competition, Anna discussed her idea with a *Business Link* advisor who suggested that business development was not a good basis for a start-up:

> You're never going to make any money out of this, there's no money in it. How are you going to scale this up? There are only so many hours in the week and you're not going to be able to survive.

Anna revaluated what she might do and began to offer freelance marketing consultancy, which involved writing marketing plans for very small businesses. After about one year Anna had so much work that she decided to take on an employee and the company then became more formalized. Currently, *Active Profile* is based in Liverpool Science Park and offers a wide range of services in the area of public relations and marketing. The company has grown steadily in the last eight years, now employs eight staff and had a turn-over of more than £500,000 in 2012. *Active Profile* has developed an extensive client base in three main areas: property and regeneration, science and technology, and professional services and finance.

## FIT CO.

*Fit Co.* was first established by a personal trainer who wanted to use his expertise in fitness to start a gym. However, while he was well known and respected in the industry, he lacked business experience. His real passion was in delivery fitness, not running the business. He encouraged an old school friend to join him. Together they were able to take responsibility for different parts of the business, and acquire a new gym to expand the opportunities to deliver classes and attract membership for the gym.

## FUME CO.

This was a small fume cabinet company manufacturer in the Northwest of England. The owner struggled for many years to achieve any growth, and his products were not known for quality or on-time delivery. He hired a new manager with experience in both manufacturing and sales to help address the problems. Bringing in this expertise helped to turn around this nascent firm and develop it into a small manufacturing company with a reputation for on-time and quality products. New systems and experience helped to grow turnover from £800,000 to £4.5 million, slowly over five years.

## INNOSPACE (MANCHESTER METROPOLITAN UNIVERSITY BUSINESS SCHOOL)

*Innospace* was established in 2007 by staff from the *Centre for Enterprise* at Manchester Metropolitan University Business School to provide incubation space for graduates from all faculties of the University (Jones *et al.* 2008). The quotations from graduate entrepreneurs in *Innospace* were collected by PingPing Merkel during her doctoral research. The first objective in establishing *Innospace* was to provide graduates with support for the creation of knowledge-based businesses. The second objective was to encourage a 'community of practice' among those based in the incubator. Nascent entrepreneurs were provided with 12 months accommodation and access to knowledge, expertise and support available from MMUBS as well as other organizations within the Manchester City-region. Within 6 months of launch *Innospace* had attracted 74 graduate entrepreneurs. *Innospace* is hosted within a self-contained floor of a Grade II listed building less than two minutes' walk from Manchester City Centre. *Innospace* continues to promote graduate entrepreneurship in MMU and details can be found at the following website: www.innospace.co.uk.

## JAZOOLI

While still at school Sam Wilson began to buy and sell mobile phones on *eBay* to supplement his pocket money. Sam's brother Ben formerly established *Jazooli* in 2008 while taking a year out before going to University and the business was run from Ben's bedroom in the family home for the first nine months of operation. Ben began to source accessories for electronic goods directly from China, and because higher volumes demanded more space, their parents agreed to convert the family's garage into a storage unit. By October 2009 the business was doing so well that it was decided that Martin, their father, should join *Jazooli* on a full-time basis. On completing sixth form in 2010 Sam also joined the company on a full-time basis and they moved to a 2,500 square-foot warehouse with better transport links for deliveries and mail collections. The business continued to grow and four full-time staff had joined the company by May 2012 as well as three part-timers. In the first year of operation (2008) business turnover was £70,000 and this increased to £1.6 million in 2011. Business activities extended from mobile phones and accessories for tablet computers to include electronic cigarettes.

## MACHINE CO.

The owner of this company started with a small machine shop. The industry was changing with the introduction of CNC machines and so were customer expectations. As a supplier to the aerospace industry, which was under financial pressure the company was in danger of losing the small amount of business they had. However, their customer helped set up a supplier development project, which they joined, and the owner embedded new continuous improvement systems he learned on the programme into the business. Academics from a nearby university as well as consultants provided other expertise that the owner was lacking in quality management and tooling procedures. He was also able to show the system to prospective customers as evidence of the legitimate manufacturing practice in the business, and he won new clients that reduced his reliance on one main customer and thus spread the risk. He managed to grow the business from £500,000 to £1.8 million in annual turnover, by leveraging weak ties and embedding new systems.

## PACKAGING CO.

*Packaging Co.* was the second new firm for the owner who had previously owned a small contract packing business selling pre-packaged 'kits', such as for bicycle repair. His first business failed and the packaging firm was in a similar area of expertise. The owner-director's strategy was to develop business opportunities by first proving his firm's capability through successful 'small jobs', with a view to getting larger contracts. Through this strategy, the firm grew slowly over 8 years from 3 to 12 employees, and from £0.2 million to £0.65 million in turnover. A local competitor business came up for sale, and the owner managed to purchase the business to expand through acquisition, and he moved the business to these 'new' premises. However, he did not hire any new management, and he struggled to cope with both the merger and the development of more complex manufacturing scheduling. The owner was constantly trying new methods or ideas: he introduced a new management information system, he changed the management structure and he attempted a range of options to manage efficiencies, staff involvement and to develop the business. He learned about these ideas from his business contacts, but he always tried to achieve them on his own. Despite a number of initiatives, the firm struggled to reach its potential. It eventually failed.

## PPE CO.

This small firm was established by a husband and wife team. The husband had worked at *BNFL Ltd*, and he used his experience and relationships to establish a small manufacturing facility for personal protective equipment (PPE), including protective non-slip boots, protective tenting and a more versatile protective suit. For a number of years this was a very small affair, but over time, the husband (technical director) leveraged his relationships and addressed some of the problems he had experienced while working in protective equipment at *BNFL*. He embedded these solutions into product lines. Over five years he grew the firm to £800,000 in annual turnover. His relationships, and growing reputation as a solution provider, allowed him to win a contract as a PPE supplier to *BNFL*. As part of the contract, *PPE Co.* were required to value-engineer existing supplies, which required rationalization and improvement of PPE products. Part of this process involved taking on manufacturing assembly work of products they co-innovated with supply network partners, and it also required that they encourage suppliers to innovate products to meet the demanding standards required in the nuclear industry. In 18 months, turnover grew from around £800,000 to approximately £3.5 million, and the number of staff grew from 8 to 32. Despite its rural location with poor transport connections, which limits access to technical networks and educational institutions, *PPE Co.* established relationships in their business network to enable the development of the firm into a successful and innovative small firm.

## SPARK REVOLUTIONS LTD

Phil and Alan established *Spark Revolutions* to offer website design and consultancy services. *Spark Revolutions* is based on Liverpool Science Park and now comprises five individuals who cover a broad area of expertise. Both developers have deep knowledge sets and achieved first-class degrees in their respective disciplines. This allows *Spark Revolutions* to be focused on innovation and not be constrained by a narrow knowledge base. *Spark Revolutions* have worked for *Apple* in their headquarters in California and are SAP qualified ERP consultants. *Spark Revolutions* create robust systems while also implementing stunning visuals by leveraging the latest technologies. *Spark Revolutions* work closely and efficiently with all their clients and customers. The company combines with *Ashgrove Marketing* to offer a broad range of scaleable solutions comparable to those provided by larger organizations while maintaining the innovativeness and flexibility of a small business.

## WIGAN RECYCLING

It was while working at a community partnership project that Paul's interest developed in the area of recycling. After seeing the potential to develop his interests into a social venture, Paul started conversations with local hospitals, schools and universities for possible collection of redundant computers for his business. With the stocks in hand, Paul found an old derelict supermarket that he hired free of charge to set up his computer recycling business, *Wigan Recycling*, in early 2009. Despite all the cost-saving measures employed, he ended up building £20,000 worth of debt on credit cards, which he later settled with a grant he received from the Liverpool City Council. He later entered into negotiations with a local recycling company to share their staff on a part time basis and this, along with free support from his family and friends, helped the business to expand its operations outside of Liverpool.

# Chapter 1

# Introduction: dynamic entrepreneurial learning capabilities

## 1.1 INTRODUCTION

The topic of entrepreneurship has grown in importance over the last 15 years. There are now many textbooks dealing with entrepreneurship, business start-up and the management of small firms. At the outset, our intention was that this book should adopt a different approach from those already offered to students. Our focus is considerably narrower than the writers of most textbooks. Here we concentrate on what we regard as the most important period associated with an entrepreneurial venture: the decision to start a business and the first 12 months of operation. We focus all chapters in this book on how nascent entrepreneurs obtain, mobilize and apply their resources in this crucial period. Very few entrepreneurs will be concerned with employees at this stage and we do not spend time discussing issues related to small firm management. Most new entrepreneurs should concentrate on managing themselves and mobilizing their resources rather than trying to deal with the complexity of employment-related issues. At the same time, the principle of this book is that the 'blue-print', or template, established in the immediate pre- and post-start-up phase will have significant implications for the future of the business (Baron *et al.* 1999). Hence, we stress the importance of 'dynamic entrepreneurial learning' and the need to create new businesses based on the principles of dynamic capabilities. There has been much intellectual effort expended on defining the term entrepreneur (see for example Shane 2012). We adopt a very general definition in which an entrepreneur is someone who is attempting to start his or her own business, or those who are currently managing their business (Aldrich and Yang 2012).

The second focus of this book is summed-up in the title of this particular chapter. While there are a number of critics who find little evidence of 'entrepreneurial learning', our approach is based on the principle that learning is central to long-term success of start-up businesses. There is certainly evidence that supports the view that there is a positive relationship between higher levels of human capital and entrepreneurial success (Davidsson and Honig 2003, Kim *et al.* 2006). For example, the concept of 'absorptive capacity' is based on the principle that possession of knowledge makes it easier to recognize the value of new information and apply it to commercial ends (Witt 2004, de Jong and Freel 2010). While Cohen and Levinthal (1990: 129) were referring to learning in R&D-based organizations, the concept of absorptive capacity was firmly based on the principles of cognitive learning: 'accumulated prior knowledge increases both the ability to put new knowledge into memory, what we would call the acquisition of knowledge, and the ability to recall and use it.' Building resilience into start-up businesses means that young and inexperienced entrepreneurs must develop the ability to make the best of their own skills and knowledge. However, they must also have the social skills to mobilize the resources of those 'close ties' belonging to their immediate networks of family and friends.

The authors have been teaching and researching entrepreneurship for a considerable amount of time. At the same time, our thinking about entrepreneurial learning has been influenced particularly by the work of Allan Gibb and by the contribution of the late Jason Cope. The title of the book very much reflects our debt to Jason who coined the term dynamic entrepreneurial learning (Cope 2005). Learning from critical incidents (crises) or even from failure is a crucial element of Jason's contribution to our understanding of the way in which entrepreneurs learn in practice (Pittaway and Thorpe 2012). We believe that such principles can be applied in the classroom by encouraging students to engage in a process of active learning. We acknowledge that conventional lectures still have a place in terms of transmitting ideas, 'facts' and theories about entrepreneurship. However, we argue that real learning will only take place if students engage in activities that give them some experience of undertaking tasks associated with entrepreneurship. Such experience can take a variety of forms including vicarious learning from experienced entrepreneurs, engaging in computer simulation games or experiencing real business start-up guided by organizations such as Young Enterprise (see Chapter 3).

## 1.2 LEARNING OBJECTIVES

- ■ To identify why entrepreneurship is growing in importance.
- ■ To describe the nature of the learning approach advocated in this book.
- ■ To explain the differences between routines, heuristics and habits in relationship to new venture creation.

## 1.3 GROWING IMPORTANCE OF ENTREPRENEURSHIP

Entrepreneurship has become a topic of major importance to politicians and to those involved with higher education. In the United Kingdom, the advent of a new political agenda became apparent with the first Thatcher government of 1979, which began to promote the idea of an enterprise culture within the UK (Anderson *et al.* 2000). Similar changes were also occurring within other developed countries as the 'post-war' consensus between politicians of the left and right about the role of the State and commitment to public spending based on Keynesian economic theory began to disintegrate. A political realignment with the emergence of New Labour under the leadership of Tony Blair meant the politicians of the left were as enthusiastic about entrepreneurship as previous Conservative governments. Both Blair and his successor as prime minister, Gordon Brown, were keen to ensure that the UK was 'the best place in the world to start a business'. This phrase is still being used by the present Conservative government led by David Cameron. However, growing interest in entrepreneurship as an alternative to paid employment is not simply associated with developed countries such as the UK (see Chapter 11). According to the GEM (Global Entrepreneurship Monitor) studies, 'factor-driven economies' (the least developed), such as Ghana and Zambia, have extremely high levels of entrepreneurial activity (see www.gemconsortium. org for more information). Efficiency-driven economies, including China, Argentina and Brazil, also have levels of entrepreneurial activity that far exceed levels in the innovation-driven economies such as the UK, US, France and Germany. As discussed in Chapter 11, it is important to consider the distinction between opportunity-based entrepreneurship and necessity-based entrepreneurship. Necessity-based entrepreneurship, which is usually very low value, accounts for a greater proportion of entrepreneurial activity in less developed economies. Therefore, it is not simply the level of entrepreneurship that is important, but also the extent to which such activity contributes to National economic and social well-being.

Despite growing interest in entrepreneurship, the failure rates of new businesses remain extremely high. Baron *et al.* (1999) proposed that all entrepreneurs begin with a blueprint that informs their approach to the process of building a business. Drawing on a survey of 76 technology-based companies in Silicon Valley the authors identified five basic employment models (engineering, star, commitment, bureaucracy and autocracy) based on three dimensions: attachment, selection and coordination/control (Baron *et al.* 1999). Such blueprints are associated with a number of factors including the entrepreneur's business strategy and the influence of key resource-providers (Baron *et al.* 1999). Aldrich and Yang (2012: 1) extend these ideas by suggesting that a key reason for failure is that the majority of young people attempting to start their own businesses have not acquired 'the blueprints and associated tools they need to build organizations'.

The first and most important of those tools is knowledge: what entrepreneurs need to know and how they apply that knowing. Aldrich and Yang (2012) suggest that there are three interrelated personal 'dispositions' associated with entrepreneurial actions, which they describe as routines, habits and heuristics. The term routine was developed by Nelson and Winter (1982: 97) and it refers to 'regular

**3**

and predictable patterns of behaviour'. Latour (1986) differentiates between ostensive routines (abstract patterns) and performative routines (specific actions). From the perspective of a nascent entrepreneur, ostensive routines encompass such activities as the need to produce a well-researched business plan as a means of engaging with resource-providers. Performative routines concern those actions entrepreneurs undertake to obtain and analyse the data necessary to convince potential funders that their business idea is worthwhile.

Habitual behaviour is an essential element of human activity as well as the underpinning of future 'organizational routines' (Hodgson 2009). Individual habits are the basis on which nascent entrepreneurs enact emerging routines in their new businesses (Aldrich and Yang 2012). As pointed out by Baron (2008) emotions and feelings are central to the habitual responses made by entrepreneurs to key decisions during business start-up. Therefore, in considering the ways in which students make the transition to entrepreneurship it is important to encourage reflection on the efficacy of those habitual behaviours that influence development of their 'business models' (see Box 1.1).

The third element identified by Aldrich and Yang (2012) is heuristics, which are distinctive from habits. With regards to nascent entrepreneurs, it is suggested that they must make the best use of information appropriate to their particular situation. Hence, simple 'rules of thumb' inform decisions when individuals are short of both time and resources. This suggests that effective nascent entrepreneurs do not waste time and effort trying to achieve optimal solutions. Rather, they accept that they will have to compromise and make the best of the resources they have available. As we discuss in later chapters, this approach fits very well with what we describe as entrepreneurship based on bootstrapping and bricolage.

It is widely accepted that routines are essential to the effective operation of established organizations (March and Simon 1958, Nelson and Winter 1982, Cohen and Bacdayan 1994, Pentland and Feldman 2005). According to Pentland

## BOX 1.1

I guess the hard work was always in me and just took a while to come out. From about 11 or 12 when my mum started doing her master's she worked 16 hours a day non-stop and still does. I am like that, people email me at 10 p.m. and they have a response within 5 minutes and I think if you own your own business you should expect to be on call 24 hours a day. If you don't deal with problems there and then you don't care enough about what you do.

[Ben Wilson, *Jazooli*]

**BOX 1.2**

When you start off you have no idea how to price things and it's impossible to find out about market averages. You haven't got a clue how long it's going to take to develop a product; you go off best-guesses and sometimes they are just wrong. There've been a few times when we've priced ourselves out of the market, even undercharged, been way off the mark, got caught in the enthusiasm trap, and it's not the best thing we could have done.

[*Spark Revolutions*]

*et al.* (2012), repetitive patterns of action form the basis of all routines. In the context of a new business venture, the entrepreneur's habitual behaviours and heuristics (rules of thumb for problem-solving) will combine to establish some rudimentary routines concerned with activities such as the pricing of their products or services (see Box 1.2).

Entrepreneurs who understand the need to overcome *ad hoc* approaches to pricing and costing, as well as other business activities, are more likely to be successful in the longer term. Routines are based on a 'substrate of individual habits' acquired as a result of influences from family, education and early work experiences (Aldrich and Yang 2012: 13). Subsequently, entrepreneurial choices about the nature of their 'business platform' will form the basis of organizational routines as the firm becomes more established (Davidsson and Klofsten 2003). Routines will be refined via a process of variation and selection as entrepreneurs identify approaches that work best for their businesses. As discussed in Chapter 4, a range of knowledge, skills and capabilities are associated with the early stages of starting a business and form the basis on which new entrepreneurs embed the appropriate routines into their commercial activities.

While we acknowledge that functional and technical skills are important in most start-up businesses it is also essential that nascent entrepreneurs develop their social competencies (Holt and Macpherson 2010, Tocher *et al.* 2012). Entrepreneurs must create routines based on activities associated with boot-strapping and bricolage, which are central to the acquisition, reconfiguration, integration and exploitation of the resources required to establish their businesses. As the business grows, bootstrapping and bricolage should become embedded routines in the fabric of the firm to ensure that it remains responsive and agile by maintaining a lean approach in its operating strategy (Timmons 1999). For example, RSL, a small, entrepreneurial manufacturing firm, adopted a number of relatively straight-forward routines that helped to improve the overall business performance and these are summarized in Table 1.1 (Jones and Craven 2001b). As these basic routines became established in the firm it was possible to introduce more

**Table 1.1** Developing new routines

| | Actions taken in RSL |
|---|---|
| Scan trade journals | Carefully examine trade journals and supplier catalogues for new product ideas |
| Develop customer contacts | Build strong relationships with customers to identify their existing and future needs |
| Attend trade shows | Initiate informal discussions with staff from competitors to stimulate new product ideas |
| Competitor price check | Examine competitor prices as a basis for estimating their cost-base |
| Encourage supplier input | Involve suppliers in early stages of new product development – helping to reduce costs |

sophisticated routines associated with a new product development committee and the 'reverse engineering' of competitor products (Jones and Craven 2001a).

As we discuss in the next section, linking entrepreneurial actions to those routines that form the basis of a successful business platform fits with contemporary perspectives on entrepreneurship, which are known as the practice-based approach (De Clercq and Voronov 2009). The practice-based view of entrepreneurship rejects the idea that some individuals have intrinsic attributes (such as tolerance of ambiguity, risk-taking and the need for achievement) that mean they will be more likely to become entrepreneurs (McClelland 1962). The alternative view is that entrepreneurship is a set of social practices that are influenced by broader structures, institutions and societal norms (Lounsbury and Glynn 2001).

## 1.4 A PRACTICE-BASED APPROACH TO ENTREPRENEURIAL LEARNING

As we discuss in Chapter 3, early approaches to entrepreneurial learning were based primarily on cognitivism (Kohler 1925, Piaget 1926) and behaviourism (Thorndike 1913, Pavlov 1927, Skinner 1938). Gradually there have been moves to adopt approaches that incorporate experiential and social learning. Our understanding of entrepreneurial learning has certainly been influenced by David Kolb's experiential learning theory (ELT). As Kolb (1984) acknowledges, his own ideas owe a strong intellectual debt to Jean Piaget's contribution to the understanding of cognitive development. The work of social psychologist Kurt Lewin on group dynamics also influenced the development of ELT. In particular, Lewin's (1951) action-research approach to planned change ranging from small groups to complex organizations has had 'the most far-reaching practical significance' (Kolb 1984: 8). Kolb also acknowledges his intellectual debt to the work of American philosopher John Dewey. Recent interest in the 'practice turn' has revitalized interest in Dewey's contribution to the fields of philosophy and education (Raelin 2007). Kolb (1984) argues that Dewey's commitment to experiential learning meant that he was the most influential educational theorist of the twentieth century. Dewey, along with Charles Sanders Pierce and William James, was one of three scholars associated with founding the pragmatism school of philosophy. Pragmatism is based on the idea that theory and practice are linked in a process of mutual reinforcement. Practice informs theory, enhanced theory improves practice, the adoption of new practices further aids theory development. The important issue as far as we are concerned is that it is essential to identify the social practices that underpin the actions of nascent entrepreneurs as they attempt to establish new business ventures (Anderson *et al.* 2010).

Emergence of the practice perspective was based on attempts to resolve tensions between contrasting explanations of social phenomena based on either agency (individual action) or structures such as class, family and education (Bourdieu 1977, Giddens 1987). Gradually the practice perspective has been adopted in the study of strategy (Whittington 1996), management (Samra-Fredericks 2003), organizational learning (Lave and Wenger 1991), small firms (Stringfellow and Shaw 2009) and entrepreneurship (Steyaert and Katz 2004, De Clercq and Honig 2011, Karatas-Ozkan 2011). De Clercq and Voronov (2009) set out an explanation of entrepreneurship from a practice perspective based on Bourdieu's (2002) concept of habitus (see Box 1.3). As discussed in Chapter 3, individual dispositions at the micro-level are linked to the macro-level ('the field') by habitus at the meso-level. Perhaps the most useful applications of Bourdieu's ideas concerns the four types of capital that individual entrepreneurs draw on to pursue their objectives in setting-up a business (Karatas-Ozkan 2011):

## BOX 1.3

Habitus focuses attention on the values, dispositions and expectations of social groups that are acquired through the activities and experience of everyday life. Habitus refers to the elements of culture that can be identified in the day-to-day practices of individuals, groups, societies and nations. It includes the habits, skills, styles and tastes that form the basis of the non-discursive knowledge on which the taken-for-granted assumptions of various social groups are founded.

- ■ **Economic capital** refers to the financial resources to which a nascent entrepreneur has access – can include debt and equity funding;
- ■ **Cultural capital** concerns the socialization processes associated with education and training as well as other forms of work-related experiences;

- **Social capital** refers to the resources (physical and emotional) that can be acquired via the nascent entrepreneur's various network ties (strong and weak);
- **Symbolic capital** is the sum of the other three forms of capital as it is central to the entrepreneur's ability to legitimize themselves and their business in the eyes of potential stakeholders.

The various forms of capital are used by individuals to legitimize their identity as entrepreneurs and provide credibility for the various social practices associated with acquiring the resources to start a new business (De Clercq and Voronov 2009). Karatas-Ozkan (2011) uses this framework in a detailed case study of a new business venture established by five nascent entrepreneurs. She concludes that learning experiences associated with the various forms of capital are mobilized by a range of entrepreneurial practices related to starting a new business (Table 1.2).

According to Raelin (2007), higher education is dominated by pedagogical approaches that adhere to the Cartesian principle that separates theory and practice. Objectified knowledge is based on *facts* that are established through the collection of *positive* empirical data. Consequently, learning in higher education relies on the transfer of objectified knowledge from lecturer to students via theories and frameworks. In entrepreneurship education, objectified facts include the psychological attributes associated with entrepreneurs such as risk-taking, tolerance of ambiguity and the need for achievement. Those whose approach is informed by a social constructionist (Berger and Luckmann 1966) epistemology reject the idea that social phenomena can be defined by objective facts. Rather, social constructs such as 'entrepreneurship' differ according to their location in time and space in relationship to a particular culture. To give an extreme example, the way in which a young male entrepreneur based in Silicon Valley understands and practises entrepreneurship will be very different from the understanding and experience of

**Table 1.2** *Routines and entrepreneurial practices*

| Routines | Entrepreneurial practices |
| --- | --- |
| Identify business opportunities | Develop a 'feel' for the market and existing competitors |
| Acquiring resources | Use social networks as a basis for identifying and acquiring relevant resources |
| Managing oneself | Develop practical rules of thumb to make best use of own resources (time) |
| Managing business functions | Learn to balance various activities associated with a new business: operations, finance, customers, suppliers, etc. |

a middle-aged African woman engaging in subsistence agriculture to feed her family. Raelin (2007) argues that an 'epistemology of practice' has major implications for the integration of class-room based learning and work-based learning. Individuals should be encouraged to construct knowledge in conjunction with their lecturers and other students. So, for example, rather than being provided with objectified knowledge about the problems associated with starting a business students must be given the opportunity to gain first-hand experience of such problems. They should also be encouraged to learn by reflecting on their experiences at the individual and group levels. Hence, students' learning from others in a social environment is mediated through both theories that are presented in the classroom and through the norms associated with knowledge-sharing within groups (Vygotsky 1978).

Activity theory (Engeström 2001) has been widely adopted to develop a better understanding of organizational learning. Jones and Holt (2008) use activity theory to examine the ways in which entrepreneurial ventures change during their early years of operation. They use three case studies to illustrate the inherent messiness associated with the transition from conception of business ideas to their actual gestation. In particular, the study indicates a range of factors such as pro-activity, risk-taking, heightened self-confidence, vision and the use of heuristics and rules of thumb, which are used by entrepreneurs to identify and exploit new opportunities. During business start-up, new business owners form their entrepreneurial identities within social and cultural environments that include family, professional and policy communities. Entrepreneurs have to organize their knowledge and actions within existing structures such as business planning, marketing, limited liability and intellectual property rights (Jones and Holt 2008).

Adopting a practice-based view of learning has substantial implications for those engaged in entrepreneurial education. Instead of concentrating on individual traits and cognitions, there is more focus on socially embedded experiences and relations. As Higgins and Elliott (2011: 353) point out, 'practice as a pedagogical approach to entrepreneurial education' means that 'individual learners are encouraged to understand a situation by connecting knowing and doing'. This also means that students must be encouraged to adopt an active, rather than a passive, approach to learning by engaging in the knowledge creation process. A further advantage is that the interaction of experience and practice helps students develop the appropriate critical thinking and communication skills that are a prerequisite for entrepreneurial success (Higgins and Elliott 2011). The ability to remember 'facts' and to describe appropriate theories such as Corbett's (2005) conceptualization of how experiential learning informs opportunity recognition and exploitation are important elements of any course/module offered in higher education. As well at the objective/explicit knowledge associated with known facts and theories about entrepreneurship, students should be encouraged to develop their tacit knowledge associated with the development of sense-making

**9**

abilities related to the 'reading' of social situations and adoption of the appropriate (formal or informal) language (Lee and Jones 2008, Cornelissen *et al.* 2012).

## 1.5 SUMMARY AND KEY LEARNING POINTS

In Chapter 2, we discuss the evolution of theories related to entrepreneurship. In its early stages, the field was dominated by individualist approaches associated with psychology (McClelland 1962) and macro-level approaches associated with economics (Kirzner 1973). Gradually, a range of theorists introduced approaches that were based on a more social understanding of entrepreneurship. Many writers have incorporated ideas associated with social network theory and social capital theory to challenge ideas associated with the entrepreneur as heroic individual (Conway and Jones 2012). For example, based on the process perspective, Steyaert's (2007) concept of 'entrepreneuring' has begun to have an impact on our understanding of entrepreneurship. Of course, the entrepreneurial learning perspective also draws heavily on the importance of the entrepreneur's engagement with other social actors (Cope 2005, Rae 2005, Macpherson and Jones 2008, Jones *et al.* 2010b). Although Sarasvathy's effectuation theory has its roots in Simon's (1959) ideas about information processing, her work also incorporates a strong social element via the entrepreneur's social networks (whom I know).

We acknowledge that traditional views of entrepreneurship (McClelland 1962) cannot be entirely discounted because there is no doubt that some individuals, such as Sam and Ben Wilson[1], are *natural* entrepreneurs in the same way that other young people have an affinity for music, sport or science. We also acknowledge the importance of an internal locus of control to successful entrepreneurship (Rotter 1966, Mueller and Thomas 2001); locus of control refers to the extent to which individuals believe that they are in control of events in their own lives rather than being subject to external forces (see Box 1.4).

---

### BOX 1.4

Before this I was a completely different person, most people would say that I was lazy, didn't try hard at school. I could have done much better but I took school as a stepping stone. GCSEs, they were stepping stones, and A Levels. I always got what I needed and was offered a place at University. I declined for a year and set this up. As soon as I set this up I watched TV programmes like *Dragons' Den*, I would read articles and things and I just took from that all I needed was hard work, determination and common sense.

[Ben Wilson, *Jazooli*]

---

At the same time, we are firmly committed to the idea that people can learn entrepreneurship and that individuals can even be encouraged to develop the motivation to start their own businesses. In part, this can be explained by ideas related to self-efficacy – those who believe they have mastered the appropriate skills are more likely to undertake a particular task (Bandura 1997, Smith and Woodworth 2012).

Although we claim that our approach is very different from most textbooks because of our focus on the early stages of entrepreneurship, there is one way in which the book is conventional. We have tried to plan the book so that the reader's understanding of entrepreneurship is cumulative, building from the basics of accessing the essential resources to the application of such resources to develop a growing business. We start by exploring theories that underpin the approach to the book (Chapters 2 and 3), followed by a discussion about the types of skills (Chapter 4) and the role of networks and social capital (Chapter 5) in starting a business. Thereafter, we concentrate on acquiring and developing intangible and tangible resources (Chapters 6, 7 and 8). We develop our discussion into the application and reconfiguration of those resources though dynamic capabilities (Chapter 9) and discuss the changing challenges for growing a business (Chapter 10). Chapter 11 is a 'stand-alone' section that deals with the policy issues associated with entrepreneurship. Therefore, we suggest that students will gain most value from this book by approaching the text in a relatively linear fashion. We have also adopted a writing style and approach that is perhaps a little more academic than many textbooks, which place greater emphasis on accessibility. This is because the book is very much driven by a research-based approach and we have tried to incorporate contemporary ideas and emerging knowledge about entrepreneurship (see Chapter 2). While we remain convinced that entrepreneurship is an appropriate topic for study in Higher Education, we are also committed to the idea that the conventional lecture/tutorial format simply does not work in entrepreneurial education. As we have briefly outlined above, a strong practice element is an essential criteria for encouraging students to develop their under-standing of whether or not they have the skills, competencies and commitment to become entrepreneurs. The key points from Chapter 1 are as follows:

- Entrepreneurship is important whatever the national level of economic activity.
- Routines, heuristics and habits provide the 'blue-print' for the creation of any entrepreneurial business.
- As a new business begins to operate then bootstrapping and bricolage should become embedded routines.
- Bourdieu's four types of capital (economic, culture, social and symbolic) are important for any young entrepreneur when setting-up a new business.

## 1.6 DISCUSSION QUESTIONS

■ What are the most important factors that have influenced politicians' views on the significance of entrepreneurship?

■ Why do so many new businesses fail?

■ What key 'dispositions' do you possess?

■ In what ways does the practice-based perspective differ from more traditional approaches to entrepreneurship?

# Chapter 2

# The changing nature of entrepreneurial theory

## 2.1 INTRODUCTION

As briefly discussed in Chapter 1, there is increasing interest in the topic of entrepreneurship. Governments around the world have been keen to promote entrepreneurship as a way of responding to the decline of old industrial sectors as well as capturing the benefits from the emergence of new information and communication technologies (ICT). The academic study of entrepreneurship and new venture creation has also grown rapidly over the last 40 years. Landström *et al.* (2012) identify a number of key figures who defined the intellectual basis for future generations of academic researchers. It is widely acknowledged that Richard Cantillon (1732/1931) first used the term entrepreneur in his *Essai Sur la Nature du Commerce en Général* where he outlined the importance of individual property rights, economic interdependency and the concept of arbitrage. Jean-Baptiste Say owned a cotton-spinning mill as well as being Europe's first professor of economics, and the entrepreneur was central to his explanation of how the economic system functioned. Say's (1880) ideas were also important because he recognized that human industry (knowledge) was the third factor of production in addition to land and capital (Pittaway 2012).

Although Adam Smith (1776) did not use the term entrepreneur in *The Wealth of Nations*, his work was important in developing a deeper understanding of how a capitalist market economy operated. Joseph Schumpeter (1934) is by far the most important influence on contemporary understanding of the role played by entrepreneurs in capitalist economies. Even those with an extremely limited knowledge of Schumpeter's writing will be able to cite the crucial role of 'creative destruction' as the engine of economic change. *The Theory of Economic Development* (Schumpeter 1934) remains the most important publication in the entrepreneurship literature (Landström *et al.* 2012). There have, of course, been a number of other significant contributors to entrepreneurship during the course of the twentieth century and these include: Frank Knight (1921), Ludwig von Mises (1949), Israel Kirzner (1973), and Fredrich von Hayek (1990). The most widely known work other than Schumpeter's is almost certainly that of David McClelland (1961), whose ideas about entrepreneurial traits, such as the need for achievement, risk-taking and a tolerance of ambiguity, still have a seductive appeal to students. However, research on traits has been inconclusive and, in contrast, many recent scholars have focused on the ambiguity and complexity associated with firm emergence (Baker and Nelson 2005, Steyaert 2007, Sarasvathy 2008). It is the historical and institutional settings that actors occupy, rather than specific psychological traits or particular resource bundles, that determine entrepreneurial performance (Katz and Gartner 1988, Gartner and Shaver 2012).

Landström *et al.* (2012) argue that there have been three phases of entrepreneurship research since the 1970s. The *take-off phase* was stimulated by Birch's work in the US and the Bolton report in the UK. The *growth phase* of the 1990s involved both creation of a research infrastructure and greater fragmentation as a new generation of researchers questioned the earlier economic assumptions. From 2000 onwards, *the maturity phase* has incorporated much greater understanding of the phenomena of entrepreneurship with the emergence of various sub-groups who have continued to question the dominance of economic and psychological approaches to the study of entrepreneurship (Landström *et al.* 2012: 1156). A key article by Shane and Venkataraman (2000), which represents the traditional, largely economic, view of entrepreneurship, was followed by a series of important publications that discussed a number of alternative views related to how entrepreneurs operate in practice.

In this chapter, we examine individuals and opportunity identification, before opening the discussion out into new venture creation and exploring recent theoretical developments. We finish with a discussion about various practice-based theories that examine the context, ambiguity and variety of pathways to entrepreneurship in the early days of venture creation. The theoretical debates help to contextualize the remainder of the book, and provide grounding for some of the key debates associated with the study of entrepreneurs engaged in the process of establishing new businesses.

## 2.2 LEARNING OBJECTIVES

- Explain the differences between opportunity identification and opportunity creation.
- Explain the significance to entrepreneurial practice of the distinctions between the causal and effectuation theories of entrepreneurship.
- Evaluate the implications of entrepreneurship process theories for understanding new venture creation.

## 2.3 INDIVIDUALS AND OPPORTUNITIES

In addition to advances in the theoretical understanding of entrepreneurship, which are discussed below, there have been some very important empirical studies (Landström *et al.* 2012). Research carried out by Birch in the US and the Bolton Commission in the UK laid the foundations for future empirical studies. David Storey's *Understanding the Small Business Sector* was the outcome of a major research project funded by the UK's ESRC (economic and social research council). Storey (1994) provided an in-depth account of research findings related to the birth, growth and death of small firms. This remains the only major study of entrepreneurship and the management of small firms carried out in the UK. In the US, Saxenian's (1996) book, in which she examined the phenomenon of technology-based small firms in Silicon Valley and Route 128, was influential in identifying the role of culture in promoting entrepreneurship. There are also a large number of US studies that draw on the Panel Study of Entrepreneurial Dynamics (PSED I and PSED II) and these are summarized by Gartner *et al.* (2012) as well as work associated with the Global Entrepreneurship Monitor (GEM) studies (Kelley *et al.* 2011). According to Gartner and Shaver (2012), the PSED and GEM studies provide conclusive evidence that entrepreneurs are not born with specific attributes that distinguish them from the broader population.

The traditional view of entrepreneurship, described by Sarasvathy (2001) as the causal approach, adopts a linear perspective on the process of discovery, evaluation and exploitation of new ideas (Shane and Venkataraman 2000). Within this field, early studies (McClelland 1961, Brockhaus 1980, Chell *et al.* 1991) focused in on the psychological traits of successful entrepreneurs in the belief that these distinguished them from the wider population. Alternatively, the resource-based view in management studies (Barney 1991) suggests it is the arrangement of resource bundles internal to businesses that drives competitive advantage. This logic has developed into strategic entrepreneurship studies that analyse how competitive entrepreneurial opportunities are discovered and resources allocated to new business ventures (Hitt *et al.* 2001a, Zahra and Dess 2001). Reflecting on these developments, Shane and Venkataraman (2000) introduced a distinct unifying construct into the domain of entrepreneurial study by focusing on the nature of opportunities. In contrast to Gartner (2006), who suggests that entrepreneurship is characterized by its messiness, Shane and Venkataraman (2000: 218) believe that the entrepreneurial process can be encapsulated in a relatively straight-forward definition:

> the field involves the study of *sources* of opportunities; the *processes* of discovery, evaluation, and exploitation of opportunities; and the set of *individuals* who discover, evaluate and exploit them.

There are a variety of ways in which business opportunities can be surfaced: new uses for existing resources; new products from existing resources; new resources for existing products; openings created through regulatory or demographic changes (Shane and Venkataraman 2000: 220); creation of new information; and exploitation of market asymmetries (differences in information about potential opportunities) across space and time. Variations in the ability of individuals to exploit new opportunities are attributed to 'entrepreneurial alertness' (Shane and Venkataraman 2000, Kirzner 2009). Individual alertness depends on intuition and heuristics, as well as access to appropriate information, and these factors determine who will become an entrepreneur (Shane 2000). According to such writers, the nature of opportunity is a 'concrete and real' space in a market that is ripe for exploitation. Focus on the nature of opportunity reduces the earlier emphasis of entrepreneurial traits such as the need for achievement and risk-taking (McClelland 1961). While they shift the focus onto other individual characteristics, such as alertness and foresight, the entrepreneurial ability to discover, evaluate and exploit new opportunities, is retained (Shane 2000, Shane and Venkataraman 2000).

Recently, Shane (2012) has argued that he was responsible for establishing the process perspective as the dominant approach in entrepreneurship (Shane and Venkataraman 2000, Venkataraman et al. 2012). He does, however, disagree with critics who believe that his model is based on a planned sequence of events that follow-on from opportunity identification. For example, he suggests that activities associated with the exploitation of an opportunity are simply 'sub-processes' that could occur in any order. Shane also takes issue with those who suggest that his view of entrepreneurial opportunities as objective phenomena is misguided (Alvarez & Barney 2013, Arend 2013). Instead, he argues that there is a clear conceptual distinction between opportunities and business ideas. It is acknowledged that business ideas are entrepreneurs' subjective interpretation of the resources required to pursue a particular opportunity (Shane 2012: 15). Nevertheless, Shane's model (2003) is a deliberate attempt to combine the individual and environment perspectives on entrepreneurship (Figure 2.1). Hence, the model combines individual psychological attributes and demographic factors (age, education, experience) with environmental factors (sector and the macro environment). The underpinning ethos of the model is that entrepreneurs are driven by the profit-motive to identify and exploit opportunities. This illustrates the so-called causal approach in which opportunities are identified and then the entrepreneur acquires the resources needed to exploit that opportunity.

An alternative approach to the opportunity identification view is that potential entrepreneurs use their knowledge and experience to create opportunities (Gartner et al. 1992, Macpherson and Holt 2007). The linking of experience and the creation of new opportunities can be traced to the work of Edith Penrose (1959) who laid the foundations for the resource-based view of the firm (Barney 1991).

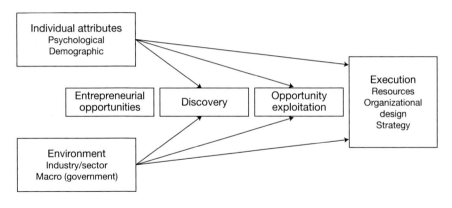

**Figure 2.1**
Shane's causal model

The legacy of Penrose can be found in a range of approaches to understanding the entrepreneur–opportunity interface: entrepreneurial embeddedness (Anderson and Jack 2002, Anderson and Miller 2003), entrepreneurial learning (Rae 2004, Cope 2005, Rae 2005) and entrepreneurial practice (Katz and Gartner 1988, Sarason et al. 2006, Fletcher 2007). Penrose (1959) is important because she rejected views of entrepreneurs being rational economic actors in favour of the idea that opportunities are created (rather than discovered) during the day-to-day practices of being in business.

The work of Penrose and Gartner provides the foundation for the so-called 'narrative turn' in entrepreneurial studies. Three related themes in entrepreneurial narrative research have emerged in recent years. First, a number of scholars suggest entrepreneurial practice is a narrative pursuit through which actors create their life-stories (Rae 2005, 2004, Rindova et al. 2009, Garud and Giuliani 2013). Second, others focus on the metaphors (Cornelissen and Clarke 2010), plots (Hamilton 2006) and clichés (Down and Warren 2008) that are commonly employed when actors talk about their entrepreneurial actions. Third, entrepreneurial storytelling and narratives articulate images of new business ventures, which emphasize their formality (Gartner et al. 1992) and their legitimacy (Lounsbury and Glynn 2001, Zott and Huy 2007) rather than the informality and uncertainty usually associated with start-ups. There is a common focus on how opportunities emerge via exchanges made between creative actors and the historical and institutional settings in which they operate. Sarasvathy's (2001, 2008) effectuation theory is also a narrative approach to understanding how entrepreneurial opportunities develop in actors' imaginations. Sarasvathy (2008: 13) suggests that opportunities emerge from a combination of history, and identity: 'who actors are, what they know, and who they know'. The effectual principles of design and creation in turn are propelled by the transformation of existing

**17**

realities as actors attempt to create something from a limited set of resources. Effectuation enables prospective entrepreneurs to act in the face of *goal ambiguity* because opportunities emerge through practical engagement and experience. Sarasvathy's effectuation theory is described in more detail below.

## 2.4 NEW VENTURE CREATION PROCESSES

Most writers take Low and Macmillan's (1988: 141) seminal definition of entrepreneurship as the 'creation of a new venture' as their starting point. This definition suggests that entrepreneurship is a process that takes months, or even years, rather than being an instantaneous event. Katz and Gartner's (1988: 433) work is important here because it concentrated attention on to the processes by which 'an organization evolves from nothing to something'. What this means is that it is necessary to develop a better understanding of the 'territory between preorganization', before nascent entrepreneurs have initiated their venture, and the actual creation of a new organization (Katz and Gartner 1988). Gartner (1985) developed a conceptual framework that describes new venture creation as an interaction between the environment, the organization, entrepreneurial behaviour and the process of business creation (Figure 2.2). Gartner's (1985) work was a direct response to the continuing focus on identifying particular entrepreneurial traits. This prompted a shift to much greater interest in the process-related aspects of entrepreneurial behaviour (Gartner *et al.* 1992). According to Gartner (1985) there are six processes associated with business creation and organizational emergence:

■ locate/identify a business opportunity;
■ accumulate resources;
■ market products or services;
■ produce products or services;
■ build the organization;
■ respond to government (regulation/taxes) and society (the market).

From this perspective, the challenge is to understand exactly how new organizations are created, enacted (Weick 1995) or socially constructed (Berger and Luckmann 1966). The shift from the identification of an opportunity to a functioning business represents a quantum rather than an evolutionary change. Entrepreneurs attempting to set-up new businesses must 'talk and act "as if" equivocal events are non-equivocal' (Gartner *et al.* 1992: 17). In existing organizations, non-equivocal events are based on the routines and repertoires that individuals undertake that have meaning for other organizational actors (see Chapter 1). Organizational emergence is concerned with the entrepreneur generating a set of appropriate interactions that are convincing for actors such

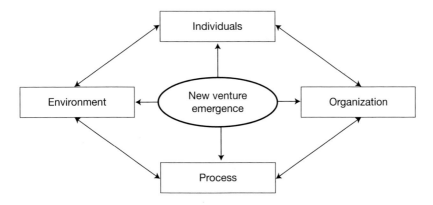

**Figure 2.2**
*Gartner's model of organizational emergence*

as potential customers, suppliers and employees as well as resource-providers such as bankers, venture capitalists or business angels.

Starr and Fondas (1992) utilize theories of organizational socialization to illuminate the role of entrepreneurs in emerging organizations. Socialization is a useful concept because it specifies attitudinal and behavioural changes as well as revealing role relations between the entrepreneur and key outsiders who act as socializing agents (Starr and Fondas 1992). A similar theme is pursued in a later paper in which Larson and Starr (1993) critically examine the role of network relations in organization formation. The network model has three stages that are important for the acquisition of the critical resources needed to start a new business. As pointed out by Kanter (1983) these resources include information, technical knowledge, capital, physical resources, as well as symbolic support such as endorsement, political backing, approval and legitimacy.

- **Stage one** – focuses on essential dyads; relationships including family, friends and business contacts provide the basis for any entrepreneur seeking essential resources for a new firm. Effective entrepreneurs concentrate on the critical dyads by 'culling' those unlikely to provide sufficient resources to the venture.
- **Stage two** – converting dyads to socioeconomic exchanges, is concerned with changing 'one dimensional' (social or economic) exchange processes into two dimensional exchange processes (social and economic).
- **Stage three** – activities becomes more formalized through as functions such as finance, marketing and production are established. Development of organizational routines means that there is increasing interdependence with a number of key customers and suppliers who stabilize the network. Increasingly, relationships are not reliant on the entrepreneur's personal links but become part of repeated exchange cycles that typify established organizations.

**19**

More recent studies confirm the importance of entrepreneurs recognizing that different resources can be accessed via strong and weak ties. Strong ties (essential dyads) are crucial in the early stages of business start-up. In the longer-term, entrepreneurs must develop their weaker ties if they want to access the resources necessary to build a sustainable business (Lee and Jones 2008). Other studies demonstrate there are clear links between the ability of entrepreneurs to extend their networks and the financial performance of early-stage businesses (Jones and Jayawarna 2010).

While a wide range of authors have proposed frameworks for the process of new venture creation (Gartner 1985, Greenberger and Sexton 1988, Katz and Gartner 1988, Vesper 1990, Mazzarol *et al.* 1999), there is little evidence to suggest a common pattern of events. Carter *et al.* (1996) draw on Weick's (1979) theory of organizing as the conceptual basis for their exploration of business start-ups. The process of new business creation is analogous to the concept of 'enactment', which refers to the generation of specific patterns of interlocking behaviours among individuals (Weick 1979). The study was based on the analysis of two existing data-sets (Curtin 1982, Reynolds and Miller 1992, Reynolds and White 1997), which provided a total of 71 nascent entrepreneurs. Interviews identified a list of 14 'precursor behaviours' associated with new venture creation that were categorized according to the time between initiation and completion (3 month period up to 5 years). Precursor behaviours included: prepared plan, invested money, bought/rented facilities, devoted full-time. The authors were able to discriminate between three distinct groups (started, still trying and given-up). Those still trying were differentiated from the other two groups by being less likely to have obtained financial support or bought equipment. Second, those who had given-up were less likely to have obtained financial support or developed models or prototypes (Carter *et al.* 1996: 158).

In explaining these results, the authors summarize each of the three groups. Successful entrepreneurs were more aggressive in making their business tangible to others by obtaining equipment, finance, organizing their team and in establishing a legal entity. Those who gave-up were quite similar in their activities to the first group, but their early enthusiasm soon dissipated. Emphasis on the development of a 'model' suggested that 'testing' may have indicated that the concept/idea did not work in a way that matched the entrepreneurs' expectations. The 'still-trying' group seemed to lack motivation because they had undertaken fewer activities and those activities were 'internal' such as saving money and preparing a business plan. Significantly, they put much less effort into the more 'external' activities likely to make the business real to others.

In terms of advice to individuals considering starting a business, it would seem that the results provide evidence that nascent entrepreneurs should aggressively pursue opportunities in the short-term, because they will quickly learn that these opportunities will either reveal themselves as worthy of start-up or as poor choices that should be abandoned.

(Carter *et al.* 1996: 163)

Reynolds (2011) recently re-examined precursor behaviours by interviewing a representative sample of those in the process of starting a business. The results are summarized in Table 2.1 and provide some insight into the way in which US entrepreneurs establish new businesses. The main precursor of setting-up a business was 'serious thoughts about business' for 99 per cent of entrepreneurs. A total of 11 precursor behaviours were new in the 2011 survey (not mentioned in the 1996 study) and these included 'began talking to customers', 'use of physical space' and 'collect competitor information'.

**Table 2.1** Start-up activities

|  | Survey 2011 (%) | Survey 1999 (%) |
| --- | --- | --- |
| Serious thoughts about business | 99 | 99 |
| Invested own money | 79 | 68 |
| Began talking to customers | 76 | NA |
| Developed model/prototype | 65 | 35 |
| Initiated business plan | 64 | 56 |
| Use of physical space | 62 | NA |
| Collected competitor information | 62 | NA |
| Created inventory | 59 | NA |
| Generated income | 56 | NA |
| Phone book/internet | 55 | NA |
| Defined market | 54 | NA |
| Bought facilities/equipment | 53 | 50 |
| Examined regulatory requirements | 53 | NA |
| Promoted good/services | 49 | NA |
| Business bank account | 39 | NA |
| Registered business | 36 | NA |

Mueller *et al.* (2012) describe a rather different approach to identifying what entrepreneurs actually do when engaged in business start-up. This study is based on a detailed observation of six entrepreneurs engaged in the process of business start-up, which has similarities to Mintzberg's (1973) classic study of managerial work. The six businesses had been established between 3 and 12 months at the time of the study. Work undertaken by the entrepreneurs was characterized by 'brevity and high levels of fragmentation' (Fritsch and Mueller 2004: 1004). Actions undertaken by the entrepreneurs were organized under three headings:

- **activities** – primarily concerned with exchanging information, undertaking analytical and conceptual work and networking/maintaining relationships (75 per cent[1]);
- **functions** – marketing, sales, PR; product/service development; administration; finance; environmental monitoring (62 per cent);
- **exploitation/exploration** – the former refers to activities that are aimed at improving efficiencies within the business (65 per cent); the latter involves activities focused on experimentation and innovation (33 per cent).

## 2.5 THE ENTREPRENEURIAL PROCESS

One of the common elements that underpin these academic attempts to understand new venture creation is that entrepreneurship is described as a process rather than a single event. In fact, questions about the activities in which entrepreneurs actually engage during business start-up are central to the interest of academics and policy-makers. Low and MacMillan (1988) set out a detailed account of the activities associated with business creation that still influences entrepreneurial scholars. In recent years, a number of new theoretical approaches have been developed in an attempt to provide a better understanding of the behaviours that are associated with the entrepreneurial process. As Fisher (2012) points out, these new theoretical perspectives have taken very different approaches to the traditional causal explanation of how new ventures are created. In the causal approach, entrepreneurs follow a linear process of opportunity identification and evaluation, the setting of goals to exploit that opportunity, and the identification of means by which to achieve the goals. In contrast, the process perspective pays attention to the actions undertaken by entrepreneurs, which are based on an interrelated set of creative activities.

Evolutionary perspectives have certainly strongly influenced the process view of entrepreneurship. Nelson and Winter (1982) developed the concept of organizational routines that have been influential in understanding how existing firms change as well as how new firms are created (see Chapter 1). The work of Aldrich (1999) extended the evolutionary approach by introducing ideas related to variation, selection and retention. Moroz and Hindle (2012) identified 32 'scholarly works' that focus on the entrepreneurial process and examined four of those 'theories' in greater depth: Gartner (1985), Bruyat and Julien (2001), Sarasvathy (2001) and Shane (2003). In their conclusions Moroz and Hindle (2012: 811) suggest that there are some important points of agreement based on their analysis of the four process models:

- The relationship between individual and opportunity is crucial (not all entrepreneurs can exploit all opportunities).
- Time matters as opportunities do not last for ever and market receptiveness changes.

■  Action is absolutely crucial to the exploitation of any opportunity.
■  Understanding the context in which the entrepreneurial action takes place is essential.

According to Fisher (2012: 1020), over the last decade a range of new theoretical perspectives have outlined the behaviours associated with the entrepreneurial process: effectuation theory (Sarasvathy 2001), entrepreneurial bricolage (Baker and Nelson 2005), the creation perspective (Alvarez and Barney 2007) and user entrepreneurship (Shah and Tripsas 2007). In addition, there is a largely European approach that draws on the practice perspective and is known as 'entrepreneuring' (Steyaert 2007). Based on a detailed study of six entrepreneurial ventures, Fisher (2012) attempts to establish whether traditional theory (the casual model) or more modern behavioural theory (effectuation and bricolage) provides the better explanation of real-life entrepreneurial activities. A cohort of six web-based companies[2] founded in the early 2000s were analysed using multiple data sources and Fisher (2012) attempted to match the data to the behaviours associated with each theory. Only two of the start-ups, *Flickr* and *Trip Advisor*, adopted approaches to business start-up that fitted with causation theory: the entrepreneurs identified and evaluated the opportunity, gathered the required resources and then began to exploit the opportunity. There was no evidence that any of the other four start-up ventures adopted behaviours associated with causation. Although effectuation and bricolage are largely independent theories, there are many consistencies in terms of entrepreneurial behaviours during business start-up. Fisher (2012: 1024) concludes that there are four strong similarities associated with the two modern process theories:

1   Existing resources are important for the exploitation of opportunities.
2   Action helps overcome resource constraints.
3   Community is the catalyst for venture emergence.
4   Resource constraints are a source of creative innovation.

Fisher (2012) goes on to suggest that 'the behaviours associated with effectuation and bricolage appeared to be more representative of what entrepreneurs do in building their businesses'. The findings of this study have many practical implications for the way in which the majority of entrepreneurs actually start new businesses. Certainly, contemporary theories including effectuation and bricolage underpin the approach that we adopt in this book.

## 2.6 THE PROCESS OF OPPORTUNITY CREATION

Based on a study of 20 start-up companies in the Swedish mobile internet industry, Sanz-Velasco (2006: 267) suggests that in most cases the opportunities were 'rudimentary' and in need of further development. Hence, even in a strongly technology-based sector the idea of opportunity creation/development was more appropriate than the idea of opportunity discovery. A more recent study based on a random sample of 114 nascent entrepreneurs also found support for the view that opportunities are based on the entrepreneurs' subjective perceptions rather than having an objective reality (Edelman and Yli-Renko 2010). The study also demonstrated that those entrepreneurs who actively engaged in 'venture-creation activities' are more likely to establish successful firms. As Edelman and Yli-Renko (2010: 850) go on to state: 'It is through these efforts that entrepreneurs reduce subjective uncertainty regarding opportunities and mobilize resources to start a venture.' In this section, we examine effectuation in more detail in addition to two other approaches that were not discussed by Moroz and Hindle (2012): entrepreneuring (Steyaert 2007) and bricolage (Baker et al. 2003).

## 2.6.1 Entrepreneuring

Process theorists argue that entrepreneurship is dominated by equilibrium-based theories, which focus on entrepreneurial performance (Steyaert and Katz 2004, Steyaert 2007). As a consequence, entrepreneurship is perceived as an activity that can be defined in terms of profit and status. In contrast, Steyaert (2007) uses the verb entrepreneuring to focus attention on entrepreneurship as a deeply processual activity involving social creativity, dialogue and imagination. As an open-ended concept, entrepreneuring extends the possibilities for understanding entrepreneurial experience through the creative perspective represented by effectuation theory (Sarasvathy 2001, 2008). To make sense of the notion of relationality, Steyaert uses the term prosaic to capture the ordinary everyday experience of entrepreneurial practices. Intertextualities extend entrepreneurial practice away from isolated actors to involve conversational processes of 'co-authorship' (Steyaert 2004: 9). Entrepreneurial practices and opportunities cannot be reduced to objective entities because they are always unfinished and constantly emerging during the process of entrepreneuring (Steyaert 2007, Weiskopf and Steyaert 2009). To engage with entrepreneurial prosaics and experience as 'becoming', processual research is promoted as the narrative analysis and discursive interpretation of entrepreneurial storytelling (Steyaert 2004, Johannisson 2011). Weiskopf and Steyaert (2009) conclude that entrepreneurial practice becomes a subversive form of social creativity that is characterized by movement, life and change so that 'selves' are always unfinished.

## 2.6.2 Bricolage

The term bricolage means making the best use of the resources you have in your possession. According to Baker and Nelson (2005) *bricoleurs* use resources in ways for which they were not originally intended in a process they describe as 'creative reinvention'. In entrepreneurial terms, bricolage means that individuals use the resources to which they have access in a creative way to uncover and exploit new business opportunities. In attempting to exploit opportunities by adopting a bricolage approach, entrepreneurs can use a combination of five activities:

1 **physical inputs** – making use of unwanted materials;
2 **labour inputs** – encouraging customers or suppliers to work in the business;
3 **skills input** – encouraging the use of amateur or self-taught skills;
4 **customers/markets** – supplying products or services that would otherwise be unavailable;
5 **institutional/regulatory environment** – not seeing rules and regulations as constraining.

(Fisher 2012)

The ideas underpinning bricolage are linked to the work of Penrose (1959) who suggested that resource environments are idiosyncratic to the individual entrepreneur or firm. What this means is that resources, equipment or even skills that are worthless to one entrepreneur can be extremely valuable to someone else.

Baker and Nelson (2005) note that bricolage relies on scavenging resources in order to extract use from goods that others do not value or do not intend to use. Importantly, entrepreneurs who target this activity at a particular problem (selective bricolage) are more likely to be successful. While bricolage provides a way of recombining and reconfiguring resources, the solution has to be embedded into the firm's existing routines if it is to provide long-term rents. Baker and Nelson (2005) contrast this with 'parallel bricoleurs' who move between projects responding to customer expectations and obligations. Notwithstanding the differences between these types of bricolage, they both rely on experimentation or improvisation in order to trial and test solutions; in so doing resource combinations are broken down and/or reconfigured. In that sense, bricolage helps entrepreneurs to explore and exploit new opportunities that might otherwise be too expensive to investigate by more traditional means (Miner *et al.* 2001, Garud and Karnøe 2003, Baker and Nelson 2005, Desa 2012). The process of entrepreneurial bricolage is illustrated in Figure 2.3.

## 2.6.3 Effectuation

Sarasvathy (2001) set out what she describes as an alternative approach to the traditional causal perspective. According to Sarasvathy (2001: 250) all nascent entrepreneurs begin with three categories of 'means': their own traits, tastes and abilities; their particular set of knowledge; and their social networks. Hence,

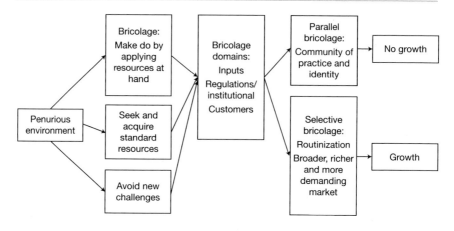

**Figure 2.3**
*Entrepreneurial bricolage*

'effectuation' is 'a tool for problem solving when the future is unpredictable, our goals unspecified or simply unknown, and when the environment is not independent of our decisions' (Sarasvathy 2004: 525). The key point in effectuation theory is that entrepreneurs begin with the means in their possession rather than beginning by establishing a set of end goals. The process is illustrated in Figure 2.4 in which the actual means at the entrepreneur's disposal influence their possible courses of action (that is, the type of business that they can establish). Effectual entrepreneurs engage in activities associated with starting their business and allow longer-term goals to emerge as they exploit the means under their control. The basic premise is that opportunities are *actively created* rather than being identified before the business is started as per the Shane model. Goals evolve over time as the business develops rather than being established at the outset. The factors that underpin effectuation theory are as follows (Fisher 2012: 1024):

- Start with means rather than end goals (bird-in-hand principle).
- Apply affordable loss rather than expected returns (risk little, fail cheap).
- Leverage relationships rather than carrying competitive analysis (crazy quilt principle).
- Entrepreneurs exploit rather than avoid contingencies (lemonade principle).

The theory of effectuation is based on Simon's (1959) decision theory, which indicates that rather than trying to predict future trends in an uncertain environment it is more effective to acquire information through experiential and iterative learning. Sarasvathy (2001) argues that one of the main benefits of an effectuation approach is that entrepreneurs who fail will fail very early and with much lower levels of investment than if they had pursued an opportunity based on the causal

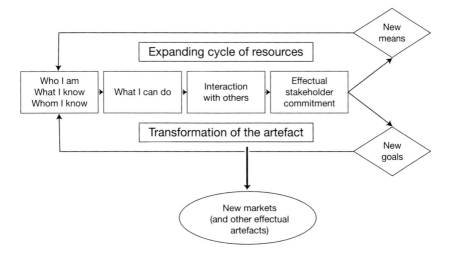

**Figure 2.4**
*Effectual entrepreneurship*

approach (Read *et al.* 2011, Perry *et al.* 2012, Sarasvathy 2012). As noted in Section 2.5, there are very strong similarities between the effectual and bricolage approaches to starting a business. In Chapter 9, we bring these ideas together to outline our own process of business creation.

## 2.6.4 Summary and example

The idea of opportunity creation fits well with the approach to entrepreneurship and business start-up adopted in this book. Very few new businesses started by young people taking courses in higher education will exploit the kind of market opportunities that are described by writers such as Shane and Ventakaraman. Even if they were able to identify an objective opportunity, the chances of them obtaining the necessary financial resources will be extremely unlikely. Adopting an approach in which young, nascent entrepreneurs make the best of the resources to which they have access means they will have more chance of success and they will be exposed to much less risk of financial loss. An example of how a substantial, fast-growing business can be established using this approach is described in the box below.

There are some important provisos to make about the *Jazooli* case. First of all, Sam and Ben had parents who were willing to support their venture by letting them convert a bedroom and then the family's garage into a store-room for the business. Second, their father, Martin, had a long history of self-employment and it is certainly well established that those who come from such a background are more likely to start their own businesses. Third, Martin supported Sam and Ben

**BOX 2.1**

Sam Wilson began buying and selling mobile phones while still at school and at that stage had no intention of setting-up a business. Gradually, Sam began to increase the amount of money that was generated by his on-line trading and in 2008 *Jazooli* was established as a company by Sam's brother Ben who took a year out before going to university. For the first nine months of operation Ben ran the business from his bedroom in the family home. After completing sixth form in 2010 Sam also joined *Jazooli* on a full-time basis. The business continued to expand and *Jazooli* moved to a large warehouse and now employs seven full-time staff and three part-timers with a turnover of £1.6 million in 2011. Business activities have extended from mobile phones and accessories for tablet computers to include electronic cigarettes.

The *Jazooli* story is a great example of opportunity creation. Rather than starting out with a clearly articulated business idea Sam began by trading mobile phones to supplement his pocket money. When Ben started to work in the business he realized that they could increase their margins by sourcing goods directly from China – instead of buying and selling on *eBay*. Gradually, as business activity increased, Ben, Sam and their father Martin began to adopt a more strategic approach to managing the business.

by providing them with the business experience that he had gained during 20 years of self-employment (see Box 2.1).

## 2.7 SUMMARY AND KEY LEARNING POINTS

The precursor to the setting-up any new business is the would-be entrepreneur's ability to locate an appropriate business opportunity. The debate about whether entrepreneurs identify or create opportunities is one of the most important topics in the study of entrepreneurship. Neo-classical economic theory is based on the concept of market equilibrium, which is maintained by the 'invisible hand' of market forces (Renko *et al.* 2012). While temporary disequilibrium resulting from changes in supply or demand may lead to some entrepreneurial opportunities, in general there is no place for entrepreneurs in neo-classical theory. While Schumpeter's work was located in neo-classical theory, he suggested that major technological change could lead to market disequilibrium and provide significant entrepreneurial opportunities (creative destruction). In recent years, the Austrian school has been influential in defining the nature of entrepreneurial opportunities.

As we discussed above, the work of Shane and Venkataraman is the most important in bringing this view into the mainstream of entrepreneurship research. The Austrian view of markets is that they are in a constant state of disequilibrium and are characterized by dynamic competition. Entrepreneurial opportunities are created as a result of these constant disturbances to the market. The nature of those opportunities is that they have an objective reality, a reality that is distinct from the entrepreneurs who identify them as new business opportunities. Those subscribing to this view are described by Sarasvathy (2001) as the 'causal school'.

The alternative view rejects the idea that profitable opportunities are 'out there' waiting to for entrepreneurs to discover them. Those who focus on the creation of opportunities do not accept that entrepreneurs base new businesses on clear objective opportunities. Sanz-Velasco (2006) suggests that the differences between 'discovery' and 'creation' are reflected in differences between what Sarasvathy (2001) describes as 'causation' and 'effectuation'. The creation perspective proposes that, during the emergence of the firm, entrepreneurs' activities actually create the opportunities that they exploit. As discussed above, such a perspective draws heavily on the ideas of Penrose (1959) and Weick (1995). These theorists see the process of opportunity creation as a 'sensemaking process' in which entrepreneurs slowly develop an image of how they might start a new business. That 'image' influences entrepreneurial behaviours during an iterative process involving the matching of perceived means and perceived ends. Thus, the creation perspective is based on the principle that entrepreneurs make decisions based on their own subjective judgements rather than the evaluation of objective environmental factors (which underpins the causation perspective). The creation perspective is linked to the three more recent process theories of entrepreneurship (discussed in the previous section). Baker and Nelson (2005) use the terms improvisation and bricolage to explain how opportunities are 'created and enacted idiosyncratically' by entrepreneurs making the best of limited resources. Sarasvathy's (2001) effectuation theory provides the intellectual bedrock for what we regard as a more realistic perspective on the entrepreneur–opportunity interface. For most entrepreneurs, the information available when they are considering starting a new venture is both incomplete and overwhelming. As described by Read et al. (2011: 5), data are confusing and conflicting, which means that entrepreneurs generate opportunities from a number of possibilities.

Therefore, the approach adopted in this book fits with the opportunity creation and effectuation/bricolage perspectives. We are certainly willing to acknowledge that on some occasions entrepreneurs do identify objective opportunities and then follow a conventional causal approach to the exploitation of that opportunity. However, such cases will, we suggest, be in a minority, as most young entrepreneurs will adopt a more effectual approach to entrepreneurial development. Key learning points in this chapter are:

- There are substantial differences between the traditional causal approach to understanding entrepreneurship and the bricolage/effectuation perspectives.
- The trait-based approach has largely been superseded by the narrative approach based on the work of Gartner.
- Understanding the difference between opportunity identification and opportunity creation is fundamental to benefiting from this book.
- The work of Edith Penrose (although written more than 50 years ago) is central to understanding the links between the entrepreneur and an opportunity.

## 2.8 DISCUSSION QUESTIONS

- To what extent has the 'trait-based' approach contributed to theories of entrepreneurship?
- What is the significance of Scott Shane's work to our understanding of entrepreneurship?
- What are the most common behaviours associated with an entrepreneur starting their own business?
- Can you briefly outline three process theories of entrepreneurship?
- What are the main principles of effectuation theory?

## 2.9 FURTHER READING

Steyaert, C. (2007) '"Entrepreneuring" as a Conceptual Attractor? A Review of Process Theories in 20 Years of Entrepreneurship Studies', *Entrepreneurship and Regional Development*, 19(6), 453–477.

Read, S., Sarasvathy, S., Nick, D., Wiltbank, R. and Ohisson, A.-V. (2011) *Effectual Entrepreneurship*, London and New York: Routledge.

# Chapter 3

# Learning to be an entrepreneur

## 3.1 INTRODUCTION

Whether or not entrepreneurs are 'born or made', and the extent to which entrepreneurship can be taught, are two of the most persistent questions posed to those engaged in teaching enterprise-related subjects. We acknowledge that some individuals are extremely entrepreneurial from a very young age. Our view is that entrepreneurship comprises a set of skills that can be acquired by any reasonably motivated student. However, a number of authors have tried to establish that there is a genetic component to entrepreneurship (Nicolaou et al. 2008). Shane et al. (2010) examine links between genetics, the big five[1] and the likelihood of becoming self-employed by comparing a large sample of twins (monozygotic and dizygotic). However, the authors admit that they were only able to identify a 'modest association' between two of the big five personality characteristics (extraversion and openness to experience) and the propensity to become an entrepreneur. Rather than relying on an entrepreneurial gene, an alternative explanation is that some families endow their children with attributes such as self-discipline and conscientiousness as well as good habits, including critical self-reflection and awareness of cognitive shortcuts (Aldrich and Yang 2012). Aldrich and Yang (2012) go on to say that such social learning provides continuity in entrepreneurship across generations and is more important than specific entrepreneurial knowledge. We believe that the context and the influence of key individuals including parents are likely to be more important than any genetic predisposition towards entrepreneurship (see Box 3.1).

Simply explaining key theoretical concepts such as opportunity identification or resource acquisition by means of conventional lectures is not an appropriate way to learn about entrepreneurship (Pfeifer and Borozan 2011). Effective entrepreneurship education must include a practical element in which students are able to apply ideas to which they have been introduced via lectures, tutorials or independent study. There are a number of ways in which this can be done that vary from computer simulations such as *SimVenture*, to actually starting a real

---

## BOX 3.1

Sam has probably told you it started off as a bit of hobby – but then it became evident, very early on, that it was something more than a hobby. I think he was about 13 when we discovered what he was up to – it started with second-hand mobile phones that he knew he could buy and sell. It became evident the amount of money he was making was becoming quite significant and I said to him, I think you should make this into a proper business. I like to think I have a bit of an entrepreneurial spirit myself because I have been self-employed for 20 years. So whenever I have seen anything in the boys I have always tried to encourage it, and that happened with Sam. Even when he was at primary school he got into a bit of trouble for selling pens.

[Martin Wilson, *Jazooli*]

---

business in programmes run by organizations such as *Young Enterprise*, as well as extra-curriculum activities including initiatives such SIFE (students in free enterprise) and student societies (Liverpool Enterprise Network Society – LENS). In this chapter, we intend to demonstrate what is known about enterprise education and entrepreneurial learning (Byrne *et al.* 2013). We then examine the implications for students of entrepreneurship in terms of the knowledge they need to acquire as well as their expectations about how such knowledge is acquired. The starting point is based on the view that there are a number of skills or competencies that are associated with effective entrepreneurship. However, the ability to list or recite a set of competencies, no matter how sophisticated, will not in itself turn undergraduate or postgraduate students into successful entrepreneurs. Learning has a strong social element and engaging in activities designed to encourage the sharing of knowledge and understanding is an essential element of the approach advocated in this book. We begin by outlining some of the most recent models of entrepreneurial learning.

## 3.2 LEARNING OBJECTIVES

- To explain why approaches to entrepreneurial learning have changed in the last 15 years.
- To describe the principles of the Kolb learning cycle.
- To explain how social learning and cognitive learning contribute to a better understanding of entrepreneurship.
- To identify the benefits of active learning and simulation in terms of enhancing entrepreneurial learning.

## 3.3 MODELS OF ENTREPRENEURIAL LEARNING

Until quite recently, courses offered by universities that dealt with entrepreneurship or the management of smaller firms were rare in the UK. In the US, the teaching of entrepreneurship has a much longer tradition and the first course was established in 1947 (Katz 2003). In terms of the number of institutions offering courses in entrepreneurship, the field had reached maturity by the beginning of the twenty-first century. This is further demonstrated by convergence in the topics of US textbooks dealing with entrepreneurship and small business management (Katz 2008). US enterprise education has also been strongly promoted by leading institutions such as the Kauffman Foundation (www.kauffman.org) and Babson College (www.babson.edu). Kauffman has an extensive research programme designed to provide an in-depth understanding of what drives innovation and economic growth in entrepreneurship. Babson is also involved in entrepreneurship research via the Global Entrepreneurship Monitor (GEM), the Diana Project and the Trans-generational Entrepreneurship Practices (STEP) project.

From around 2000, interest in entrepreneurship has grown very rapidly and most UK institutions now offer courses that deal with business start-up. Growth in teaching of entrepreneurship can be explained by increasing legitimization of the topic as an area of academic study. Allan Gibb's pioneering work focused on understanding the process of starting a new business (Gibb and Ritchie 1982). The authors begin by rejecting conventional 'trait' theory and, instead, argue that entrepreneurship is a social process that involves a series of transactions as individuals gain experience. Interestingly, the importance of family, friends and career development as well as primary, secondary and further education are noted as being influential (for a detailed summary see Gibb, 2002). This view fits very closely with the importance of the entrepreneurial 'life-course', which is discussed in Chapter 6. In his 1996 paper, Gibb examines the role of Business Schools in providing education for entrepreneurs and owners of small businesses (Gibb 1996). Gibb stressed the importance of entrepreneurship for creating new jobs and enhancing economic growth. In terms of entrepreneurial learning, Gibb focuses on the importance of an 'action learning' approach that actively engages students. Action learning is usually conducted by small groups in which participants share their experiences to solve work-related problems. Members of action learning sets are encouraged to challenge the assumptions that limit performance at the individual, group and organizational levels (see Kolb 1984, Revans 1980, Raelin 2007, Rae 2012). An extensive review of the literature considers UK and European responses to the challenge of enterprise education (Gibb 2002). Most recently, Gibb (2011) examines a programme designed to develop the skills of enterprise educators via the International Entrepreneurship Educators Programme (IEEP). A persistent theme in the literature is the central importance of entrepreneurs acquiring and developing the skills, heuristics and frameworks necessary to meet

**33**

the changing demands of a growing business (Breslin and Jones 2012; also see Chapters 4 and 10).

The importance of understanding the context in which entrepreneurial learning takes place has also been stressed by other key authors (Cope and Watts 2000, Rae and Carswell 2001, Cope 2005). As indicated in Chapter 1, Kolb's ideas about experiential learning have been very influential in the field of entrepreneurship (Figure 3.1). In developing the learning cycle, Kolb[2] drew extensively on the work of Dewey (1938), Lewin (1951) and Piaget (1951). The experiential learning cycle is based on the principle that knowledge is created by a combination of two dialectical processes: making sense of experience (prehension) and applying that experience (transformation). The prehension dimension varies from abstract conceptualization (comprehension) to concrete experience (apprehension). The transformative dimension varies from active experimentation (extension) to reflective observation (intention). These four basic learning modes can be summarized as follows:

- **Abstract conceptualization** – focuses on the 'scientific' ability to use logic, ideas and concepts as a way of understanding particular physical or social phenomena.
- **Concrete experience** – emphasizes an artistic and intuitive approach (rather than a science-based approach) based on dealing with real situations in an intuitive manner.
- **Active experimentation** – focuses on directly influencing other people as a way of changing particular situations through a process of doing rather than observing.
- **Reflective observation** – focuses on understanding ideas and situations through a process of careful observation (rather than a focus on taking action).

Combining the two dimensions (Figure 3.1) illustrates four distinct and elementary forms of knowledge (Kolb 1984). The essential idea underpinning the learning cycle is that knowledge creation and knowing requires the transformation of experience and the ability to be able to make sense of experience (prehension):

- **Convergent knowledge** is created by the combination of comprehension (abstract conceptualization) and transformation through extension (active experimentation).
- **Accommodative knowledge** is created by the combination of apprehension (concrete experience) and transformed by extension (active experimentation).
- **Divergent knowledge** is created through apprehension (concrete experience) and transformed by intention (reflective observation).
- **Assimilative knowledge** is created through comprehension (abstract conceptualization) and transformed by intention (reflective observation).

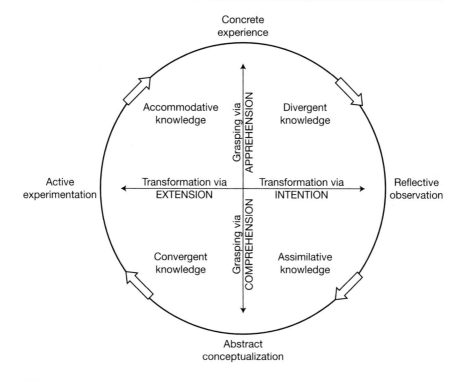

**Figure 3.1**
*Kolb's learning cycle*

Kolb's model has been used as the basis of a 'learning style inventory' (Honey and Mumford 2001), which classifies learners into four types: activist, theorist, pragmatist and reflector. This is certainly a useful device for encouraging students to think about the way in which they learn. For example, 'theorists' learn best from the presentation of abstract ideas about entrepreneurship such as differences between opportunity identification and opportunity creation (Shane and Venkataraman 2000). Alternatively, 'activists' learn best by actually trying out new things rather than listening to lectures dealing with various aspects of 'entrepreneurial theory'. Pragmatists are more concerned with trying things that actually work while reflectors learn best from observation.

The various learning style inventories based on Kolb's cycle have been criticized by a wide range of writers (see Manolis *et al.* 2013). For example, test–retest experiments indicate that the scales do not reliably measure learning styles. Manolis *et al.* (2013) developed what is described as a reduced learning style inventory (RLSI), which they suggest is superior to earlier measurement instruments. The authors argue that their instrument provides a more holistic measure of student learning styles. We suggest, however, that the benefit of such learning style

**35**

inventories is not based on the extent to which they objectively measure an individual's particular approach to learning. Rather, learning style inventories can be used to encourage students to reflect on their responses to the various forms of pedagogy used in the teaching of entrepreneurship. Hence, rather than being a fixed psychological attribute, 'learning style' is something to which students can adjust according to the context and the topic they are studying. As we discuss in the following section, effective entrepreneurial learning has both cognitive and social elements (Cope and Down 2010).

It is argued that Kolb's experiential learning theory (KELT) is based on the principles of cognitivism in which thinking is separated from experience and action. As Holman *et al.* (1997: 139) argue in this model the learner is seen as an 'intellectual Robinson Crusoe'. Drawing on activity theory (Vygotsky 1978, Bakhtin 1981), the authors suggest that learning should be understood in the context of the learner's social relations (see Chapter 1). Learning is a process of 'argumentation' in which activities associated with thinking, reflecting, experiencing and action taking are mediated by the social, cultural and historical context in which the learner is situated (Holman *et al.* 1997). Kayes (2002), in particular, suggests that critics of KELT have not paid enough attention to the influence of Vygotsky's social constructivist learning theory. More recently, Kolb and his colleagues explicitly extend KELT to account for social processes as well as cognitive processes (Baker *et al.* 2005). The authors propose that conversational learning helps learners construct new meaning and transform their collective experiences into knowledge and knowing (Baker *et al.* 2005: 412). While it is suggested that there are five dialectics associated with conversational learning theory, we concentrate on the two dimensions that are the basis of ELT: apprehension–comprehension and reflection–action.

■ *Apprehension and comprehension (concrete experience and abstract conceptualization).* The core dialectic of apprehension and comprehension means that knowledge is based on concrete knowing and abstract knowing (Kolb 1984). There is constant tension between subjective, intuitive and emotional understanding and objective, abstract and rational understanding (this can be summarized as right brain–left brain thinking). In terms of entrepreneurial learning, this dialectic can be represented by, on the one hand, encouraging students to explore their previous experiences of entrepreneurship (perhaps through TV programmes such as *Dragons' Den*) and consider how that experience has influenced their perceptions of what it is to be an 'entrepreneur'. On the other hand, students can be presented with data related to numbers of start-ups per year, the proportion that obtain external finance as well as conceptual ideas such as resource-dependency theory or resource-deficiency theory. Promoting class conversations based on resolving the tension between students' feelings about entrepreneurship and more abstract theories/data related to entrepreneurial activity promotes much deeper learning.

■ *Extension and intention (reflective observation and active experimentation).* The second dialectic of extension and intention means that there is a tension between the application of new knowledge (action) and a sense-making or meaning-making process (reflection). Experiential learning approaches must create conversational space to help learners resolve the tension between action and reflection. In terms of entrepreneurial learning resolving this dialectic means students must engage in active experimentation by, for example, generating ideas for a potential new business. This should be combined with group (not individual) reflections on their experiences related to idea generation and encouragment to engage in conversations about the implications for their own understanding of what it means to be a nascent entrepreneur engaged in creating a new business.

This broader understanding of the experiential learning cycle is described as follows by Taylor and Pandza (2003). The four elements of the model (theorizing, action, experience and reflection) all take place within a social context. Therefore, it is essential that entrepreneurship courses provide plenty of opportunities for students to share their knowledge and understanding. Conventional activities such as preparing a business plan or participating in a simulation game (such as *SimVenture*) can easily be organized to accommodate social learning activities. Consequently, as we illustrate in Figure 3.2, the focus shifts from a concentration on cognitive learning (as described in the traditional Kolb cycle) to social learning as group activities encourage discussion and reflection as students move through the four stages of the model.

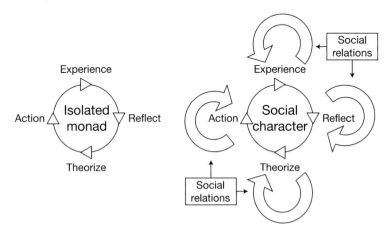

**Figure 3.2**
*Extending Kolb's experiential learning cycle*

Cope's (2003) influential work draws heavily on heavily on KELT to stress the importance of basing entrepreneurial learning on an action-oriented process of co-participation (Politis 2005, Pittaway and Cope 2007). According to Cope (2005) there are five key areas that should be of concern in terms of entrepreneurial learning (Table 3.1). We have structured these five factors in a hierarchy because we believe that any well-planned course should provide students with the opportunity to learn about themselves and the extent to which they have the attributes (persistence and resilience) to become entrepreneurs. Second, (see Chapter 4) we see the acquisition of appropriate social skills as crucial to effective entrepreneurship. Therefore, the opportunity to learn about the nature and management of relationships is central to establishing businesses with real potential for growth. Learning about (the) business and learning about the environment and entrepreneurial networks are equally important to students of entrepreneurship. Finally, learning about small business is less important during the nascent entrepreneurship stage. Clearly, as the business becomes established, acquiring broader managerial skills such as human resource management or leadership will contribute to the longer-term success of the firm (Chapters 4 and 10).

In terms of 'learning in practice', Cope and Down (2010) attempt to 'accommodate' the cognitive and social learning approaches to entrepreneurship education. They build on the work of Marshall (2008: 419) who suggests that the cognitive and practice perspectives are complementary because they provide a deeper understanding of 'how unfolding social realities are constituted and enacted'. Cope and Down (2010) also draw on Burgoyne's (1995) attempt to reconcile the cognitive and social perspectives on learning (Figure 3.3). The model illustrates the fact that nascent entrepreneurs do not make decisions or undertake tasks related to starting their businesses in isolation from other social factors. Participation refers to the active encounters that are the basis of effective entrepreneurial learning. Such encounters can be formal elements of a module in

**Table 3.1** Entrepreneurial learning tasks

| Learning tasks | Associated activities |
| --- | --- |
| Learning about oneself | Evaluating strengths and weaknesses in terms of aptitude for entrepreneurship |
| Learning to manage relationships | Developing appropriate social skills to build relationships with resource-providers |
| Learning about the business | Improving understanding of how the business works – making a profit |
| Learning about the environment and networks | Building relationships with stakeholders, customers, suppliers and competitors |
| Learning about business management | Acquiring the skills and knowledge necessary to grow the business |

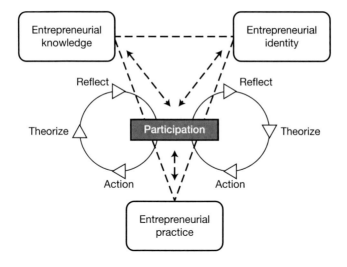

**Figure 3.3**
*Combining entrepreneurial cognition and practice*

which students are expected to engage in group-work: for example, brainstorming business ideas or preparing a business plan. Encounters can also be informal based on students' conversations outside the classroom (perhaps using social media) or their engagement with entrepreneurs, owner-managers or employees of smaller firms (this could occur as students engage in part-time work in a bar or restaurant). This idea of 'conversations' informing various activities associated with the learning cycle fits with the approach proposed by Baker *et al.* (2005).

Entrepreneurial knowledge is obviously a key issue for most undergraduates and postgraduates who are unlikely to have had direct exposure to the issues associated with small businesses. For such students, their understanding of entrepreneurship will be informed by the media via programmes such as *Dragons' Den* or through new-style entrepreneurs such as hip-hop star Jay-Z who made the transition from drug dealer to high-profile businessman (Greenburg 2011). Alternatively, it is well established that those who come from entrepreneurial families will generally have been exposed to the day-to-day problems of managing a small business (Zellweger *et al.* 2012). Consequently, this group may have a much clearer understanding of what it takes to become an entrepreneur. As we indicated above, encouraging conversations among students about their different understanding of what it means to be an entrepreneur can be an enriching experience.

Identity refers to the extent to which the 'self' is recognized in the entrepreneurial process (Burke 2006). As pointed out by Down and Warren (2008) entrepreneurial identity is shaped as a result of interaction between the individual, the venture and broader cultural influences. From a pedagogical perspective, entrepreneurial identity focuses attention on the way in which belonging to a community of practice provides opportunities for students to learn how to be an entrepreneur. For many, this will be a discomfiting experience in which they must make the switch from the 'passivity' of being a student to the action associated with being an entrepreneur.

Entrepreneurial practice is not simply about doing things (capabilities); it also concerns learning the appropriate social skills such as negotiation with suppliers, customers, funders and other stakeholders. Rae (2004) suggests that immersion in practice enables entrepreneurs to develop a theory of what works that can be described as know-how, know-what and know-who (Dohse and Walter 2012). In a study of fast-growing businesses set-up by young entrepreneurs, Hickie (2011) notes that 11 of the 15 participants in his study had developed informal ventures while still at school. This might be something that is difficult to replicate in the classroom with students who have had little practical exposure to entrepreneurship. However, some practices can be replicated by encouraging students to engage in meaningful tasks such as writing and presenting a business plan or setting-up a business. What is crucial about such activities is that the participants must be encouraged to reflect on the whole experience to help them link practice, learning and identity through participation in a community of practice.

The work of French social theorist Pierre Bourdieu is the basis of a recent attempt to locate entrepreneurial learning within the context of a multi-layered relational framework. Karatas-Ozkan and Chell (2010) distinguish between the micro, the meso and the macro levels based on a detailed, longitudinal study of two start-up businesses. The value of this approach is that the orientations and dispositions of individuals (micro) are located within the context of their relationships and social networks (meso) and the broader institutional context, which includes regulatory factors as well as market and sectoral influences. For example, although recent graduates in the UK, France, China and India face similar difficulties in starting new businesses (lack of resources/experience) they will also be faced with societies in which the support and approval for entrepreneurial activity will be very different. In Chapter 11, we discuss the GEM studies that distinguish between three stages of economic development (factor-driven, efficiency-driven and innovation-driven). Similarly, those starting businesses that require limited amounts of experience or specialized knowledge face very different problems from those of a young scientist or engineer attempting to establish a technology-based business. These ideas are summarized in Figure 3.4, in which the three levels of entrepreneurial learning are identified. Cognitive learning is a central element of business education whether at the undergraduate or postgraduate levels. An individual's 'absorptive capacity' will influence their ability to learn and apply new ideas and new ways of thinking. At the same time, it is central to the perspective adopted in this book that learning has a strong social element. In the classroom, this means that group exercises such analysing case studies or

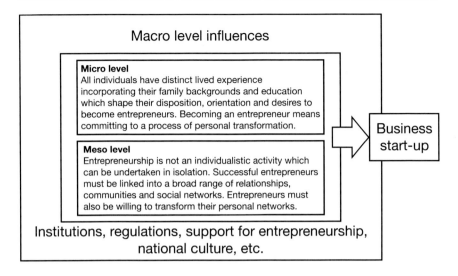

**Figure 3.4**
*Entrepreneurial learning model*

undertaking business planning exercises are an extremely powerful form of learning. Outside the classroom, this means learning from our experiences as consumers (spotting potential gaps in the marketplace) as well as learning vicariously from more experienced entrepreneurs. Equally, the influence of the context in which individuals are considering starting their business will have consequences for the success or failure of those businesses. For example, there are likely to be far more business opportunities in rapidly growing economies, such as China, Brazil or India, than there are in developed economies, such as France or the UK, which are experiencing very low-levels of growth (see Chapter 11).

## 3.4 UNIVERSITIES AND GRADUATE INCUBATION

In the early years of the twenty-first century a number of UK reports stressed the importance of universities making a bigger contribution to economic growth (DTI 1998, DTI 2000, DfES 2003, Lambert 2003, HMT *et al.* 2004). Incorporation of the 'third mission' (Clark 1998, Van Vught 1999, Lambert 2003) in which universities are an integral part of regional economic development has formalized a process that has been occurring for some time in the US (Etzkowitz 1998, Henry 1998). In addition, changes to UK government funding regimes promoted 'the third mission' to the very top of the agenda for vice chancellors (Woollard *et al.* 2007). For example, involvement with the New Entrepreneur Scholarship (NES) enabled a number of universities to develop innovative programmes designed to support individuals from disadvantaged backgrounds start their own businesses (Jayawarna *et al.* 2011).

Etzkowitz (2003) uses the term 'entrepreneurial university' to describe those institutions committed to regional economic development. It has been adopted by academics and policy makers to describe universities that effectively deliver on their 'third mission'. As such, developing a more entrepreneurial culture can be regarded as the essential mechanism through which universities become effectively involved in economic development (Fairweather 1990, Liu and Dubinsky 2000, Hagen 2002). Etzkowitz and Leydesdorff (2000) describe the evolution of tripartite relationships between university, industry and government through the Triple Helix III model, which, they claim, most countries are trying to achieve. Other work on university–industry links emphasizes the role of higher education institutes in regional systems of innovation as the primary driver of economic development (Bercovitz and Feldman 2006). There is a large degree of agreement with the view that active relationships within the triple helix system help to develop an entrepreneurial culture within universities (Etzkowitz et al. 2000). Increased understanding of the role that universities play in economic development provides a useful framework to assist managers and administrators create strategies for their institutions to become more entrepreneurial (Woollard et al. 2007).

In addition to the 'third mission' and engagement with business, an increasingly important element of any enterprising university is a strong commitment to enterprise education (Pittaway and Cope 2007) and the support of graduate entrepreneurship through the provision of incubation facilities (McAdam and Marlow 2008). The UK government, like most other developed and developing countries, has encouraged the creation of business incubation to enhance technology transfer from universities as a way of improving economic performance (Cooper and Park 2008, McAdam et al. 2009). US universities have also been heavily involved in the development of business incubators. Such incubators enable universities to engage in technology transfer as well as providing support for nascent entrepreneurs (Rothaermel and Thursby 2005, Qian et al. 2011). This emphasis on incubation has also coincided with an increase in university courses designed to promote entrepreneurship to undergraduate and postgraduate students (Herrmann et al. 2008). Pittaway and Cope (2007), based on their systematic review of the literature, suggest there are areas where there is a critical mass of knowledge related to enterprise education. These areas include, 'student propensity, pedagogy, management education development and work on the enterprising university' (Pittaway and Cope 2007: 498). The authors also suggest that there are significant gaps in the knowledge base including a lack of studies that provide a better understanding of the impact of enterprise education on the 'performance' of those who chose to pursue entrepreneurial careers.

Enterprise education is aimed a 'achieving a learning culture' that will equip greater numbers of students to engage in business start-up activities (Kothari and Handscombe 2007). This commitment to enterprise education is based on the idea that entrepreneurship can make a real economic difference by creating new firms and new jobs as well as innovating new products and services. The authors describe the role of Sheffield's White Rose Centre for Enterprise (WRCE) in embedding enterprise skills within the University's curriculum. Science Enterprise Challenge (SEC) helped promote the importance of links between universities, enterprise education and business (Handscombe 2003). SEC has now been reinvented as 'Enterprise Education UK' and continues to promote the benefits of student entrepreneurship. Champions of academic enterprise suggest that student education needs to shift away from a traditional learning mode of study to an approach that immerses students in enterprise activities (Gibb 2011). For example, Lourenço and Jones (2006) describe the importance of adopting an approach to enterprise education that uses more active learning techniques such as roleplay, fieldtrips and scenario planning alongside conventional classroom pedagogy.

Enterprise education is only effective if it encourages some members of the student population seriously to consider starting their own businesses. Many universities now offer incubation or 'hatchery' facilities to help students make the transition into entrepreneurship. Recent graduates engaged in business start-up have a number of significant disadvantages including, of course, the likelihood that they will have substantial debts accumulated during their studies. Most are unlikely to have real business experience and they will have limited networks and lack credibility with resource-providers. Incubation can help overcome such liabilities in a number of different ways. For example, being based in a university incubator is consistent with the idea that entrepreneurial learning is experiential in nature. Incubation provides an ideal opportunity for learning-by-doing as well as social learning through engaging with others who are involved in the start-up process (see Box 3.2). Becoming part of a 'community of practice' (Lave and Wenger 1991) helps nascent entrepreneurs acquire knowledge and engage in active learning. In addition, incubation provides access to key knowledge brokers such as the incubation manager who can link young and inexperienced entrepreneurs to those with greater experience as well as potential resource-providers in the form of larger companies, business angels and, eventually, venture capitalists.

In a study of university technology business incubators, Patton and Marlow (2011) argue that to gain real benefit entrepreneurs have to actively engage with support offered by incubation managers. Equally, managers have to work hard to ensure that incubators provide an integrated service to those engaged in business start-up. Battisti and McAdam (2012) examine how graduate entrepreneurs develop their social capital while based in university science incubators. They found that family and friends were the most important resource-providers for graduates at the start-up stage. More surprisingly, these close ties still dominated after more than two years of incubation. This suggests that the incubator managers provide a limited brokerage role in helping inexperienced entrepreneurs link into broader networks.

**43**

**BOX 3.2**

There are a few other businesses at *Innospace* similar to mine and I got to be good friends with another guy and we chat every day at lunch about different things and ideas and bounce things off each other all the time. I do the same with Richard even now; do you know Richard from *Make your Move*? Well I helped him develop his site and he had been working with BT and I helped him sort that out. So I have worked with both of those people kind of on and off. For example, say I was stuck on something or needed advice on the best way of doing something then he could ask me or I could ask him and we could talk about the pros and cons of each idea. I mean none of us minded disclosing any information about our clients because we knew we got on well and I didn't even feel I was in competition with any of them. I think there are like four web design companies who came in and although you should probably see them as competition, I didn't.

[Phil Jones, *Innospace*]

## 3.5 ROLE OF ACTIVE LEARNING AND SIMULATION

As indicated above, there has been a shift away from simple models of the individualistic entrepreneur who is blessed with specific traits (risk-taking, internal locus of control, need for autonomy) that differentiate them from other members of the population. A broader understanding of entrepreneurship has prompted more sophisticated approaches to teaching and learning. The socially situated view of learning increasingly influences the way in which teaching is actually delivered in the classroom. Entrepreneurship education was originally based on the transfer of knowledge and information, which followed the 'traditional' university pedagogy (Harris *et al.* 2000). In this approach, students were perceived to be passive receivers of wisdom from their lecturers and professors. Allan Gibb was an early advocate of a 'mixed' approach to learning that focused on developing enterprising behaviours, skills and attributes (creativity, self-confidence, motivation; Gibb 1987). Such an approach to entrepreneurship education adopts a 'transformative methodology', which means that learners are engaged in constructing and owning their own learning (Sterling 2001). In contrast to lecture-based courses in which knowledge is passed to passive learners, enterprising approaches emphasize the use of experiential and action learning through which knowledge is constructed by learners in the process of 'doing' (Lourenço and Jones 2006).

There are a number of ways in which more enterprising approaches can encourage active learning among students. Probably the most widely used approach is to invite experienced entrepreneurs as guest speakers to inspire students to start their own businesses. Preparation of business plans (either individually or in groups) is also widely used to promote more active learning as students are required to obtain and analyse information related to the market, consumers and competitors. Business simulation games have been adopted as 'tasters' for potential students or to embed elements of a particular module/course. *SimVenture* is an increasingly sophisticated game that enables students to obtain a better understanding of the complexity associated with starting and running a business. The authors have used *SimVenture* as an integral element of the learning process on undergraduate courses for more than seven years. Currently, *SimVenture* is used on an M.Sc. module known as Entrepreneurial Decision Making (a core module on an M.Sc. Entrepreneurship at the University of Liverpool Management School). The module is based on a mixed approach (as described above) as it includes traditional lectures, group-work, case studies and a number of core sessions in which students use *SimVenture*. The module includes three sessions each of three hours in which students work together in teams of three or four. The objective is to provide them with insight into the complexity of decision-making during the start-up process (see Box 3.3).

Evidence from the literature confirms the effectiveness of business games simulation and indicates that students gain real benefits in many aspects of entrepreneurial decision-making, including finance and business planning (Gabrielsson *et al.* 2010, Huebscher and Lendner 2010). Giving students opportunities to engage in entrepreneurial activities via business simulation fits with a 'constructivist'

## BOX 3.3

In *SimVenture* (www.simventure.co.uk) players take on the role of entrepreneur in managing time and money to develop the business and resolve the issues that arise over the course of a game. The player makes decisions and receives feedback in monthly cycles. Any number of decisions can be made each month in four key business areas: organization; sales and marketing; finance; and operations. Based on these decisions the simulation responds each month and shows the number of enquiries, orders and sales generated – which determines the flow of money into the business.

*SimVenture* is designed to respond to best practice principles. Players who research markets, competitors and customers carefully and then analyse the data and take appropriate actions will always do better than those who use guesswork to drive decisions. The virtual company is managed on a month by month basis allowing learners to develop their business from start-up for a maximum of 36 months.

---

## BOX 3.4

The most positive thing I gained from *SimVenture* is that is gives you a 360 degree view of the business. There are practical things in business which you don't read in theory – for instance, data problems, getting payments from customers and getting a reminder letter about a legal case. Things like getting a different supplier and how to deal with problems as they happen. These are very practical things that you are not taught about in class. It is a 360 degree process looking at recruitment, what gaps you have in your business – what skills you are looking for. These were the most positive experiences of *SimVenture*.

[Anurag, Liverpool entrepreneurship student, 2012]

---

approach to learning. That is, students are encouraged to create their own understanding of specific situations as a result of combining their own previous knowledge with their experience of engaging with the simulation (see Box 3.4).

During the simulation itself, lecturers/instructors should act as facilitators of students' 'learning-by-doing'. In addition, students should be encouraged to undergo 'double-loop' learning as they acquire new knowledge and understanding as well as new skills, such as decision-making. Argyris (1992) distinguishes between single-loop learning in which a fault is corrected to align performance to expected outcomes and double-loop learning in which an individual (or organization) examines the 'governing variables' which influence a particular activity and, therefore, attempts to deal with the problem at a deeper level. For example, rather than thinking about how to improve an existing service (single-loop learning), the entrepreneur could consider whether it was really necessary to offer that service (double-loop learning). Based on a sample of more than 2,000 students, Huebscher and Lendner (2010) conclude that business simulation promotes real learning and complex entrepreneurial thinking. Students in the sample indicated that they obtained real benefits in terms of developing a better understanding of entrepreneurial thinking/action, strategy, marketing, problem-solving and team-work. The authors also indicate that simulation games are useful for sensitizing non-business students to the nature of entrepreneurial action. Our own experience of using *SimVenture* is that simulation games are best used as part of a blended learning programme, which certainly should include some time in which students are encouraged to reflect on what they have learned from the simulation. The importance of combining experiential learning and reflection is confirmed by Ahn (2008) who conducted a study based on three groups of students who played the game individually:

- **RO** – reflective observation group (after playing the game students were asked to reflect on their decision-making).
- **RO+AC** – reflective observation and abstract conceptualization (these students were asked to list the concepts/theories which related to their decision-making before they reflected on their decision-making).
- **CG** – control group (were asked to evaluate performance of the company – without reflection).

The RO+AC group rated the 'educational efficacy' much higher than the RO group and the CG group scored lower than either of the other two groups. The RO+AC group also had higher levels of 'fun and excitement' while playing the game and found it technically much easier than the other two groups. According to Ahn (2008) these results confirm the value of actively engaging students in Kolb's experiential learning cycle. The results substantiate our own experiences of combining *SimVenture* with conventional lectures for introducing appropriate concepts and theories as well as periods of guided reflection in which students are actively encouraged to link theory and practice. In addition, learning is enhanced when the simulation game is played by small groups (three or four) of students rather than individually. They should then be encouraged to discuss and reflect on their decisions as the game progresses.

## 3.6 CLUBS AND SOCIETIES

In addition to courses related to entrepreneurship and the management of small firms, many universities encourage students to join enterprise societies and participate in initiatives such as Students in Free Enterprise (SIFE[3]), European Federation of Junior Entrepreneurs (JADE), Young Enterprise or IBM Challenge. According to Pittaway *et al.* (2011), the number of entrepreneurship clubs and societies is used to assess the quality of educational programmes in US universities. Many enterprise educators also see clubs and societies as a way of encouraging informal learning that adds value to conventional pedagogy in the classroom. In the UK, clubs and societies are generally managed by students themselves and are usually affiliated with Student Unions. Clubs can be important for introducing students to the idea of entrepreneurship via activities such as: the chance to meet successful entrepreneurs; networking events to engage with the local business community; and participating in seminars and competitions. Some institutions offer students the opportunity to participate in investment funds or investment clubs, which involve the buying of stocks and shares or the chance to invest in start-up companies (Pittaway *et al.* 2011: 40) – see Box 3.5.

Pittaway *et al.* (2011) carried out a study in the UK to evaluate the effectiveness of clubs and societies in enhancing entrepreneurial learning. The authors conclude that clubs and societies are an important component in encouraging students to

**BOX 3.5**

At the University of Liverpool Management School, students participating in a second year entrepreneurship module have to engage in a business start-up as well as conventional lectures. *Young Enterprise* provide the expertise to help 20 groups of 10 students identify a business idea and set up a company to exploit that idea during one semester (12 weeks). In 2012 the winning group went on to participate in an event organized by *Young Enterprise* and supported by *Santander*. This group, with their business idea 'The Unofficial Student Survival Guide', won the Merseyside Overall Start Up Company of the Year 2012.

engage with entrepreneurial learning. Such learning tends to be experiential and social as students engage with practical activities and share their understanding with more experienced entrepreneurs. Participants in the study had a range of motivations for engaging in clubs and societies and these included: help starting their own business, developing transferrable skills, gaining practical experience and, more surprisingly, enhancing their curriculum vitae to improve employment prospects (Pittaway *et al.* 2011: 52). This may be because many students see entrepreneurship as something to consider in the future when they have gained real-life business experience. However, students identified real benefits from engaging in clubs and societies: gaining experience and learning-by-doing were regarded as more useful than classroom-based teaching. Second, the opportunity to engage informally with other students and practitioners can create a genuine 'community of practice' in which knowledge and understanding are enhanced for all participants (see Box 3.6).

Clubs and societies are an extremely important aspect of enhancing students' experience of studying entrepreneurship as part of a formal university course. In particular, such activities provide students with opportunities to engage in concrete

**BOX 3.6**

SIFE at the University of Liverpool engages in a number of activities that help students develop their entrepreneurial and organizational skills and knowledge. For example, one project involved supporting Abokali Sumi, an ex-MBA student at the University of Liverpool, to establish a social enterprise to enable small fruit and vegetable producers in Nagaland access customers in the major Indian cities.

experience and active experimentation that not only enhances learning through abstract conceptualization (classroom-based learning), but also encourages much deeper reflective learning. Hence, students have the opportunity to combine Kolb's (1984) two dialectical processes: making sense of experience (prehension) and applying that experience (transformation) (see Section 3.3).

## 3.7 SUMMARY AND KEY LEARNING POINTS

The sub-title of this book, *Creating dynamic entrepreneurial learning capabilities*, indicates that we see entrepreneurial learning as something that is cumulative. This means that learning in the classroom must be combined with learning from experience for those who want to make a success of their entrepreneurial careers. We have demonstrated how the understanding of learning has evolved over the last 30 years to the extent that there is now a much more sophisticated understanding of how entrepreneurs acquire the appropriate skills and knowledge. We have also stressed the central importance of experiential learning to improve the skills associated with entrepreneurship. As we have discussed in this chapter, there are a number of ways in which the experience of being an entrepreneur can be partially replicated in the classroom: inspirational talks by successful entrepreneurs; business start-up activities incorporated into courses/modules (see Box 3.5); using simulation games such as *SimVenture*; as well as actively engaging in clubs and societies such as Liverpool Enterprise Network Society (LENS) or SIFE. However, we believe that there is no substitute for engaging in real-life entrepreneurial activity as described in Box 3.7. From the above discussion the key learning points are:

■   Kolb's experiential learning cycle is the basic tool for understanding the principles of real entrepreneurial learning.

## BOX 3.7

It all began when I was about 13 years old and I started selling mobile phones on eBay for about £10. That's where it began because you can see the money you are making and you think, 'I can do this, it's easy.' So I started buying and selling grander things, anything I knew I could sell on eBay and it just started from that really. It developed further when I started looking on eBay for good deals and eventually you start thinking, there have to be suppliers somewhere and that is how it led on really – just doing a little bit and then taking a big step in buying.

[Sam Wilson, *Jazooli*]

- In recent years entrepreneurial learning has evolved so that most effective approaches combine cognitive, behavioural and social learning.
- University incubators provide an ideal environment in which to create communities of practice for those nascent entrepreneurs actively engaging in the process of new business creation.
- Simulation is an important pedagogical tool that helps inexperienced students gain experience of the decision-making activities associated with new business creation.
- Those students who are committed to a career in entrepreneurship should use a wide-range of learning opportunities, including engaging in clubs and societies as well as their work experience.

## 3.8 DISCUSSION QUESTIONS

- What are the main weaknesses associated with the cognitive approach to learning?
- How does conversational theory extend the ideas associated with Kolb's learning cycle?
- How does Bourdieu's work contribute to the understanding of entrepreneurial learning?
- What are the links between an 'entrepreneurial university' and enterprise education?
- Why are business simulation games important in developing real entrepreneurial learning?

# Chapter 4

# Knowledge, skills and capabilities

## 4.1 INTRODUCTION

Being successful in occupations requires certain knowledge, skills and capabilities, some of which we acquire as we engage in work. Starting a new venture is no different. In this chapter, we examine the knowledge, skills and capabilities that might make it more likely such a venture will succeed and grow. Some scholars suggest that there are key functional and analytical skills all entrepreneurs should have at the outset, such as those necessary to balance a budget, read a balance sheet and cope with legal requirements. There may also be key technical knowledge and the skills necessary to deliver the product and/or service produced by the firm. Some consider expertise in such key knowledge domains to be essential for ventures to function efficiently and effectively.

In addition, the key skills necessary to start a business and to manage a growing one are not necessarily the same, since managing as a sole trader is very different from managing and leading staff, as well as brokering new business. In this regard, often overlooked by entrepreneurs and researchers are the 'soft' and social skills necessary to engage with employees, customers, potential investors and suppliers. These are necessary to support creativity in developing and generating business ideas, but also to reach out beyond the firm to the wider network where many resources necessary to continue the development of the venture reside. It is important to be able to set up a production line, or customer service protocols, to manage quality and to lead teams and delegate work. However, engaging with staff and others outside of the business requires 'impression management' and communication skills that may be necessary to broker and maintain the relationships to acquire additional resources and support from external customers, suppliers and investors.

This chapter proceeds by considering skills necessary at start-up. Attention then turns to the types of knowledge, skills and capabilities identified by research necessary to develop and resource the business as it grows, and how an entrepreneur might acquire them. Finally, we consider the role of cultural entrepreneurship and the skills necessary to engage others in the development of the venture.

## 4.2 LEARNING OBJECTIVES

- ■ To describe the role of knowledge, skills and capabilities as essential resources applied to create a new venture.
- ■ To analyse the relevance of particular functional, technical, personal skills and knowledge necessary to create a new venture.
- ■ To explain how the entrepreneur must change and learn as the venture grows.
- ■ To evaluate the role of soft skills in enabling venture creation and growth.

## 4.3 SKILLS AND KNOWLEDGE: RESOURCES AT START-UP

At the beginning of a new venture, as discussed in Chapter 6, every potential entrepreneur will bring with them a set of skills gained over their life course through education, work experience, or even from managing a venture previously (Jones and Jayawarna 2011). A lone entrepreneur will have a limited set of skills, while a management team may bring a wider variety of capabilities and experience. Depending on the sector, ambition of the entrepreneur and the scope of the firm, potentially at least, the necessary skills will vary. It is important to consider, therefore, what skills are available at the outset and what the nascent entrepreneur might need now, and in the future, and why certain skills are important.

There has been some research to identify exactly what skill sets provide the best opportunities to create a successful firm. Studies generally apply the resource-based view of the firm (Barney 1991), also discussed in Chapter 6, to explain how the entrepreneur's or founding management team's capabilities and human capital have a fundamental influence on the performance of the firm. However, the results are inconclusive and it is advisable to approach this subject with caution. The issues are complex. Studies that have been conducted range across a broad assortment of contexts in terms of sector, geography, economic climate, institutional regulation, gender and so on. Studies also use a variety of measures for success – for example, profit, turnover or number of employees – and are not necessarily comparable.

The inconclusive results may be because of the different measures used and different contexts investigated. It is worth considering also that such measures may not accord with the criteria of success entrepreneurs themselves apply. For some, success is growing a business only to the point where it provides a comfortable living, rather than a larger, perhaps even a publicly listed, company. The ambition or motivation to achieve the latter will require a particular and very different skill set from a lifestyle business. Nevertheless, and despite this range of caveats, it is still important to consider the types of knowledge, skills and capabilities that may be relevant when starting a new venture.

## 4.4 DEVELOPING THE OPPORTUNITY

Schumpeter (1934: 81) suggested that entrepreneurs are rare and he argued that 'the carrying out of new combinations is a special function, and the privilege of a type of people who are less numerous than all those who have the "objective" possibility of doing it'. This means that entrepreneurial skills are perceived to be a unique set of capabilities that allows only some to both identify opportunities and to take advantage of them (Penrose 1959). Some authors argue that opportunity recognition and exploitation are the defining skills necessary to become an entrepreneur (Shane 2000, Venkataraman 2004). By this, they mean the ability to leverage existing knowledge and experience and to apply both to a new setting by identifying a gap in the market. This means that setting up a new venture requires experience of a market, the willingness to make use of that knowledge and the alertness and ability to make use of signals in the market to recognize an opportunity (see Figure 4.1). Opportunity recognition and setting up a new venture, then, require imagination, creative and innovative skills, at the outset.

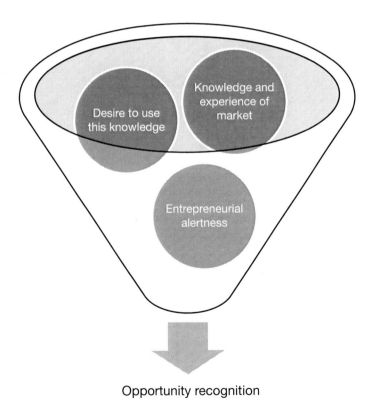

Opportunity recognition

**Figure 4.1**
*Opportunity recognition*

Certainly, if an entrepreneur is going to redefine a market or create a completely new product, then a high level of innovation and creative skills seems to be important. It is hard to imagine how successful ventures that authors use as case studies, and are taught in entrepreneurship schools, and are identified in the business press – such as Google, Apple, Microsoft, Facebook and so on – could have been successful without the self-belief and creativity to deliver innovation. That said, many new ventures are set up not with the intention of re-inventing the marketplace, but with the purpose of leveraging a niche in the market and to create enough returns to meet the needs and aspirations of the nascent entrepreneur. Indeed, many new ventures are not necessarily truly innovative, and they may take an existing idea and refine it and/or deliver a better customer experience. After all, it is difficult to see what is truly innovative about Richard Branson's Virgin Group businesses that he has developed over the years in the music, soft drinks, finance, and travel industries, yet many consider him as a role model for the successful entrepreneur. John Schnatter, who owns Papa John's Pizza with around 3,000 stores worldwide, has made a very successful business, but did his business re-invent the market?

Sarasvathy (2001, 2008) – see Chapter 2 for a fuller discussion – proposes the concept of effectuation as an alternative way of considering how new ventures emerge from contingencies and available resources. In this regard, she uses the concept of effectuation to suggest that entrepreneurs can deploy the means at his or her disposal – available resources, the entrepreneur's personal characteristics and the ability to exploit contingencies – to shape outcomes. While opportunity recognition is about identifying a gap in the current market and creating a new product to fill that gap, effectuation suggests that ventures emerge when potential entrepreneurs develop solutions to problems that then create the potential for new opportunities to develop over time. Sarasvathy thus provides insight into the emergent nature of new ventures by showing how an individual entrepreneur, or team, can take what they know and resources they have available to solve a problem (Read and Sarasvathy, 2005). As they do this, if they limit their exposure to risk and leverage the contingencies available in the environment and through their networks (and perhaps also an unexpected event or good fortune), they eventually form a venture (see Figure 4.2). The difference between the approaches is that an effectual entrepreneur seeks to take their opportunity as an uncertain future unfolds, whereas the opportunity recognition approach suggests entrepreneurs predict what the future will be.

This suggests that rather than innate skills and abilities held only by a few (as proposed by Schumpeter), the principles of effectuation can be taught and applied by anyone who is motivated to start a business. Entrepreneurial expertise is not a set of traits, characteristics or success factors, but a way of problem solving that can be learned (Sarasvathy 2008). An entrepreneur uses the human capital available to them (resilience, prior experience and education) to make sense of problems

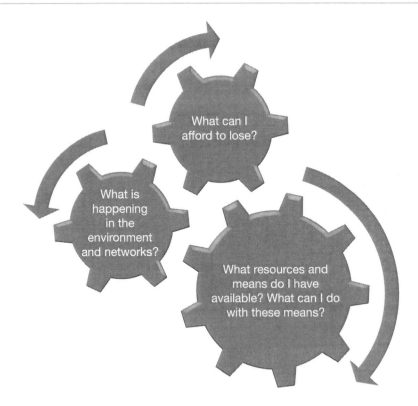

**Figure 4.2**
*Effectuation*

and contingencies. New venture owners thus demonstrate their 'knowledge-in-practice' (Orlikowski 2002) as they solve problems and create their business. In other words, whether one takes a view that entrepreneurs find or create opportunities, having a thorough understanding of their available human capital is an essential consideration when deciding what type of firm to create, or what type of market to enter (see Box 4.1).

## 4.5 MANAGING EARLY STAGE GROWTH: APPLYING KNOWLEDGE, SKILLS AND CAPABILITIES

As the venture grows, the skills and knowledge necessary to manage will change and entrepreneurs must learn to adapt and apply new skills. If this growth is slow, then the development process of the entrepreneur may not be as crucial; however, the faster the growth process, the more challenging it is likely to be to keep pace with the necessary attributes to create and manage a successful firm. In Chapter 10, we examine and critique a range of approaches to understanding growth in

**55**

## BOX 4.1

Two owner-directors of a personal protection equipment manufacturer and supplier (*PPE Co.*) had experience working for BNFL. It was during this time that the technical director realized that the PPE equipment he used performed poorly; it was cumbersome and uncomfortable. Recognizing an opportunity, the technical director set about designing a new protective suit. Working with a variety of materials allowed the technical director (TD) to build experience of material properties. He was able to develop a technical specification (strength, flexibility and performance) and the commercial director (CD) was able to engage a supplier to develop a suitable material. Manufacture of these suits also required a special production process that the technical director developed in-house to ensure bonded seams maintained strength and stretch properties.

> It's a product that we've actually developed and manufactured from scratch for the nuclear industry, because there was nothing in the market place that could fulfil what they wanted. So we found materials and then we couldn't find the equipment and [the technical director] is an instrument technician by trade. So he built the machines. I found the materials and we actually have a production line where it's totally unique.
>
> (CD)

Using business networks, the directors gained access to BNFL and convinced them of their suit's superior performance and won a contract as a supplier. Buoyed by their initial success, the technical director then set about developing other PPE products. Their initial product range included the suits, protective non-slip over boots, chemical absorption pads and booms, and the manufacture of just-in-time bespoke containment tenting. Their products established them as a competent supplier of reliable and practical PPE. It was this reputation and their network of PPE industry contacts that helped them to secure an initial contract as a single-source supplier of PPE to BNFL. They grew from their initial development of the PPE suit to a multi-million dollar business within six years by leveraging their experience and the contacts in their network.

new ventures, and we also discussed the way in which entrepreneurs learn in Chapter 3. In this chapter, however, we will focus specifically on research that examines the knowledge and skills that may be necessary to develop the firm.

## 4.5.1 Generic skills and competencies

Early learning research focused on the person (entrepreneur) and the development of their managerial knowledge (know-how) (Curran 1986, Stanworth and Curran 1991). At this time, research focused on the key entrepreneurial attributes and traits and the managerial skills appropriate for running a successful business. Entrepreneurial capabilities may be rare and inimitable, but research suggests that entrepreneurs cannot accrue profit unless managerial human capital is available to provide specialist functions and processes designed to make the most of opportunities available. Indeed, Penrose (1959) was clear in her analysis of growing firms that this required both the ability to spot opportunities, but also be able to make appropriate use of available resources to exploit such opportunities. Smith and Miner (1983), for example, suggest that managing a growing business is subtly different, and they note important differences between 'entrepreneurial' and 'management' motivation. They define managerial activity as according with the desire or willingness to implement systems of bureaucracy. Based on a comparative sample of 38 entrepreneurs and 294 managers at a variety of levels in corporate organizations, they suggest that the motivation to 'manage' was lower in entrepreneurs. This, they argue, is an advantage when spotting and acting on opportunities, but may become a distinct disadvantage if they do not have the ability to put in place the structures essential to manage a growing business.

Studies have proposed a range of skills needed by new entrepreneurs to set up and run their business. It seems that, these ideas, at least implicitly, are influenced by the idea of a 'recipe' for the management of entrepreneurial firms. The term recipe is most widely known through the work of Spender (1989) who suggested that there are particular 'guides to action' associated with specific industries or sectors. Hence, when considering the development and skills needed by entrepreneurs there is a concern with identifying and applying 'generic' recipes for firms (Sharifi and Zhang 2009). Man et al. (2002), for example, identify six competency areas necessary for managing a growing business from the academic literature.

The concept of 'entrepreneurial competencies' is also used widely by Government Agencies and business support organizations to justify particular programmes and to detail frameworks for economic development of the sector (Mitchelmore and Rowley 2010). Many textbooks also provide an 'identikit' of the model entrepreneur (see for example Stokes and Wilson 2010: 51), drawn together from a range of resources. Guides, such as the Management Charter Initiative standard, were written for entrepreneurial managers and presumed that the skills and knowledge needed to run an entrepreneurial firm were universal (Mangham 1985, Martin and Staines 1994, Sadler-Smith *et al.* 2003). These attributes are also defined in a range of tools and standards to support an entrepreneur's development, such as the enterprise qualification competence framework (SFEDI 2012), and in national vocational qualification standards in the UK (Matlay and Hyland 1997). See Table 4.1 for a generic list of 'entrepreneurial competencies' that are suggested by the literature.

Despite significant efforts to identify lists of appropriate entrepreneurial skills and competencies, evidence for direct links to improved performance has been ambiguous (Storey 2004, Beresford and Saunders 2005). Much of this research has focused specifically on how entrepreneurs develop their management capabilities and the links to success. While there have been studies that identify some links, there have been as many that find none, or where the results are unclear (Jayawarna *et al.* 2007a). Storey (2004), for example, has consistently argued that the link between entrepreneurial learning and performance is tenuous and that policy support for such activity is inappropriate. From the entrepreneur's perspective, while they recognize that business and management skills are important for success they also perceive their own skills as adequate (Carter *et al.* 2004), and often complain that the support systems provided are inappropriate for their needs (Beresford and Saunders 2005).

Despite the lack of clarity in the research, it is probably safe to say that general functional skills and competencies, such as marketing, financial control, sales,

**Table 4.1** *Generic competencies*

| Competency | Behavioural expectation |
|---|---|
| Entrepreneurial | The ability to keep abreast of potential changes in the market in order to recognize and exploit market opportunities |
| Relational | The ability to motivate others, to engage with them to build trust, establish networks and to persuade others to join in the venture. Effective communication, symbolic management and rhetorical abilities |
| Conceptual | The ability to absorb and make sense of complex information and to interpret its meaning, or be innovative in reformulating ideas based on such information |
| Functional | The ability to develop and operate management systems necessary to run the business. This involves controlling and allocating all its resources, human, technological and financial |
| Technical | These are specific key competencies that depend on technical product or service knowledge in order to deliver the primary revenue stream for the business |
| Resourcefulness | The motivation, commitment and resilience to problem solve and to apply creative solutions given limited resources and capacity |

Source: This list is developed from a number of papers and studies described above.

strategic planning, customer relationship management and personnel management might be appropriate in running and developing any firm. Specific technical knowledge of the product or service would also seem sensible in order to understand the firm's potential and new developments within the marketplace. Despite the lack of conclusive evidence of specific competencies that improve performance, it is appropriate to assume that, once a firm is established, entrepreneurs will need to continue the process of competence development. This will be required in both functional and technical skills (either through experience or education) to manage the firm's growth. Despite this general principle, the argument for a 'perfect' set of generic skills is less convincing (see Box 4.2).

## BOX 4.2

The managing director (MD) of BRWL, a machining company, had had an Aerospace manufacturer as its main customer for a number of years. However, the MD detected a shift in that relationship as a result of economic pressures in the industry. Although the MD of BRWL felt he was making savings and improving product quality to meet his customer's requirements, he could not provide evidence to his customer.

> They were looking for good business strategy you know. What are you doing to cut cost? How much scrap do you produce? I knew in my mind that we'd made cost savings but I couldn't produce evidence ... My knowledge of what was going on in the company was all word of mouth you know. I knew we had scrapped a job yesterday but by tomorrow that was all forgotten. ... I knew I wasn't performing well in these audits.

He relied on the informal systems that had been in use since he started the firm. It was clear to the MD that, if he was going to maintain his major customer in the long-term, he would need to provide competitive year-on-year improvements and he would need to develop systems to show what he had achieved. He was fortunate that his customer, concerned by the number of failed supply audits, set up a supplier development programme. This initiative was delivered by a Further Education College in collaboration with the customer. He started to use his training at the College to consider how he might improve his business, and he implemented formal continuous improvement systems and quality audits. These new skills and competencies allowed him to retain the customer. He was also able to show potential new customers his professional approach to quality and cost efficiency, which allowed him to increase his customer base and to grow the business.

## 4.5.2 Exploiting innovation and creativity

There is a tension, potentially at least, between the need to develop skills and capabilities that focus on managing the firm – such as quality control, financial management and personnel management – and the need to develop those that support continued innovation and creativity. The latter is necessary if an entrepreneur is to continue to develop their product portfolio and to respond to market changes.

This tension between exploiting existing knowledge and exploration of new opportunities was first defined by March (1991). Technical knowledge may be required to identify a gap in the market, or to innovate and design specific products, but this advantage would be quickly lost if entrepreneurs cannot provide sufficient capability to lead production and change (Kakati 2003). This means that the development of new processes or products can only create long-term profits if systems and capabilities are shared throughout the organization and institutionalized into new systems and routines (Crossan *et al.* 1999, Jones and Macpherson 2006). For example, as discussed in Chapter 2, Baker and Nelson (2005) note the difference between parallel and selective bricolage (the practice of making do with resources discarded or unused by others) among entrepreneurial firms. In their study, they argue that parallel bricolage is a habituated process of making-do and a *modus operandi* for some entrepreneurs. However, selective bricolage means pursuing particular problems, or opportunities, and ensuring they generate long-run rents by embedding the outcomes in new processes and routines. Jones and Macpherson (2006) argue similarly in their empirical study of three mature firms undergoing periods of renewal. In these firms, they noted that new systems and processes allowed the sharing of knowledge and the delegation of responsibility to enable entrepreneurs to institutionalize innovation. Put simply, while innovative and creative skills are necessary to be able to create opportunities, functional leadership and management capabilities are necessary to be able exploit those opportunities. This exemplifies arguments provided by Penrose (1959) that particular entrepreneurial and management capabilities are required in order to both understand *and* capitalize on potential within the market place.

It seems then that a firm can only grow if entrepreneurs can combine and balance innovation and management skills and capabilities. This has been conceptualized as ambidexterity (Birkinshaw *et al.* 2009), the ability to pursue two paths simultaneously (see Table 4.2). It is a challenging repertoire for large firms let alone for a single individual; it is clear, in any case, that the deployment of innovation requires others in the firms to develop the appropriate skills and competencies to be able to deliver efficient and effective processes. It is perhaps no surprise, therefore, that a study by Freel (2005) identified that the most innovative firms in his study of 1,345 SMEs invested more in developing the skills and capabilities of their staff. In other words, lists of competencies tend to focus

**Table 4.2** *Innovation and management: potential tensions*

| Exploitation focus | Exploration focus |
| --- | --- |
| Selection | Risk-taking |
| Implementation | Innovation |
| Refinement | Creativity |
| Efficiency | Experimenting |
| Control | Flexibility |
| Standardization | Variation |
| Proficiency | Play |
| Productivity | Search |

on the entrepreneur's abilities, but making the most of innovation and creativity requires attention and development of knowledge, skills and capabilities available across the venture. We discuss further the *dynamic capabilities* to be able to develop and renew the operational capacity of the venture in Chapter 9. However, below we also discuss the role of experience, education and training.

### 4.5.3 The role of experience and informal training

Given the unconvincing results regarding links between competence and performance, discussed above, theory and research have continued to develop. Attention has turned from trying to establish causality between education and performance and has begun to focus more on how entrepreneurs actually navigate and cope with the vicissitudes of starting and running a business.

In terms of how entrepreneurial skills might develop, Rae and Carswell (2001) use the life stories of entrepreneurs gathered through in-depth interviews to suggest that, while entrepreneurial activity may be dependent on specific capabilities developed during earlier careers (such as through technical knowledge and functional training), it is also developed through successful and failed activities and through interaction with others. These experiences are combined and organized to construct personal theories, or an 'entrepreneurial discourse', which, with self-confidence and belief, may result in business or personal success. These findings echo those of Cope (2010) and Rae (2004) who both confirm in their studies that experience and entrepreneurial capability co-evolve.

Rae (2004) suggests that an entrepreneur develops a theory of action as they are exposed to 'learning episodes' or experiences over time. Each new experience and interaction potentially develops their theory of action, but they are specific to both the entrepreneur and the context. This means that any understanding of an entrepreneur's success at managing a growing business through recognizing and developing opportunities must be cognizant of the situated and contextual nature

**61**

of their participation and experience. It is unlikely that such skills and opportunities will be the same for other situations, although they may be similar to a certain extent. Cope (2003, 2005) has been particularly influential in emphasizing that venture trajectories are strongly influenced by the context within which individuals manage their enterprise. In essence, using case studies in six firms, he demonstrates how situated and context-dependent experiences can create profound changes in the way entrepreneurs negotiate the development path of the firm. He argues that we need a more nuanced appreciation of how fundamental change develops from the intense and discontinuous experiences that entrepreneurs have in the day-to-day management of their business.

This means that entrepreneurial resources and competencies are not necessarily transferable, or replicable, but are embodied in the entrepreneur and embedded in the context of the enterprise. Whether we take the view that the attitude and perception necessary to develop and exploit opportunities can be taught, or only developed through situated experiences, this dimension of human capital is identified by Kakati (2003) as 'entrepreneurial quality'. This is defined as the broad range of capabilities necessary to be able to translate resources in to rents, by adopting *appropriate strategies* to develop opportunities. What is being suggested here is that what is appropriate, or might work, will be dependent to a significant amount on context, or perhaps on what Storey (2011) argues is blind luck. This resonates strongly with the concept of effectuation, as proposed by Sarasvathy (2001, 2008), where entrepreneurs are able deploy available resources to exploit specific contingencies, and this is how the venture emerges.

Here it is important to consider the role of 'sensemaking' (Weick 1995) in defining the responses by entrepreneurs to the challenges they face, and how their repertoire of available actions is continually being developed. Weick argues that sensemaking is a skill of negotiating the meaning of everyday practical experiences by comparing the available cues against the available cognitive resources, developed from prior experiences and education, to make sense of, and enact, a response. When faced with new situations, where prior experience fails to provide a solution, there is the opportunity to create new outcomes and, by enacting their responses, to make sense in new ways. In doing so, they create new traces (evident in new systems, material objects and so on) and entrepreneurs are thus deeply embedded in the environments in which they practise their craft: 'They act, and in doing so create the materials that become the constraints and opportunities they face' (Weick 1995: 31). This means that experience creates their 'entrepreneurial discourse', 'repertoire' or 'industry recipe', which they then employ when managing responses to the events they face when managing the firm (Spender 1989, Rae and Carswell 2001). Experience is a key ingredient of future action and thus highlights how a previous business failure might potentially be a useful antecedent for a future venture (Cope 2010).

## BOX 4.3

A Box Manufacturer, Pack Co, attributed his management style and processes to previous experience he had gained both in industry and in other businesses he had managed. Before he decided to start his own business, the owner-director had been in a senior sales and marketing position for a large packaging process and design company. In this job, he observed how his chairman retained tight fiscal control. These were principles that he applied to his own business and they were reinforced through experience as he operated within very tight profit margins. Thus, the owner-director spent a significant amount of his time on financial management to ensure that efficiencies were taken where possible.

> When I used to work for (the large packaging company), which was a 15/20-million-pound business, it was done exactly the same way. The chairman signed all cheques and he was the one that analysed all the margins, and if it was out he'd ask the questions. He'd make sure it was never out and that's exactly the same principles that I apply. All my jobs are costed. There's no way in the world that we would ever do anything knowingly that makes a loss. I would rather not take on the order.

Experience is a fundamental resource influencing the development trajectory of the firm, and is itself developed further over time while managing the firm. This has led some to argue that prior business experience, and even failure, provides new venture owners with more likelihood of success. Furthermore, research implies that knowledge resource requirements and configurations will change over time and, therefore, that a generic competence approach, while still important, does not address the specific challenges faced by an entrepreneur as they struggle to make sense of their own situation and enact their response. This suggests that policy makers may need to target their agenda at the specific challenges faced by entrepreneurs rather than delivering generic skills and competence solutions, although these generic approaches are not without merit, as we see in Box 4.3.

### 4.5.4 Entrepreneurial education and formal training

There are significant sources of evidence that suggest entrepreneurs do not value formal management, or employee training (Carter *et al.* 2004). Indeed, given the discussion in the last section we can perhaps see why this is the case. However, just because they may prefer informal training and learning from experience, does not mean that formal training does not have value (Jayawarna *et al.* 2007a).

It is often argued that a lack of relevant knowledge and skills at start-up, and in the early stages of development, is a significant reason for the high failure rate in new ventures, for example, Beresford and Saunders (2005), who go on to argue policy can address this weakness by providing educational support prior to, and in the first three years of, start-up. Indeed, many initiatives implemented by the UK Government that were designed to encourage start-ups and to improve the growth performance of entrepreneurial firms have emphasized management development (Fuller-Love 2006). A review of the literature by Fuller-Love shows that, on balance, management development programmes are effective for entrepreneurial firms. The main benefits appear to be survival and growth, reduction in failure and improvement in performance. The skills required include leadership and management, developing management systems and techniques and team building. In a specific study that examined the effects of a new enterprise scholarship scheme on business success, results indicated that regional grant aid and training for entrepreneurs from socially deprived areas did have a positive economic impact (Jayawarna *et al.* 2011). However, the authors do stress that their findings are not definitive and that the education process and human capital may mediate rather than directly affect success.

The development of generic competence maps, such as national vocational qualifications and skills reports, such as Bolton (1971), has influenced the content of entrepreneurship education in the UK. In the USA, the Small Business Administration (SBA) provides advice for new venture owners that covers key functional areas such as preparing a business plan, finance, marketing, legal requirements and internationalization. The list is similar at the Australian Government Small Business Enterprise Centres. In all of these approaches, competencies and/or defining key functional disciplines have significantly influenced the content of training and education programmes provided through government services, independent providers and higher education institutions. This has allowed the development of 'kits' and advice on how to prepare a business plan, and review business strategy and specialist financial information. In all of these countries, business start-up kits are available online from government-sponsored or approved agencies.

However, there has also been a relatively recent change in policy that accords with the growing body of research, discussed above, that advocates a more nuanced approach to entrepreneurship education. In the UK evidence from a more sophisticated programme (LEAD – Leadership, Enterprise and Development) developed by the Institute for Entrepreneurship and Enterprise Development at Lancaster University (www.lums.lancs.ac.uk/departments/entrep) and delivered in conjunction with 12 other organizations in the North of England, has provided targeted (as well as generic) education to entrepreneurs (Gordon *et al.* 2011).

## BOX 4.4

At BRWL, as noted above in Box 4.2, the development of continuous improvement capabilities was the key factor in winning work from their customer and in expanding the customer base. While the MD was able to not only demonstrate what he had been doing informally, his college course allowed him to develop new ideas and to improve the quality of his employees' skills.

> Well there's this college and they're telling me that all big companies use these tools and techniques and I thought, they can't all be wrong, you know. It was a realization that these must work for them to be so popular and I started to cherry pick and listen to what could work in BRWL ... I started to experiment, measuring things and trying new techniques and to encourage my staff to record and measure what they were doing. I also got in a 'set up reduction' consultant to train the staff. That helped and then they were coming to me with ideas.

This formal training allowed the MD and his staff to gain experience in quality and continuous improvement techniques used in large firms. They improved the machining systems and reduced set up times. The supplier development programme allowed the MD to learn new management techniques. By developing his own experience and learning new techniques at college, he was able to improve and formalize continuous improvement within the firm.

This programme creates close relationships to increase trust and social capital among participants, which in turn supports business development (Jones and Macpherson 2013). University staff and business experts deliver the content, in part at least, through mentors and master-classes addressing their specific needs. In the USA, the SBA has adopted the mentoring role and recent UK Government policy provided a brokering service to experts through business advisers for entrepreneurs, which had mixed success (Mole and Keogh 2009). In keeping with this individual and context sensitive education, Gibb (2009) advocates action learning, an approach that requires entrepreneurs to address real problems they face with the support of an action learning set (a group of peers) and a set facilitator. However, he also recognizes that the institutional norms of education providers and policy support make it difficult to achieve in practice.

The research that supports the role of education and training in developing successful businesses is ambiguous. However, much of this research has focused on the relationship to firm performance, and ignored the wider context and other contingent factors that might influence the relationship (Bryan 2006). Past education and experience create intellectual capital, and it is this resource that entrepreneurs use in order to make sense of ambiguity; increased cognitive capacity and ability will have implications for behaviour and actions (Wiklund and Shepherd 2003a), and a broader range of education and experience is likely to allow a wider range of possible responses (Bood 1998). Since education and training, all things being equal, improve available human capital, this is likely to provide a wider repertoire of possible responses when faced with challenges by all staff within the firm. Whether such formally developed skills and capabilities actually result in better performance will depend on contingencies and context. Also, while many entrepreneurs say they prefer informal learning, this does mean that formal education is not important in increasing the intellectual capacity of the entrepreneurs and their staff. We discuss the theme of entrepreneurial education further in Chapter 3, particularly in terms of its role in facilitating venture start-up (see Box 4.4).

## 4.6 MANAGING OTHERS AND CULTURAL ENTREPRENEURSHIP

An issue worthy of further consideration is that, given the range of knowledge skills and capabilities necessary to create a successful business, all of these are unlikely to be readily available or embodied in one individual. New entrepreneurs will need knowledge, resources and capabilities from others inside and outside the firm's boundaries, which they must borrow, appropriate and integrate into the venture. Even sole-traders need to engage with customers, suppliers and other institutions if they are to be successful. We discuss the role of networks and social capital in Chapter 5, and there are relevant discussions in Chapter 3 about social learning. All of these chapters highlight that many resources exist outside of the firm and that appropriate knowledge, skills and capabilities are held by others within the firm. As such, relationship management is a key aspect of managing a venture. Entrepreneurs must enlist the support of others to join their firm, to buy their products/services and help them operationalize their ideas (Anderson 2005).

This has led to an interest in what Lounsbury and Glynn (2001) define as 'cultural entrepreneurship'. They go on to argue that this is a process to help create and transmit an identity that others might see as legitimate in order to benefit from and engage with institutional capital and other resources. Spender (2005) suggests that the immaterial and symbolic elements of firms carry meaning. Sensemaking is a skill of negotiating the meaning of everyday practical experience with others (Weick 1995), and through the skilled presentation of symbolic and immaterial entities entrepreneurs can participate purposively with others to make collaborative engagement possible (Clarke 2011, Holt and Macpherson 2010). A similar competence is labelled as 'narrative sensemaking' by O'Connor (2002), by which she means that an entrepreneur is able to represent the firm in a coherent narrative through interconnected plot lines that make sense, and are connected, to others and other organizations. Understanding new venture creation as a performance, or narrative, shows how entrepreneurs must convince others that their ideas and proposals have merit, and provide credibility such that others will be willing to invest time, money and effort into the venture (O'Connor 2002, Anderson 2005).

For example, in a study of three entrepreneurs, using ethnography techniques, Clarke (2011) found that they used visual symbols: to present an appropriate scene to stakeholders; to create a professional identity and emphasize control; and to regulate emotions. These visual symbols included props, settings, dress and expressiveness, and entrepreneurs 'actively seek to make sure that stakeholders experience positive emotions by carefully managing their surrounding visual environment' (Clarke 2011: 1384). She argues that the more experienced entrepreneurs were more adept at this, and that such skills of symbolic management were important for securing appropriate support for their ventures. Another study examines micro-level interactions and highlights the use of both speech and gestures by entrepreneurs to convince others of the viability and legitimacy of their business (Cornelissen *et al.* 2012). These authors note that entrepreneurs use metaphors in both of these communication modes in the early stages of the commercialization of a venture. By doing so the entrepreneurs attempt to emphasize their own agency and control, but also the predictability and taken-for-granted nature of what is a novel venture.

Taking a different approach, Baron and Tang (2009), in their Chinese study, argue that skills associated with social perception, expressiveness, and self-promotion influence new venture performance, although this is mediated by the success in obtaining information and available resources. These social skills, they argue, are micro-level factors that eventually have a macro-level effect on the performance of the business. Their findings 'point to a process in which entre-preneurs' social skills influence their effectiveness in obtaining crucial resources, and these resources, in turn, influence new venture performance' (Baron and Tang 2009: 300). Such micro-level skills are important, not just for entrepreneurs, but for all actors within the business that cross boundaries, since these 'boundary spanning' roles are important in facilitating access to resources such as knowledge (Jones 2006). In short, specific social skills, such as political skills, emotional sensitivity, impression management, social adaptability and persuasiveness, can influence the quality of interactions, which in turn influence the ability of entrepreneurs to engage successfully with others when establishing and managing a new venture (Baron and Markman 2000, Tocher *et al.* 2012). This understanding of 'cultural entrepreneurship' is conceptualized in Figure 4.3.

In this section, we have highlighted how soft skills and competencies are necessary to gain access resources outside of the firm, but also to help manage

**67**

**Figure 4.3**
Cultural entrepreneurship

stakeholders within the enterprise. In essence, research into symbolic management, cultural entrepreneurship, rhetorical skills and narrative performances suggests new venture creation is as much about 'impression management' as it is about specific functional and technical knowledge.

## 4.7 SUMMARY AND KEY LEARNING POINTS

The subject of knowledge, skills and capabilities used to create and run new ventures is complicated. Research has not provided unequivocal answers. There are even those who argue that, since the evidence of a link between knowledge, skills, learning and performance is so weak, we should not provide policy support to ventures. The ambiguity of findings does question whether it is appropriate for educators and policy developers to define competence and skills lists when considering approaches to venture development. However, given the complex nature of this issue, perhaps it is not that educators and support agencies should discard such lists, but that all involved in the support and development of new ventures need to be sensitive to the fact that generic capabilities may not always be appropriate in different contexts. Stakeholders may need to be sensitive to the specific circumstances, resources and ambitions of individual ventures rather than developing blanket and generic approaches (Jones *et al.* 2010b).

Nevertheless, despite this ambiguity, when reviewing the evidence it does seem that we can identify some broad key points. From the above discussions, these are:

- Prior education and experiences may not be directly relevant to the performance of the firm, but these are key factors in providing human capital necessary to navigate the early days of venture creation.
- The broader and more varied are available skills, knowledge and capabilities, the more likely they are to provide a wider repertoire in order to cope with the challenging contexts new venture owners face.
- As the venture grows, knowledge, skills and capabilities will continue to develop through day-to-day problem solving, but they must keep pace with changing contexts.
- While informal experiences are important, formal education and training can also improve the knowledge, skills and capabilities of *all* staff and provide valuable resources for the sustainability of the firm.
- Soft skills and relationship management are a crucial part of managing all stakeholders and in navigating boundaries to allow access to other resources essential for firm survival and growth.

## 4.8 DISCUSSION QUESTIONS

- What are the range of factors that influence the skills and knowledge necessary to set up and run a new venture?
- What are the implications of different theories for defining necessary skill sets within a firm: for example, opportunity recognition and exploitation, the resource-based view of the firm, dynamic capabilities and effectuation?
- Why is it difficult to link the availability of stocks of human capital to the success of a new venture?
- What might be the potential sources of skills and knowledge that a nascent entrepreneur can bring to their business? How might they supplement these skills and address any deficiencies that they identify? Why is experience so important in making the most of existing knowledge?
- Why is it challenging to define a generic set of skills that a new venture owner might need to start a new business?

## 4.9 FURTHER READING

Sarasvathy, S. (2008) *Effectuation: Elements of Entrepreneurial Expertise.* Cheltenham, UK: Edward Elgar.

# Chapter 5

# Networks, social capital and entrepreneurial resources

## 5.1 INTRODUCTION

In this chapter, we explore the links between entrepreneurial networks, the generation of social capital and access to resources. As we discuss below, one of the key changes in our understanding of entrepreneurship has been the shift away from seeing those engaged in business start-up as 'heroic' individuals (Conway and Jones 2012). Birley (1985) was one of the first researchers to observe that the entrepreneurial ability to engage in networking was an essential skill for identifying opportunities[1] and accessing the resources necessary to develop new ventures. In the last 10 years, the study of entrepreneurial networks has become one of the most important topics for improving our understanding of the way in which new businesses operate. It is well established in that effective entrepreneurs need a mixture of both strong ties, based on family and close friends, and weaker ties based on professional and business contacts. Perhaps more importantly, entrepreneurial networks must be dynamic and the mix of strong and weak ties will change as the business becomes more established. As we discussed in Chapter 4 (skills and capabilities), developing the social and communication skills required to identify and access new network contacts is crucial for entrepreneurs who want to establish businesses that have real potential for growth.

A related issue to the interest in networks has been the emergence of social capital as an important element in understanding entrepreneurship. Social capital refers to the outputs, both tangible and intangible, that emerge from relationships between social actors. Reciprocity is a key social capital term as it emphasizes the importance of cooperation and trust between actors. At a very pragmatic level, social capital concerns the economic benefits that entrepreneurs obtain from their social networks. At a broader level, building effective entrepreneurial communities means encouraging greater knowledge-sharing among a wider range of individuals and groups. For example, as we discussed in Chapter 3, university incubators can facilitate the creation of social capital between those engaged in business start-up. In this chapter, we demonstrate the ways in which nascent entrepreneurs can

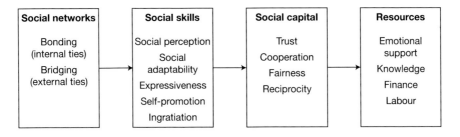

| Social networks | Social skills | Social capital | Resources |
|---|---|---|---|
| Bonding (internal ties) | Social perception | Trust | Emotional support |
| Bridging (external ties) | Social adaptability | Cooperation | Knowledge |
| | Expressiveness | Fairness | Finance |
| | Self-promotion | Reciprocity | Labour |
| | Ingratiation | | |

**Figure 5.1**
*Networks, social capital and resources*

utilize their social networks as a means of 'creating' social capital that can add real value to their businesses. In Figure 5.1, the links between social networks, social capital and the resources required by a new venture are illustrated. The effectiveness with which entrepreneurs exploit or mobilize their social networks depends, largely, on the effectiveness of their social and communication skills (see Chapter 4).

## 5.2 LEARNING OBJECTIVES

■ To explain the links between social networks and social capital.
■ To evaluate the way in which social capital helps in providing access to resources for new ventures.
■ To identify the role of social skills in creating social capital.

## 5.3 SOCIAL NETWORKS

The growing importance of social networks to entrepreneurship over the last 25 years signifies recognition that such relationships are essential for providing access to a wide range of resources (Aldrich *et al.* 1987, Cope *et al.* 2007). The basic building block of any social network is the relationship between two social actors (A and B) known as a dyad. A social network is simply a series of dyadic relationships between the entrepreneur and other individuals in their social network (Figure 5.2). The most familiar elements of a social network are those family members and close friends with whom individuals interact on a regular basis. It is generally acknowledged that family and friends are most likely to provide finance, as well as other resources, for new businesses (Mason and Harrison 1999, Bhide 2000, Brush 2002, Brush *et al.* 2002). In social network terms, such linkages are described as 'strong ties', which are favoured because they are readily accessibility to nascent entrepreneurs who find it difficult obtaining formal funding in the form of debt or equity.

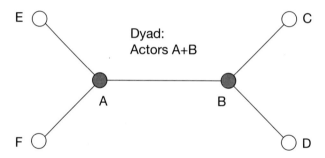

**Figure 5.2**
*Dyadic relationship*

The entrepreneur's strong ties may have limited resources and it is important that they seek additional resources from their weaker network ties. Granovetter (1973) identified the 'strength of weak ties' as crucial in providing access to more contacts and a wider array of resources (see Box 5.1). Relationship strength is important in determining the type and extent of resources that can be obtained through a network. For example, strong ties can provide funding, business-related knowledge, skills and information related to market opportunities as well as emotional support. Weak ties could be 'friends of friends' who are willing to provide the nascent entrepreneur with resources that are either free or charged at less than market price. Such resources include professional advice (legal or financial) as well as sharing office space, equipment or even employees (see Chapter 8 – 'Bootstrapping the start-up business'). As an entrepreneur becomes more experienced, their network of business relationships will grow, particularly links to customers and suppliers. These weaker ties, based on non-affective

---

### BOX 5.1

**The weakness of strong ties** – close contact with a small group of strong ties is likely, in most cases, to mean the individuals have limited access to knowledge, information and resources. While strong ties are important in the early stages of start-up they must be supplemented by weaker ties in the longer term.

**The strength of weak ties** – allow individuals access to a wider range of knowledge, information and resources. The disadvantage is that weaker ties will have less reason to share that knowledge with someone that they do not know very well. Therefore effective social and communication skills help nascent entrepreneurs mobilize weaker ties.

relationships, provide the potential for access to a range of diverse information and resources (Figure 5.3).

Open social networks, which have significant numbers of weaker ties, provide access to a wider range of unique resources. Most social actors have strong ties with other actors, particularly family and close friends, which help with the sharing of knowledge and information. There is an extensive literature that describes the process by which entrepreneurs gradually access additional resources by extending their strong ties into weaker network linkages (Larson and Starr 1993, Elfring and Hulsink 2003, Smith and Lohrke 2008). The relative importance of tie strength changes during different phases of the entrepreneurial process: emergence, newly established and maturity (Evald *et al.* 2006). Strong ties (family and close friends) play a more important role than weak ties during the emergence phase. At the 'newly established phase', it is important that entrepreneurs develop a mixture of strong and weak ties. A similar categorization also identified three distinct patterns of network development: evolution, renewal and revolution (Elfring and Hulsink 2008). The different patterns are associated with various types of start-up businesses (independent, spin-off and incubatee) and two forms of innovation (incremental or radical). The authors go on to point out that strong and weak ties are important to the emergence and growth of firms, 'although they are beneficial in different ways and at different stages of a company's development' (Elfring and Hulsink 2008: 1852).

The nature of closed (bonding) networks and open (bridging) networks is central to understanding how entrepreneurs make use of their strong and weak ties. Differences between bonding and bridging ties are similar to distinction between strong and weak ties (Table 5.1). All social actors have strong ties with other actors (family and close friends) that help promote flows of knowledge and

Closed networks

Open networks

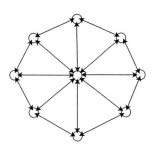
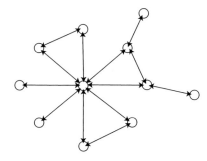

Strong ties predominate

Network open to weaker ties

**Figure 5.3**
*Open and closed networks*

**Table 5.1** *Types of network ties*

| Bonding ties | Bridging ties |
| --- | --- |
| Homogeneous ties | Heterogeneous ties |
| Horizontal linkages (similar class, age, ethnicity and interests) | Vertical linkages (different class, age, ethnicity and interests) |
| Similar moral values | Varied moral values |
| Trust and fair-play | Equivocal interests |
| Reciprocity | Negotiated reciprocity |

information. In the longer term, additional resources must be accessed by means of new network relationships. Sparse social networks, in which there are fewer direct links between actors, mean the inherent openness creates brokerage opportunities (Burt 1992). Brokerage in this context means that entrepreneurs can obtain unique or privileged information, about access to additional resources, for example. Bonding ties based on family and close friends tend to have high levels of homogeneity with strong similarities in terms of class, ethnicity and interests. Because such groups are influenced by the same social norms and regular face-to-face interaction, they tend to have similar moral values based on trust, fair-play and reciprocity. In contrast, bridging ties are more heterogeneous and often cross 'boundaries' of class, age, ethnicity and interests. As these larger groups are subject to different social norm and tend to have irregular interaction, which may be 'virtual' rather than face-to-face, they are typified by different moral values and 'negotiated' reciprocity (that is, reciprocity will be more instrumental than is typical in bonding groups).

One important early study suggested that the entrepreneur's 'identity based' (internal/bonding) ties based on pre-existing social relationships provide the main support during the early stages of business start-up (Larson and Starr 1993). As entrepreneurs become more experienced existing dyadic relationships are 'converted' into socio-economic exchanges[2] (see Figure 5.5). For example, a friend may become an investor in the company or perhaps an employee. In essence, entrepreneurs must shift to 'calculative networks' (external/bridging), in which ties based on purpose and function are more important than identity ties (Jack *et al.* 2008). What this means in practice is that nascent entrepreneurs must try to identify those people (ties) who can provide them with the resources to establish and build their businesses. Brokering links between 'structural holes' (Burt 1992) in external networks aids the identification of potential opportunities as well as providing access to knowledge, information and finance that are essential for successful growth (Lechner and Dowling 2003, Hite 2005).

There are studies that indicate 'inexperienced' nascent entrepreneurs can use more experienced intermediaries as brokers to access wider networks and resources (Burt 1992, Batjargal 2006). The findings confirm studies of incubators in which nascent entrepreneurs engaged in business start-up utilize 'boundary-spanners' to develop new network links (Hughes *et al.* 2007). Taylor and Pandza (2003) discuss the importance of 'the professional periphery', which comprises business advisors, accountants, bank managers and solicitors. These professionals can link entrepreneurs to contacts who may be willing to provide support including finance. In summary, our argument, following many earlier studies is that social networks provide access to a wide range of resources for new firms (Birley 1985, Ostgaard and Birley 1996).

There is a considerable amount of evidence that the networks of female entrepreneurs are very different from those of male entrepreneurs. In particular, female entrepreneurs tend to have networks that are dominated by strong ties. Whereas, male entrepreneurs are more willing to establish network links with people they do not know (weak ties). On the other hand, women seem to be better than men at establishing and maintaining informal, rather than formal, networks (Jayawarna *et al.* 2012). Therefore, evidence suggests that in establishing new ventures there are significant male–female variations in nature of networks and access to resources (see Chapter 8).

## 5.4 SOCIAL CAPITAL

Recognition of links between social networks and social capital has contributed to significant changes in the way that we think about entrepreneurship. Most early research concentrated on individual personality traits such as the need for achievement/autonomy, risk-taking and an internal locus of control. As we have seen above, increasingly there was recognition that entrepreneurs' contacts via their networks were important to even the most individualistic entrepreneur. It is generally acknowledged that use of the term social capital began with the work of Jane Jacobs (1965) in urban studies. James Coleman (1988) attempted to reconcile two conflicting explanations based on the distinction between social capital that benefits the individual or the wider society. In other words, is social capital something that can be owned and exploited by an individual, or is it something that can only be generated by a group or community? Developing relationships that encompass genuine shared values relies on processes of cooperation that create 'civic trust'. Putnam (1995), who became an advisor to US President Bill Clinton, claimed that the decaying of social capital was contributing to the decline of community spirit in the United States. Reciprocal relations based on mutual trust, obligations and expectations are central to the creation of social capital. Individuals help colleagues and friends because they believe that they will reciprocate and, consequently, both sides have expectations related to future behaviours. As we discussed in Chapter 3, this openness to knowledge-sharing is a particularly important feature of both entrepreneurial learning and the increase in provision of graduate incubation facilities.

Similar to social networks, approaches to social capital can be distinguished between bonding and bridging linkages. Bonding social capital (internal/strong ties) concentrates attention on the collective rather than individuals and is concerned with linkages within groups or communities. The focus is on factors such as trust, obligations and reciprocity that contribute to the building of group cohesiveness and a sense of shared goals among nascent entrepreneurs based in an incubator for example (see Box 5.2, below). Bridging social capital (external/weak ties) focuses attention on the ways in which individuals utilize their egocentric links with other social actors. In essence, bridging social capital describes the way in which entrepreneurs access resources from those who are not part of their immediate group of family and friends. These ideas are associated with two distinct views on the nature of networks and social capital (see Table 5.1, above). The first view suggests that social capital is mobilized as a result of resources that accrue to groups and individuals as a result of long-standing network relationships. Closed networks based on strong cohesive social ties create an environment that facilitates trust and reciprocal relationships (Bourdieu 1986, Coleman 1988). The other view is that the consistent norms fostered by cohesive networks limit the opportunities available to individual entrepreneurs. Hence, open networks with bridging ties between actors present far more entrepreneurial opportunities than closed networks typified by bonding social capital (Figure 5.4). According to 'structural hole theory' consistent norms fostered by strong ties limit the opportunities for entrepreneurs to access unique resources such as knowledge and information (Burt 1992, 2005). The openness associated with sparse social networks provides brokerage opportunities for those seeking to exploit 'structural holes'.

Rather than making choices about either bonding or bridging social capital, effective entrepreneurs mobilize both internal (bonding) and external (bridging) social capital to ensure they successfully acquire and mobilize the appropriate knowledge-based resources. Therefore, it is increasingly acknowledged that, rather

## BOX 5.2

Because it's hot-desking you basically meet a lot more people. The idea for MTL wouldn't have happened without *Innospace* full stop. *Innospace* gave me the opportunity to meet Neil, and without Neil, we wouldn't have that product [online workshop podcasting]. I wouldn't have had a website either. So it's the partnership with me, Neil, Dave and Val, as chains of business fundamentals. And that's really through *Innospace*.

[Phil Jones, *Innospace*]

Social capital theory
Bonding ties

Structural hole theory
Bridging ties

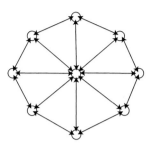
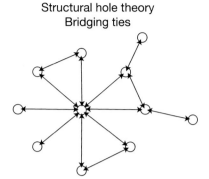

**Figure 5.4**
*Bridging and bonding ties*

than being mutually exclusive, bonding and bridging ties are important to the success of entrepreneurial ventures. Internal (bonding) and external (bridging) social capital are essential for the successful acquisition and mobilization of knowledge-based resources. As businesses begin to grow, it is even more important to balance external relationships (with actors outside the firm) and internal relationships (within the firm) (Hite and Hesterly 2001). In practice, entrepreneurs must begin to cultivate professional contacts that are useful to the survival of their business rather than relying on people to whom they have an emotional attachment. Hence, social capital can act as a form of 'glue' that bonds individuals together, or as a 'lubricant' that helps facilitate economic transactions (Anderson and Jack 2002).

The core idea on which social capital is based concerns the need for successful entrepreneurs to develop and maintain relationships with a wide range of social actors. It is therefore important that entrepreneurs reflect on the efficacy of their internal and external network relationships. Entrepreneurs also need the social skills to build and sustain bridging and bonding networks if they are to benefit from the acquisition of social capital. It seems clear that the structural and relational elements (see the following section) of social capital are likely to influence directly the intellectual capital available to owner-managers as they struggle to cope with uncertainty and ambiguity, and to make sense of existing practices and opportunities. The ability to retain and distribute this intellectual capital, and to make it more widely available within the ambit of the firm, is also important if both human and social capitals are to have more sustained and distributed benefits.

One of the most significant advances in understanding the nature of social capital was the idea that there are three underlying dimensions: structural, relational and cognitive (Nahapiet and Ghoshal 1998, Lee and Jones 2008). Structural social capital is essentially concerned with the nature of the entrepreneur's network based on size, density and diversity. As indicated earlier, smaller, closed homo-geneous social networks in which all the actors know each other well are best for sharing knowledge and information. That is because norms associated with trust, reciprocity, mutual obligations and future expectations are more likely to be created within a closed network. The disadvantage is that access to social capital is likely to be limited because the network itself will have finite resources. Larger, more diverse and heterogeneous social networks will provide the nascent entrepreneur with access to a much wider array of social capital resources (Table 5.2). However, it may be more difficult to access those resources because actors do not have the same level of obligations nor can individuals be sure about the future expectations of other actors in their network.

Relational social capital refers to the norms of trust, reciprocity, mutual obligations and expectations that influence the behaviours of those belonging to the network. Social capital is an intangible asset, which relies on goodwill between the members of a network to ensure that there are effective flows of knowledge or meaningful discussions about new ideas. Without trust between those belonging to a network, there will never be a basis for sharing valuable information such as new business opportunities or ways to improve some functional activity such as marketing or sales.

The third dimension, cognitive social capital, has received much less attention from researchers than either structural or relational social capital. Cognitive social capital refers to the way in which actors communicate via stories and narratives. Being able to communicate means we must have a 'shared language' and understand the codes that govern conversations. Clearly becoming an entrepreneur means acquiring the appropriate language in which to converse with other entrepreneurs and resource-providers. At one level, that might simply mean understanding the differences between debt and equity funding. As we explain in the next section, enhancing cognitive social capital skills means that the entrepreneur learns to communicate with other entrepreneurs as well as a wide-range of stakeholders including customers, competitors, suppliers and resource-providers (De Carolis and Saparito 2006).

Lee and Jones (2008) examined the role of cognitive social capital for two groups of nascent entrepreneurs who were attempting to access wider external resources. They based their study on two groups of students involved in business start-up programmes. Group A comprised well-qualified students undertaking a master's in entrepreneurship (high human capital). Group B comprised students from socially deprived areas who were undertaking a part-time business start-up course (low human capital) that was part of a programme known as the New Entrepreneur Scholarship (NES). The study demonstrated that both groups were effective in utilizing their bonding (close) ties to access resources. However, those with lower levels of human capital were less willing or able to 'bridge out' of their bonding ties, which limited their access to bridging resources (28 compared with

**Table 5.2** *Bonding and bridging social capital*

| Network tie | Group A<br>High human capital | Group B<br>Low human capital |
|---|---|---|
| Bonding (close) | 25 | 24 |
| Bridging (weak) | 37 | 17 |
| Bonding resources | 35 | 36 |
| Bridging resources | 55 | 28 |

55 for Group A). This is illustrated by the fact that those with low human capital on average had only 17 bridging ties compared with the 37 bridging ties of Group A. Hence, the study confirmed the importance of cognitive social capital for those nascent entrepreneurs who successfully access wider external resources.

The key point here is that there are very close links between the three forms of social capital. We can illustrate those links by making reference to the network evolution model discussed above. In the early stages of business start-up the entrepreneur's strong ties (bonding) will be the most important in providing a wide range of resources (Figure 5.5). Hence, structural social capital is key at this stage. If the business is to succeed then the entrepreneur needs to open-up the network by bridging to new network ties. This means building trust, mutual obligations and expectations with those whom the entrepreneur has recently made

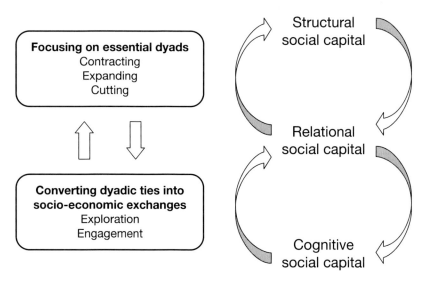

**Figure 5.5**
*Social capital and network evolution*

contact. At this stage, relational social capital becomes more important than structural social capital. Cognitive social capital is the key to building long-standing relationships with new members of the entrepreneur's network. So, the ability to construct joint narratives and stories helps turn weaker ties into strong ties, which in the long-term will have most benefits for the entrepreneur.

## 5.5 ENTREPRENEURIAL SOCIAL CAPITAL

As we have discussed in the previous sections, a key aspect of entrepreneurship is the ability to extend existing social networks in a way that provides the necessary resources to establish and grow the business. Nascent entrepreneurs have two major barriers to overcome in terms of establishing a viable new business: the liabilities of newness (Stinchcombe 1965) and of smallness (Aldrich and Auster 1986). Newness means that the entrepreneur lacks a 'track record' and the business is unlikely to have any visibility in the marketplace: potential customers will not know of the firm's existence. Smallness adds to the problems of visibility, but it also concerns the lack of knowledge, skills, information, finance and equipment, which restricts entrepreneurial businesses during start-up. The key challenge for any nascent entrepreneur is to move from an 'equivocal reality' to an 'unequivocal reality' (Figure 5.6). What this means is that entrepreneurs have to give their businesses a tangible reality if they want to succeed. They can do this in a number of ways, both physically and virtually: physically means have premises, a trading name, telephone number, a web address; and virtually includes a functional website, Facebook and Twitter accounts (see Box 5.3).

Rae (2005) developed a conceptual framework that has three elements: personal and social emergence, contextual learning and negotiated enterprise. The first element focuses on the development of 'entrepreneurial identity' based on an individual's social, educational and career experiences. Second, contextual learning is related to social networks that help develop the skills associated with developing entrepreneurial opportunities. Third, negotiated enterprise is based on the recognition that any new business venture can only be established through 'negotiated

|  |  |
|---|---|
| Equivocal reality: | Unequivocal reality: |
| Does the business exist? | The business definitely exists |

**Figure 5.6**
*From equivocal to unequivocal reality*

**BOX 5.3**

When you are trying to start a business it is important to have the kind of facilities that you have got in *Innospace*. Having access to meeting rooms and the networking areas, it's the kind of resources you might not have otherwise and I think it's also useful. It helps when you are dealing with customers or external bodies that you want to meet because its much more professional to have a place like this. Having a meeting room and have access to the projector and things like that. It's important that when you meet other people you present a professional image. It is also useful to have access to the internet, computers, the printers, filing cabinet and those types of things which allow you to develop your business whereas if you didn't it would be less professional and more difficult.

relationships' with other people (Rae 2005). Those who become successful entrepreneurs transform their experiences into new and useful knowledge. Entrepreneurs are action oriented and learning is largely experiential (see Chapter 3). Learning-by-doing is linked to what Cope (2003) describes as discontinuous events such as crises (failing to get an order or losing an existing customer) that promote higher-level (double loop) learning. Such transformational learning relies on the individual entrepreneur's mental models, which include their knowledge, experience and beliefs (Cope 2003). Our view of entrepreneurship focuses on developing the most appropriate behaviours rather than considering the individual's personality traits. The learning perspective that is adopted in this book complements the behavioural approach because, for example, it draws attention to the way in which nascent entrepreneurs mobilize their social capital.

The ability to extend personal relationships by bridging new networks is a crucial entrepreneurial skill (Larson and Starr 1993). Research demonstrates how entrepreneurs transform different forms of media into 'knowable actions' to create meaningful communication patterns during business start-up. As demonstrated above, there are close links between human capital (education and experience), a willingness to learn and the creation of social capital. Human capital theory is based on the idea that increases in cognitive ability lead to higher levels of productivity and efficiency (Chapter 6). Furthermore, human capital incorporates experience and experiential learning as well as formal education. Cooperation from actors sharing similar interpretive frameworks during communication confirms the importance of cognitive social capital (De Carolis and Saparito 2006). Entrepreneurial preparedness means that those engaged in business start-up can make use of previous experience to help acquire the skills to establish new businesses (Cope 2003, 2005). The underlying links between structural capital

**81**

(bonding and bridging) and cognitive social capital (language, codes and narrative) provide entrepreneurs with the means to access additional resources.

## 5.6 SOCIAL CAPITAL AND RESOURCING NEW VENTURES

Edith Penrose (1959) is a key figure in understanding the nature of resources that can be mobilized by entrepreneurs and owner-managers. As we discuss in Chapter 2, her seminal book was the foundation for the resource-based theory of the firm. Penrose suggested that the entrepreneur's ability to exploit opportunities depends on the configuration of their resources. Researchers concerned with the development of entrepreneurial firms have been influenced by the resource-based view of the firm (Macpherson and Holt 2007). The increasing focus on social capital has led to the recognition of how important network relationships are in providing resources for start-up businesses.

In understanding how social capital contributes to entrepreneurial resources, it is important to consider once again the distinction between bonding and bridging network ties. Bonding ties are based on relationships with family members and close friends and tend to be homogeneous. Bridging ties are often based on professional or business relationships, as well as 'friends of friends', and therefore tend to be more heterogeneous. Heterogeneity is important because it exposes the entrepreneur to new ideas, new ways of thinking and new business opportunities as well as a wider array of more tangible resources (including finance). One of the most pressing problems for the majority of young entrepreneurs is that they lack business experience and, as a consequence, they also lack linkages to wider networks of professionals who have access to additional resources. Bonding and bridging social capital enables nascent entrepreneurs to obtain both tangible and intangible resources. As we discuss tangible resources in both Chapter 7 ('Enhancing tangible resources') and Chapter 8 ('Bootstrapping the start-up business') we focus on intangible resources in this section. Although, of course, it is important to acknowledge that family and friends are likely to provide some of the financial resources required to start a new business. Intangible resources include such factors as emotional support, business advice, potential referrals, business opportunities and new relationships.

It is generally agreed that there is a positive relationship between network size and access to resources: this is known as the 'network success hypothesis' (Birley 1985, Jones and Jayawarna 2010). The network effect seems to be particularly powerful for bonding ties. The larger the network of family and close friends then the more likely entrepreneurs will be able to acquire useful resources. At the early stages of business start-up – having a large network of bridging ties does not appear to be so advantageous (Lee et al. 2011). This may be because attempting to acquire resources from weaker ties during the crucial stages of business creation distracts the entrepreneur from their more important tasks of ensuring the business is actually functioning.

Importantly, bonding social capital also seems to be significantly more important in smaller communities than it is in large towns and cities. Entrepreneurs who live in rural communities appear to mobilize social capital through their memberships of clubs and associations (sports clubs, youth clubs, civic societies and so on). It appears that for those attempting to start a rural business social capital helps compensate for the lack of formal institutions that support businesses in urban environments (Bauernschuster *et al.* 2010, Sørensen 2012). Nevertheless, there are advantages to geographical concentrations in which entrepreneurs can share knowledge and information (Pitelis 2012); this is particularly important in the case of technology-based firms (Maine *et al.* 2010).

A recent study examined the way in which social networks contributed to the performance of start-up firms that had existed for less than three years (Jones and Jayawarna 2010). The study confirmed that entrepreneurs used their strong ties to access a range of resources from their family and close friends. The study also demonstrated that weak ties were important in providing access to resources from suppliers and customers in terms of negotiating favourable trading relationships and securing working financial capital. Interestingly, the study also revealed that inexperienced entrepreneurs used experienced intermediaries to act as 'brokers' in negotiating access to wider networks and resources (the results of this study are discussed in more detail in Chapter 8). The role of network brokers is very important in understanding how nascent entrepreneurs can access a wider range of social capital. As we have demonstrated in Figure 5.5, network evolution is linked to the way in which entrepreneurs make use of their structural, relational and cognitive social capital. Using brokers who are more experienced is an effective way for those entrepreneurs who lack the necessary skills to bridge-out of their existing networks. Such brokers are important for two reasons: first, they can link new entrepreneurs into their own more extensive social networks. Second, brokers can help create social capital by using their own professional reputation to confirm the reliability of inexperienced entrepreneurs to third-party business acquaintances. In other words, trust, reciprocity, mutual obligations and expectations between the broker and their networks ties can be 'transferred' to new entrepreneurs. University incubators are an effective way of mobilizing the professional links of an incubation manager for the benefit of incubatees (see Box 5.4, below). According to Taylor and Pandza (2003) 'the professional periphery' links entrepreneurs to contacts who provide access to a wide range of additional resources (Figure 5.7).

As the topic of social skills has been dealt with in more detail elsewhere (Chapter 4) this section provides a very brief overview of the links between networks, social capital and resourcing a new business. Surprisingly, there has been a limited amount of research examining links between the entrepreneur's social skills and the success of their new venture (Baron and Markman 2003,

**BOX 5.4**

A good example is that recently Dominic (*Innospace* manager) suggested I spoke to an accountant who he knew. I was able to speak to her for about an hour and she advised me of the different ways that you go about issuing shares and how to factor in potential scenarios such as one director wanting to leave the company, as well as the legal implications of what the directors can decide on, what the shareholders can decide on and what percentages I needed to ensure a majority big enough to retain control. That directly influenced the way that we will be writing the legal documentation, the shareholders' agreement, the directors' service agreement, changing the memorandum and the articles of association. So these are essential documents that determine how the company is run, and by getting this advice we will be altering them in a way that better suits our needs.

[Phil Jones, *Innospace*]

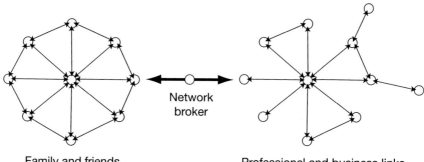

Family and friends          Professional and business links

**Figure 5.7**
*Network brokers*

Zott and Huy 2007). There is, however, research that indicates that those employees with higher-level social skills provide benefits to the individual and to the organization (Ferris *et al.* 2005, Harris *et al.* 2007). Therefore, social skills are also likely to be of considerable benefit to those engaged in business start-up. Baron and Tang (2009) suggest that there are several social skills that are important to nascent entrepreneurs:

- **Social perception** – refers to the ability to understand the motivations and attitudes of those people who are important during start-up. For example, potential working partners, employees and financial stakeholders.

■ **Social adaptability** – concerns the ability to adjust behaviours to a range of different social situations as well as being comfortable with people from different backgrounds, ages and social classes.

■ **Expressiveness** – is the individual's ability to express their feelings in an open and honest manner; that is, letting other people know how you feel about particular issues.

■ **Self-promotion** – means presenting your achievements and skills in a positive way to other people who have an influence on you and your business.

■ **Ingratiation** – the desire and the ability to encourage other people to have a positive attitude towards you by offering compliments and praise or doing personal favours.

Based on a study of 500 new ventures in Southern China, Baron and Tang established that social perception, expressiveness and self-promotion were all positively and directly linked to firm growth. Social perception and social adaptability were strong related to the acquisition of information including professional, managerial and marketing knowledge. Social adaptability and ingratiation were linked to effectiveness in acquiring resources including 'supply chain', human and financial resources (Figure 5.8). Hence, some social skills act on venture growth through access to information and resources. Baron and Tang (2009) conclude by stating that their study confirms that entrepreneurs' social skills play an important role in the performance and success of new ventures.

## 5.7 SUMMARY AND KEY LEARNING POINTS

Social networks, social/communications skills and social capital combine to provide access to a wide range of resources for nascent entrepreneurs. Resources include

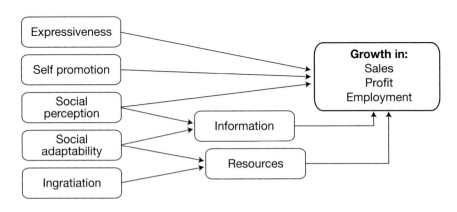

**Figure 5.8**
*Social skills and new venture performance*

tangible assets such as finance and premises (a friend's garage or a converted bedroom in your parents' home) and intangible assets including emotional support, advice and links to other business people. In the early stages of business start-up, strong (bonding) ties that include your family and close friends are of most importance. Building a business that has the potential for long-term success means linking to those weaker (bridging) ties who will provide access to a much wider range of resources. Social capital embodies the trust, reciprocity, obligations and mutual expectations about future behaviours that facilitate the benefits of belonging to a larger, more diverse social network.

Links between the three dimensions of social capital (structural, relational and cognitive) are central to understanding how nascent entrepreneurs convert/extend their strong ties into more instrumental (economic) exchanges. In effect, this means that entrepreneurs must move from relationships based on strong emotional bonds to those in which both parties have expectations of future economic and financial benefits. Ultimately, the entrepreneur's ability to use their social network as a mechanism to mobilize social capital is only of use if it provides those resources necessary to develop their business.

Key learning points are:

■ Understanding the changing nature of entrepreneurial networks is fundamental to building successful and sustainable new businesses.

■ Distinctions between bridging and bonding network ties also contribute to our understanding of how entrepreneurs access wider resources.

■ Social capital comprises three distinct but interlinked dimensions: structural, relational and cognitive.

■ The structure of networks is closely linked to the entrepreneur's human capital that helps explain differences in male and female networks.

■ The entrepreneur's social skills are a key element of effectively mobilizing social capital.

## 5.8 DISCUSSION QUESTIONS

■ How does Granovetter's work help with the understanding of entrepreneurial social networks?

■ What is the significance of structural holes in terms of accessing entrepreneurial resources?

■ What are the differences between social networks and social capital?

■ How do entrepreneurs move from equivocal reality to an unequivocal reality?

■ How does the work of Edith Penrose contribute to our understanding of entrepreneurial resources?

# Chapter 6

# Resourcing start-up businesses

## 6.1 INTRODUCTION

The resource-based view (RBV) promotes resources as central to the firm's capabilities for value-creation and long-term competitive advantage. Resource assembly occurs throughout the entrepreneurial process and it is particularly crucial at the start-up stage as it provides the basis for subsequent development of the venture. Indeed, research evidence suggests that new ventures with a larger pool of resources are more likely to survive and display higher growth potential when compared with firms operating in resource poor environments. In the new venture context, resources encompass both tangible and intangible assets as well as capabilities that are available for entrepreneurs to exploit their new business ideas. As Sarasvathy (2001: 250) points out, all nascent entrepreneurs begin with three categories of 'means'; their own traits, tastes and abilities; their knowledge corridors; and their social networks.

Traditionally the literature advocates complete ownership control of all resources if firms are to gain competitive advantage. Depending on the scale and nature of the business and the abilities and starting endowments of the entrepreneur, however, gaining complete ownership of resources is a difficult task in most new ventures. Recent literature emphasizes the importance of developing behaviours that enhance the entrepreneur's abilities to use and extract value from resources that are outside their control. 'Bootstrapping' describes the process that enables resource-constrained entrepreneurs to access resources relatively cheaply and quickly in order to create, or respond to, market opportunities (see Chapter 8 for a discussion of bootstrapping). Once built-in to the fabric of the firm through its embedded routines, bootstrapping may also provide a way to remain responsive and agile by encouraging a lean approach to the firm's operating strategy (Timmons 1999). Research also shows that not all entrepreneurs plan to grow their ventures, and therefore resource assembly is also influenced by the purposeful decisions and expectations of the entrepreneur (Penrose 1959).

In this chapter, we introduce the resource-based view of the firm and examine the key resources required for entrepreneurs who are starting and running new ventures. Burt (1992) proposed three essential resources for entrepreneurs during the venture founding stage: personal financial resources, personal skills and social resources. The importance of social and financial resources to the entrepreneur is discussed in more detail in Chapters 5 and 7, respectively. In this chapter, we pay attention to the role of human capital in the entrepreneurial process. Most importantly, human capital is the first available resource for entrepreneurs, and it leads to the development and acquisition of other types of resources important for further venture development. The chapter also includes a section that highlights the importance of recasting human capital in lifecycle terms, and emphasizes the idea that children's education has far-reaching effects that become manifest in career paths related to entrepreneurship. Finally, we provide some research evidence that explains the links between entrepreneur human capital and new venture success/performance.

## 6.2 LEARNING OBJECTIVES

■ To describe the relevance of the resource-based view to nascent entrepreneurs in their effort to accumulate appropriate resources at start-up.

■ To identify that there are different types of resources that entrepreneurs require at the early stage of business development.

■ To evaluate the role of human capital as a resource for entrepreneurs.

■ To describe childhood opportunities for the accrual of human capital required to pursue a career in entrepreneurship.

■ To analyse the evidence related to how human capital impacts on entrepreneurial potential and success.

## 6.3 RESOURCE-BASED VIEW OF THE FIRM

RBV is built on the premise that all firms comprise bundles of resources (Penrose 1959), and that resource accessibility will shape the firm's direction and ultimately determine performance (Barney 1991). Barney (1991: 101) classifies resources as 'all assets, capabilities, organizational processes, firm attributes, information, knowledge, etc. controlled by the firm that enable the firm to conceive of and implement strategies that improve its efficiency and effectiveness'. Firms with stronger resource bases are better able to survive and grow irrespective of environmental change and business decisions. Critical to the theory is that resources that are valuable, rare, imperfectly inimitable and difficult to substitute provide firms with sustained competitive advantage (Barney 1991). In a sustainable setting, substitution, duplication and imitation of resources is not possible due to the complexity associated with the processes that involve resource acquisition, management, reconfiguration and leverage (Sirmon and Hitt 2003). Therefore, it is not only the resources themselves that determine a firm's competitive position, but also how firms allocate and deploy resources for strategic activities. Because resource needs are idiosyncratic, there are variations in value-creating actions and the competitive position derived from the entrepreneur's resource base (Arend and Lévesque 2010).

More recently some writers have emphasized that while resources are necessary to deliver capability, the RBV is too static for explaining how firms create new capabilities or exploit opportunities within dynamic and changing markets (see, for example, Coen and Maritan 2011). In accordance with the dynamic-capabilities theory, 'both the skills/resources and the way organizations use them must constantly change, leading to the creation of continuously changing temporary advantages' (Fiol 2001: 692). As firms need to reconfigure opportunities through creative deployment of resources, it is the way in which owner-managers envisage and enact available resources that defines a firm's trajectory (See Chapter 9, 'Dynamic capabilities').

Chrisman (1999) referred to the accumulation of resource stocks for new venture creation as a special case of resource-based theory, because entrepreneurs begin with few, if any, stocks of resources other than their own knowledge and social networks. This knowledge is critical to make resource-related decisions and to gain access to costly-to-duplicate resources that give the entrepreneur a competitive advantage (Foss *et al.* 2008). For new ventures, initial resources are particularly important, as they not only act as a buffer against the liabilities of smallness, but they also provide strategic alternatives for the entrepreneur to develop their business.

## 6.4 TYPES OF RESOURCES

RBV is based on the potential for multiple types of resources including 'assets, capabilities, organizational processes, firm attributes, information, and know-ledge' (Barney 1991: 101) that can be categorized as either tangible or intangible (Figure 6.1). Lichtenstein and Brush (2001) identify what they describe as 'salient resources' for entrepreneurial ventures. These include: capital, social and organizational systems/structures, management know-how, technology, physical resources, leadership, culture and 'informal systems'. The authors go on to argue that, in new ventures, organizational resources evolve over a period of weeks, months and years (Figure 6.2, on p. 91, explains how the emphasis on human, social and financial resources changes when the nascent entrepreneurs set-up, run and develop their ventures). If new firms are to become established or self-sustaining then 'a series of resource acquisitions and combinations might be necessary' (Lichtenstein and Brush 2001: 41). Interestingly, Lichtenstein and Brush found in their longitudinal analysis of three firms that intangible resources

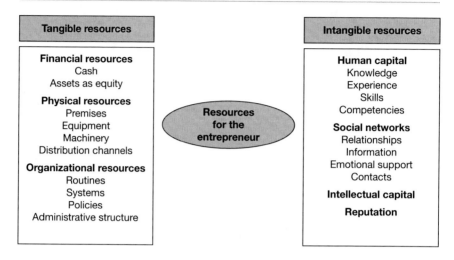

**Figure 6.1**
Resources for the entrepreneur: tangible and intangible resources

(knowledge, expertise, relationships, sales/service delivery and decision-making) were more salient than tangible resources.

## 6.4.1 Tangible resources

A firm's tangible resources include financial, physical and organizational resources (Barney 1991). In terms of financial resources, during the stages of conception and gestation, entrepreneurs rely on their own funds and those obtained from family and friends (Cassar 2004). As firms grow, there is a shift in focus from 'insider' to 'outsider' finance as investment becomes more attractive to business angels and venture capitalists (Bozkaya and De La Potterie 2008). These financial resources are generally crucial to enable the acquisition of physical resources such as premises, machinery, equipment and distribution channels (see Chapter 7 for a fuller discussion on financial resources). Organizational capital includes routines, systems, policies, and related firms' administrative structure within which other resources are applied to create value-adding activities (Penrose 1959). More specifically, these resources include a 'firm's formal reporting structure, its formal and informal planning, controlling, and coordinating systems, as well as informal relations among groups within a firm and between a firm and those in its environment' (Barney 1991: 101).

## 6.4.2 Intangible resources

Intangible resources include social networks, intellectual property, reputation and human capital resources. Social capital includes the resource stocks embedded in

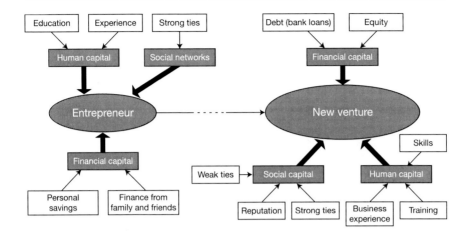

**Figure 6.2**
*Resource needs: from entrepreneur to new venture*

the social networks that entrepreneurs can access. Networks are important because friendship and kinship ties provide access to resources at less than market price or even provide resources that are simply not available via market transactions (Baker *et al.* 2003, Witt *et al.* 2008). Sparse social networks typified by weak ties also provide 'brokerage opportunities' to access unique resource-providers (Burt 1992, 2005) and therefore access to valuable resources. Entrepreneurs' pre-existing networks and the capability to bridge into new networks are both important (Lee and Jones 2008) because these shape the trajectory of a firm as they are the resources 'at hand' that entrepreneurs use when solving problems (Baker *et al.* 2003). Gaining access to value-rich networks depends on perceived legitimacy, the resources an entrepreneur has to exchange, their ability to bear the transaction costs involved in networking (Hanlon and Saunders 2007) and skills necessary for creating quality engagement (Holt and Macpherson 2010; see Chapter 5 for a discussion of social networks). Human capital resources include the knowledge, experience, judgment, intelligence, relationships and insight of people working in the firm, in particular the owner-manager/entrepreneur. Human capital delivers both functional capabilities (such as marketing), as well as the capability to innovate and solve organizational problems (Penrose 1959). Clearly, knowledge in the form of human capital is significant for the development of new technologies as well as for the delivery of those functional competencies necessary to run a business.

Although tangible resources are important for survival and growth, intangible resources are viewed as being the principal drivers of competitive advantage. Intangible resources are embedded in organizational systems and processes and are not easily acquired in factor markets. They are largely related to the knowledge

**91**

held by entrepreneurs, or the reputation and legitimacy acquired through social networks, and are therefore difficult to replicate (Diaz-Garcia and Jimenez-Moreno 2010). Transmission of such resources requires context-specific tacit knowledge because it arises from situations that are idiosyncratic and complex. Capabilities that intangible resources provide to the entrepreneur are particularly important for accessing tangible resources and managing innovatively through partnerships and knowledge exchange. According to Hitt *et al.* (2001a: 14), 'intangible resources are more likely than tangible resources to produce competitive advantage'.

## 6.5 HUMAN CAPITAL AND ENTREPRENEURSHIP

Of the wide-ranging literature that discusses the relevance of intangible assets for start-up, a special emphasis has been placed on the human capital of the entrepreneur or the entrepreneurial team. Human capital is a powerful predictor of a person's propensity to establish a new venture. It encompasses the value-creating skills, knowledge, competencies and talents acquired through formal and informal learning that reside within individuals (Becker 1964) and relates to intergenerational transmission of knowledge and learning behaviours (Roberts 2001). In addition to the human capital that entrepreneurs bring to their business, accumulation of human capital over time through training and work experience is also relevant. According to the labour-economics literature, while human capital is a favourable resource for all employment, the effects are more pertinent to some careers. Williams (2004) explains that individuals with higher stocks of human capital and varied skills are better able to make use of their resources in entrepreneurship than in salaried jobs. Teece (2011) agrees that there are strong links between entrepreneurship and human capital. He draws on Schumpeter's concept of 'creative destruction' to identify the key role of well-educated individuals in restructuring the economy:

> Whether one is focusing on creating value or capturing it, in recent decades the numerati and literati (expert talent) and entrepreneurs have become more important for the creation and management of technology in the global economy.
>
> (Teece 2011: 531)

At the same time, Teece acknowledges that the ability to create or sense new opportunities is not something that is 'universally distributed'. While *generic* human capital, such as education, knowledge and skills (acquired through formal education) can provide entrepreneurs with a relatively stable advantage over time, *specific* human capital accrued through on-the-job training and experience provides the capability for creating sustained competitive advantage. As specific human capital is inherently linked to the context of an opportunity, the associated knowledge is tacit and organizationally embedded making the firm's resource base inimitable and non-substitutable. Tacit knowledge is very relevant here, as entrepreneurship is usually developed through interaction with others (Rae and Carswell 2001) as well as from the experiences of success and failure (Cope 2011). Prior knowledge of markets and a clear understanding of how to address customer needs appear to aid this process of discovery (Shane 2000). Therefore, with time, entrepreneurs can draw upon additional human capital to gain greater diversity of skills and competencies.

Existing stocks of human capital are also the basis of sense-making resources through which appropriate actions are conceived and executed (Weick 1995). Prior knowledge does have the potential to enable and constrain the ability of individuals to conceptualize alternative priorities. While human capital comprises an entrepreneur's knowledge and experience their learning trajectories also depend on motivation and resourcefulness (Hmieleski and Corbett 2006). Learning from experience, through both reflection and reflexivity (Cunliffe 2002) enhances an entrepreneur's human capital and provides opportunities to translate experience into innovation. Managerial and technical competencies are important, but the ability and willingness to engage in critical reflection provides the creativity necessary to promote organizational learning (Cope 2003).

It is often argued that, in order for entrepreneurs to successfully manage the complexities of establishing a venture, previous education and work experience need to be supplemented by the advice and knowledge gained through networking (West and Noel 2009). Entrepreneurs must enlist the support of others to join their firms, to help make and sell their products or services, and to help them realize imagined futures (Gold et al. 2002). They must also possess the social skills to enable them to interest potential stakeholders in the new venture (Baron and Tang, 2009). Such social skills (human capital) are important for converting 'weak ties' into strong ties that provide access to valuable resources (Granovetter 1973). Previous business experience helps create intangible assets (reputation) that give owner-managers credibility with other actors and therefore the potential to access valuable resources to the venture.

Entrepreneurs must be able to convince others that their chosen direction has merit and embed that vision in shared practices (Gold et al. 2008). Analysis of entrepreneurial stories demonstrates the interdependence of the entrepreneur and employees within an institutional context (O'Connor 2002). Thus, in order to enact change, entrepreneurs must use their human capital to engage with others and foster what Sadler-Smith et al. (2001) describe as a 'learning orienta-tion'. Utilizing human capital requires entrepreneurs to collaborate with others in order to embed learning in shared activities (Macpherson and Jones 2008). It is these collaborative routines that potentially support firm-level innovation and performance.

**93**

### 6.5.1 Experience as human capital

The entrepreneur's ability to effectively engage in opportunity creation is largely influenced by previously acquired experience and abilities as well as the learning that takes place at each stage of the venture creation pathway (see Box 6.1, below). Previous experience is not only a means to acquire the knowledge and skills required to manage a new business, but it also acts as a powerful factor for accessing additional resources. While inexperienced entrepreneurs rely more on personal sources such as family, friends, and other business owners in their search for information, experienced entrepreneurs seek advice and support from more powerful and resource-rich sources (Cooper *et al.* 1995). Entrepreneurs whose business operations complement their previous employment can make use of the experience, knowledge and connections that are very relevant to the business in hand.

West and Noel (2009) provide a word of caution when they explain that the relatedness of experience to the new venture influences future performance. Politis *et al.* (2012) found that entrepreneurs with previous business experience or experience from the same industry are capable of securing and using less costly resources during the new venture creation process. Experienced entrepreneurs were also found to be practising bootstrapping in favour of traditional resource acquisition behaviours. Previous experience of the same industry in which the business is to function is considered particularly important for accessing the industry-specific knowledge necessary to become competitive (Sharifi and Zhang

---

**BOX 6.1**

I remember being very young and going to dad's office and him teaching me to do the very big A1 plans and also just being aware of the pressures he was under sometimes.

I also did a bit of work for my father at the time – he had an architect business at the time and so I did his website and did a few things like coordinating marketing activity. I probably did that for a few months – working off my kitchen table, pretty much, for most of that time and at that time I was generating enough business.

It is always around you and you are kind of aware of it – I had seen people fail, I had seen my dad fail, not fail, but the job come to a natural conclusion due to the market conditions; I had seen the businesses I had worked for when I was in University, get funding and go bump. So without that I don't think I wouldn't have learnt what I have.

[Anna Heyes, *Active Profile*]

---

2009). Such knowledge is especially beneficial to 'spot trends or generate a range of possible alternatives from which to make the best possible business decisions' (Boeker and Karichalil 2002: 821). Additionally, experiences in different functional areas can provide the entrepreneurs with a wide breadth of management skills and know-how that is essential to manage and run their own businesses (Timmons and Spinelli 2004).

## 6.5.2 Knowledge as human capital

RBV asserts that a firm's growth and competitive advantage arises from managerial knowledge (Esteve-Perez and Manez-Castillejo 2008). In addition to knowledge relevant to the business, the knowledge to identify and evaluate those resources in which to invest and how to utilize them is a key task for the entrepreneur. Knowledge acquired by entrepreneurs through their idiosyncratic information gathering behaviours is particularly useful for acquiring and deploying resources in combinations that are difficult to copy. Tacit knowledge is more important than explicit knowledge for entrepreneurs who want to build long-term competitive advantage. Initially, internal knowledge largely resides with the individual entrepreneur and is central to opportunity creation. As the business develops, externally sourced knowledge in the form of partnerships with key stakeholders is important for enhancing the firm's resource capabilities (Jenssen and Koenig 2002). To be successful, entrepreneurs must know how to integrate product specific knowledge, facts and management techniques with contextual experience (Alvarez and Busenitz 2001).

The knowledge resources necessary for entrepreneurs include an understanding of the processes involved in business creation, people management, business growth, new technologies and new product development (Brush et al. 2001). The successful pursuit of these activities will depend on the entrepreneur's understanding of the types and configurations of resources that are necessary to develop a particular opportunity. Wiklund and Shepherd (2003b) identified three types of procedural knowledge important to new venture founders: knowledge about the industry, knowledge about the type of business and knowledge about starting-up new ventures. A wealth of experience-based knowledge, developed over time, exerts a central and often pivotal influence on the entrepreneur's ability to engage effectively in opportunity recognition and the exploitation of new ideas.

Entrepreneurs' understanding of opportunities is more likely to be related to the knowledge they have already acquired through occupations, job routines, social relationships and daily life (Venkataraman 1997). For example, high-tech entrepreneurs need specialized knowledge to understand and develop unique business opportunities within highly specialized industries. As Grant (1996) proposes, knowledge is the foundation for the rent-earning potential of all resources, and, therefore, entrepreneurs need to draw in new members with new

**95**

knowledge when seeking growth opportunities (Jones and Macpherson 2006). However, for new entrepreneurs, accumulation of human capital in the form of recruiting skilled and competent staff is a difficult task due to their limited financial capabilities. Therefore, 'an entrepreneur's expanding knowledge base and absorptive capacity becomes an entrepreneurial firm's competitive advantage' (Alvarez and Busenitz 2001: 766). Here pre-existing networks and the capability to bridge into new networks are both important. The first is a structural issue dependent on the number and depth of existing network ties (Elfring and Hulsink 2003, Elfring and Hulsink 2008). The second is a capability issue that requires the skills to understand resource opportunities available in more diverse network ties (Lee and Jones 2008). For example, the ability of entrepreneurs to actively engage suppliers and customers as well as other business and social contacts can help support emerging firms (Baker et al. 2003).

At an early stage, entrepreneurs lack the necessary resources to build an internal knowledge base. Essentially, knowledge resources and capabilities need to be identified, borrowed, appropriated and integrated from outside the firm's boundaries. This is particularly important for technological entrepreneurs as the range of knowledge resources necessary to create a successful business is unlikely to be readily available or possessed by the entrepreneurs themselves. For their ventures, high performance is more likely to be achieved if a range of skills is available via a start-up team or embedded in the firm's employees. If appropriate skills are absent, it is suggested that talented expertise may be recruited (Kaulio 2003), developed within a wider managerial team (Littunen and Tohmo 2003) or obtained via external consultants or through alliance partners and other firms in close proximity (Fernhaber et al. 2009). When entrepreneurship is team-based, it is important that knowledge and skills are complementary rather than dependent on a single individual with an absolute set of skills/knowledge (Jones et al. 2010b). Brush et al. (2001) conclude that one of the biggest challenges facing new ventures is transforming the founding entrepreneur's personal knowledge of the industry, market and product into organizational resources, especially when the entrepreneur is working with a team.

## 6.6 ACCUMULATION OF HUMAN CAPITAL OVER THE LIFE COURSE

Many researchers argue that the qualities entrepreneurs bring to new ventures largely depend on resources built up through their education and experience. While those with better education and experience have greater entrepreneurial intention (Kim et al. 2006), and more chance of succeeding, their opportunity costs for foregoing employment can be higher. Consequently, potential entrepreneurs with high human capital may not start a business, or only start one with high earning prospects (Cassar 2006). Despite it being widely accepted that human capital is an essential entrepreneurial resource base, most start-ups are founded by those with limited educational qualifications (Henley 2007). This distinction could be explained by differences between necessity-based entrepreneurship and opportunity-based entrepreneurship (Valliere and Peterson 2009). Contradictions in the evidence base may also result from weak conceptualizations of how the process of accruing human capital and the experience of applying it in the labour market influence business start-up. Educational and sociological researchers focus on how social factors, including family, influence children's educational attainments (Hartas 2011). Heinz (2002) argues that an individual's future outcomes arise from personal, family and work histories rather than from achievements fixed in time. Consequently, there has been growing interest in examining learning in a wider context, including on-the-job training as well as the role of family and community groups (Eraut and Hirsh 2007). Most of an individual's personal qualities are established at early stages in life and therefore 'entrepreneurs are a product of their upbringing' and being born in a family with the 'right kind of parents' is important to the pursuit of a successful entrepreneurial career (Douglas and Shepherd 2000: 233). Conceptualization of life course pathways leading into entrepreneurship is important in this regard as it enables us to understand potential entrepreneurs as socialized agents in continual interaction with an external social world structured through complex social relations that set boundaries on opportunities (Welter, 2011, Jayawarna *et al.* 2013). For example, Jayawarna *et al.* (2013) explained how motivations for sustaining business ownership relate to social structures in complex ways, as they are experienced by individuals across life courses.

Life-course studies have also promoted awareness in the potential links between human capital acquired in childhood with entrepreneurial potential (Jayawarna *et al.* 2007b). These life-course studies explain the importance of conceptualizing age-appropriate human capital effects on entrepreneurship and suggest using life histories over an extended period. A recent study using longitudinal UK data (National Child Development Study (NCDS)) argues that the accumulation of entrepreneur human capital is a long-term outcome arising from the development of childhood cognitive abilities (education, subject knowledge, intelligence) and advantages based on family resources (parents' education, occupation) combined with the cumulative 'events' and 'opportunities' experienced during adulthood (Jones and Jayawarna 2011). Empirical results suggest that there are powerful, and previously unexplored, human capital effects that foster the development of skills and competence necessary to follow a career in entrepreneurship (see Figure 6.3 for the conceptual framework used in this study). More specifically the research emphasizes the importance of studying human capital as a resource that begins in childhood. Childhood literacy skills negatively affect business entry, which suggests some support for the dyslexia thesis of entrepreneurship; numeracy skills although important are an inconsistent determinant of entrepreneurial status. The authors

**97**

go on to argue that cognitive ability at early childhood and outstanding ability identified in later childhood are strong positive predictors of entrepreneurship. The results further note that the importance of education in facilitating entrepreneurship operates not so much through the attainment of an outstanding education, but rather through attainment of moderate achievements with a solid basic education. More surprising were the strong links between human capital acquired through apprenticeship and the entrepreneurial prospects of young people. The role apprenticeship programmes play in delivering human capital necessary to promote entrepreneurship was attributed to two factors:

1  Apprenticeship endows people with specific skills and knowledge that give them advantages in setting-up a business.
2  Drop-outs from salaried employment may start an apprenticeship as an alternative route to increase the chances of employability and therefore have higher likelihood of starting a business.

Importantly, previous ownership experience (during early adulthood) has been found to account for a substantial portion of the human capital effects on entrepreneurship. This emphasizes the importance of specific human capital for opportunity identification and exploitation as relevant to entrepreneurship. Family-related resources, such as parents with entrepreneurial experience, also facilitate the accumulation of business specific knowledge. It is certainly well established that those children whose parents are involved in small businesses are more likely

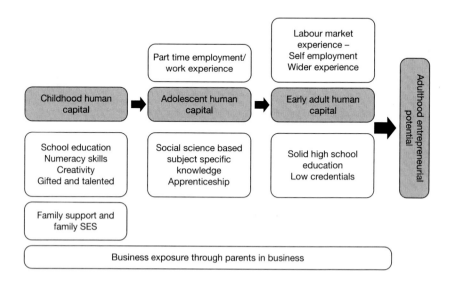

**Figure 6.3**
*Accumulation of human capital over the life course of the entrepreneur*

to become entrepreneurs themselves (Zellweger *et al.* 2011). This is generally attributed to the benefits of positive role models and early exposure to the experience of business-related activities. Work experience gained during secondary education is also a strong predictor of entrepreneurial careers in adulthood. As Burchinal *et al.* (1997) point out, early work experience provides students with a variety of resources and skills that are distinct from those acquired in other pursuits such as conventional education. This experience not only provides students with knowledge in areas such as money, banking and consumer matters, but it also helps with additional responsibilities and practical life-skills. Resources associated with early employment have close links to adult wealth accumulation and are also important for the creation of new businesses. It is legitimate that high-school employment is a stronger human capital predictor for entrepreneurship than for waged employment. Similarly, high-school employment helps to develop social networks of those with similar interests (Painter 2010), and social networks are valuable resources for future entrepreneurial endeavours. Painter (2010) also noted that an advantageous family socio-economic status (SES) could channel children with less cognitive ability into a more positive developmental pathway leading into a career in entrepreneurship. Children who grow-up in high SES families have more opportunities to convert negative human capital into positive entrepreneurial outcomes, and have more potential to nurture positive childhood human capital into positive entrepreneurial outcomes.

## 6.7 EFFECTS OF HUMAN CAPITAL ON ENTREPRENEURIAL SUCCESS

Some studies have focused on measuring the effects of human capital endowments by examining the influence of educational attainment and organizational experience on financial performance, growth and innovation. Kim *et al.* (2006), using US data from a panel study including nascent entrepreneurs and a comparison group, conclude that actual entrepreneurial entry was influenced by human capital; both educational attainment and prior managerial experience. Indeed a great deal of research in understanding success distinguishes between education and experience. According to Kim *et al.* (2006), attainment is normally a measure of the educational level (secondary or higher) rather than subject-specific, such as entrepreneurship. Few studies provide an examination of entrepreneurship education and business start-up. Those that do often consider the effects of a specific education programme on the business outcomes (Jayawarna *et al.* 2011). This study found that human capital (degree-level education) provided access to a wide network of resources for the early-stage business, which, in turn, facilitated development. It seems, therefore, that education is important, but the impact could be indirect since educational experience provides access to wider networks (see Chapter 5). A study by Colombo and Grilli (2010) focused on technology-based start-up firms also found that levels of founders' skills supported an argument of competence-based success in these businesses. Here, though, they also found that, in venture-capitalized firms, investors provided a coaching function that overrode the founder's skills deficits. In other words, human capital is still important; it does not have to belong to the venture owner, but they can 'borrow' it from others.

Other studies that have examined the transition to self-employment consider human capital resources such as the non-financial motivation to be an entrepreneur and work experience. In one study, Burke *et al.* (2002) found that non-financial motivation was influential on success for male entrepreneurs, but not for females; education and work-based human capital (experience) had similar gender differences. Wiklund and Shepherd (2003a) examined the relationship between growth aspirations and the success of small firms in 552 firms from four sectors in Sweden. They found that the cognitive resources available to a person, measured in terms of education and experience, magnified the effect of an entrepreneur's growth aspirations. In other words, motivation is not enough, and personal aspirations are realized through the human capital available to the entrepreneur, since this provides the ability to manage a growing business and, as mentioned above, to gain access to additional resources.

It might also be the case that such prior experience is both enabling and limiting. Eisenhardt and Schoonhoven (1990) address the impact of a firm's 'founding conditions' including human capital embodied in the management team. In their study of 92 high-tech firms in Silicon Valley, they found that the management team's composition, including past, shared and broader experiences, were associated with links to higher growth. They argue that, regardless of market conditions, previous managerial experience enabled a defter and more nuanced navigation of the market. Experienced teams were particularly effective in exploiting growth markets, suggesting that they could make more able strategic choices. Small differences multiplied significantly over time – that is, the effect of the human capital becomes more, not less, significant as ventures grow. Other studies have also found clear links between the founding management team's experiential and educational background and the subsequent dynamic development of the firm (Ensley and Hmieleski 2005, Hmieleski and Ensley 2007).

This suggests that the human capital available at start-up has a long-term influence on the trajectory of the firm. This is exactly what Baron *et al.* (1999) found in their study regarding the 'logics of organizing' implemented by a firm's founders. Their evidence suggests entrepreneurs influence not only organizational structures, but also the cultural fabric of the organization from the outset (Baron *et al.* 1999). They examined 76 growing technology start-ups in Silicon Valley California and found significant path-dependence in the way the firm developed from first principles, and this had a lasting effect on the intensity of bureaucracy. In essence, their findings suggest that the founder's organizational blueprints, theories or 'recipes' (Spender 1989) influence the rate of bureaucratization as the organization grows. Those firms that made early investment in 'cultural control' or softer management skills were able to economize on formal administrative systems. In other words, the early systems implemented create a culture that influences future organizational development. Such path dependencies are important since prior experience may not necessarily be relevant to developing a vibrant new firm. In that way, prior knowledge and skills gained through experience may actually impede longer-term development. Taken together, these findings suggest that the early days of a new venture are particularly important, since entrepreneurs establish systems and activities quickly that have a long-term influence on success.

So, human capital in the form of prior education and experience is not only relevant because of the way in which new entrepreneurs apply it within the firm; human capital is also important because it mediates access to wider capital resources available from external networks (Chapter 5). However, contradictions in the evidence may be related to the difficulty of conceptualizing (and testing) how human capital is both accrued and applied in the labour market and how that experience influences start-up (Unger *et al.* 2011). Nevertheless, it seems that prior education and experience potentially provide the knowledge and skills required by new entrepreneurs to establish systems, structures and relationships; these initial structures then have a long-term effect on the trajectory of the firm, since they create path dependencies. This can be both positive and negative dependent on the range of skills brought to the venture (see Chapter 4 for a discussion of entrepreneur skills and competencies).

## 6.8 SUMMARY AND KEY LEARNING POINTS

RBV has focused attention on the role of firm resources as critical inputs and as a key source of competitive advantage. Prior research suggests that those with higher capital resources are more likely to establish successful new ventures, since such capital endowments allow exploitation of the potential inherent in processes of production. Accumulation of resource stocks for new venture creation is a special case of resource-based theory as start-up resources are very limited and largely depend on the entrepreneur's original endowments (funds, education, experience, time and contacts). These entrepreneurial resources need to be combined with external resources acquired as the firm becomes established.

Primarily based on the resource-based view of the firm (Barney 1991), research on entrepreneurship has attempted to link stocks of human capital to venture founding and success. Human capital is a valuable resource for the nascent entrepreneur as it is the first and sometimes the only resource available to them at start-up. Human capital not only includes the individual's stock of knowledge and skills acquired through prior education and experience, but also their rhetorical and social skills, which are necessary to persuade others about the potential of their proposed venture. Researchers have also explored the importance of conceptualizing age-appropriate human capital effects on entrepreneurship and suggest life histories, starting from childhood, are required to fully appreciate its role.

Taken together, the key learning points from this chapter are:

■ Each business start-up is different as they possess unique bundles of tangible and intangible resources and capabilities that are acquired, developed and expanded over time.

■ Intangible resources are more important than tangible resources for entrepreneurs to achieve competitive advantage, as these resources are developed internally and competitors cannot obtain them in the factor market or appropriate the same value in a new context.

■ Human capital endowments are enhanced through experience, education and critical reflexivity, and cannot be created or deployed in a vacuum. This accumulated human capital is central to enhancing absorptive capacity, social capital and, ultimately, firm performance.

■ An individual's human capital accrued through cognitive developments and achievements in early childhood influence entrepreneurial potential in adulthood.

■ Despite the wider recognition of the importance of the entrepreneur human capital and the development of a firm knowledge base, research into the link between human capital and success is not as clear as we would expect.

## 6.9 DISCUSSION QUESTIONS

■ What are the main types of resources that entrepreneurs require at the early stage of business development? What are the implications of the resource-based theory of the firm for defining these resources within an entrepreneurial firm?

■ What are the key sources of human capital for the entrepreneur, and how do these sources help to understand the resource capability of the entrepreneur and the entrepreneurial venture?

■ What are the implications of seeing the human capital of the entrepreneur as emerging from childhood? How might the human capital acquired during childhood and parental influence in childhood education influence entrepreneurial potential in adulthood?

■ Why is it challenging to link the knowledge and experience as the human capital of the entrepreneur to new venture performance?

## 6.10 FURTHER READING

Penrose, E. T. (1959/1995) *The Theory of the Growth of the Firm*, Oxford: Oxford University Publications.

Sarasvathy, S. D. (2001) 'Causation and Effectuation: Toward a Theoretical Shift from Economic Inevitability to Entrepreneurial Contingency', *The Academy of Management Review*, (2), 243–263.

# Chapter 7

# Enhancing tangible resources

## 7.1 INTRODUCTION

New entrepreneurs have to create a resource base to invest in assets, fund business operations and support growth agendas: decisions regarding tangible resources, including finance, are critical. Many young entrepreneurs start with low levels of capitalization, and this has a major influence on the survival and growth prospects of their ventures. Existing empirical evidence provides support for the assertion that new ventures face difficulties in acquiring external finance, or the lack of financial support discourages many people from starting businesses. The entrepreneur's personal financial capabilities are often limited, and, in the absence of internal cash generation, young entrepreneurs are unlikely to have the capacity to self-fund their ventures.

There are a variety of forms of capital and several possible sources of finance, including internal equity financing (i.e., money from the entrepreneurs, their family and friends), bank loans, trade credit, government grants, business angel investment and venture capital funds. Entrepreneurs in their early stage of business start-up, however, are regularly denied finance and working capital by external investors. According to a report by the Department of Business, Innovation and Skills (BIS) less than 50 per cent of small ventures in the UK utilize any form of external finance (including credit cards and overdrafts); only 11 per cent of those ventures used bank loans (including commercial mortgage) and between 1–2 per cent attempted to obtain equity finance (BIS 2012). Banks follow conservative, risk-mitigated lending approaches and therefore tend to pick entrepreneurs that are already successful or have access to assets to provide collateral. Traditional venture capital and business angels represent only a minor proportion of the necessary capital for entrepreneurial ventures. Due to limited external finance options available to new ventures, this forces entrepreneurs to consider alternative sources including personal investments. Bootstrap financing enables entrepreneurs to access resources at 'little or no cost' (Harrison *et al.* 2004) and is a popular strategy for start-up and during the early stages of operation (see Chapter 8 for a fuller description of bootstrapping finance).

In this chapter, we give an overview of different funding options available for new entrepreneurs and discuss the various opportunities and challenges. Drawing insight from theoretical and empirical contributions to the subject of venture finance, we then consider the difficulties entrepreneurs face when accessing external finance. We discuss information asymmetries and moral hazards, which are barriers to accessing financial resources from external providers. While initial financial decisions are important for the pursuit of new opportunities, entrepreneurs need additional capital as their firm develops, and therefore financing choices and lending relationships evolve over time. We also give an overview of the resourcing requirements of three specific types of venture: social enterprises, high-technology ventures and family businesses. Finally, we evaluate the current evidence, both academic and policy, on whether or not entrepreneurs face a funding gap in the current financial market.

## 7.2 LEARNING OBJECTIVES

- To explain the challenges for the entrepreneurs to raise finance for their entrepreneurial ventures.
- To analyse different financing options for the entrepreneur.
- To describe theoretical and empirical explanations of funding gap for new entrepreneurs at start-up stage.
- To identify the lifecycle aspect of a firm's financing and capital structure decisions.
- To explain how context influences the finance choice of entrepreneurs.

## 7.3 TANGIBLE RESOURCES

The resource-based view (RBV) refers to both tangible and intangible resources as important sources of capabilities that contribute to the value-creation process. Although intangible resources (see Chapter 6) are more likely to generate competitive advantage than tangible resources (Hitt et al. 2001b), the latter are undeniably an essential entrepreneurial resource that contributes to survival and the performance of entrepreneurial activities. Tangible resources encompass financial, physical and organizational assets (Barney 1991). Financial resources generally include the cash assets that are necessary to generate products and services and to acquire other essential resources. Financial resources can come from institutional investors (primarily banks, government agencies and venture capital funds) and individual investors (the entrepreneur, family, friends and angel investors). Physical resources for the firm include raw materials, equipment, technology, premises and geographic location. Organizational assets include the firm's formal and

**105**

informal planning, controlling, coordinating and reporting systems. Both physical and organizational resources can be used as collateral to secure financial capital.

## 7.4 WHY IS IT DIFFICULT TO FINANCE ENTREPRENEURIAL VENTURES? A THEORETICAL EXPLANATION

The value and quality of an entrepreneur's ideas are difficult to judge and quantify. Without the ability to evaluate the viability of ideas, resource-providers have difficulties in judging whether entrepreneurs are capable of transforming resources into value added activities (Jing *et al.* 2011). Investments in early-stage ventures are high-risk due to liabilities of newness, lack of prior financial history, limited business experience and untested markets. Unless the risk-returns of the investment can be accurately evaluated by appropriate due diligence, resource-providers are at risk of losing their investments (Shane and Stuart 2002). In addition to uncertainty, information asymmetry also complicates resource acquisition. Information asymmetries arise when outside financiers do not have the same information about the quality of an investment as the entrepreneur. Specifically, entrepreneurs possess more information about their own abilities and the prospects of their ideas than external resource-providers (Shane 2000). Unless entrepreneurs can transfer this information and establish credibility, resource-providers cannot appraise the viability of new ventures.

Entrepreneurs are often reluctant to disclose fully information to resource-providers because of business confidentiality. Failure to communicate effectively with potential investors means that entrepreneurs face the risks of funders misinterpreting the information. This is particularly the case with evaluating technological innovations because of long product development times and the mismatch of the entrepreneur's scientific knowledge and the funder's commercial skills (Van Auken 2002). In such events, as Dowd (2009) notes, it is essential that financial investors apply precautionary contractual restrictions in order to reduce risk exposure and it is a technique deployed by all reputable financial institutions. Empirical evidence suggests that businesses that have a high risk of failure and limited cash flow tend to seek more external funding. Therefore, applying such contractual restrictions is an important mechanism for discouraging entrepreneurs with low survival prospects seeking debt finance (Vanacker and Manigart 2010).

The other difficulty entrepreneurs face when obtaining external finance is related to the moral hazard problem. Moral hazards occur in situations where 'one person makes the decision about how much risk to take, while someone else bears the cost if things go badly' (Krugman 2009: 63). Essentially, it is asserted that, because the capital risk is shared between lender and borrower, the latter takes higher risks than they would have done without external funding (Dowd 2009). It also recognized that entrepreneurs might misuse or misallocate external funding for personal benefit. In order to ensure that this is not the case, financiers introduce complicated contracts with restrictive terms and conditions that they manage through costly and labour-intensive monitoring systems. However, it is acknowledged that, while financial institutions can monitor the borrowers' activities throughout the duration of the facility, the cost of performing this role can be disproportionately high. Research also indicates that the cost of monitoring may lead to credit rationing even in circumstances where there is limited evidence of moral hazard and adverse selection (Dowd 2009).

There are a number of strategies to mitigate the problems of information asymmetry and moral hazard to improve the probability of resource acquisition by entrepreneur (Shane and Stuart 2002). These include encouraging information transfer through social ties, introduction of intensive monitoring systems and credit subject to collateral provided by the entrepreneur. Interpersonal relationships with resource-providers are also instrumental in helping entrepreneurs overcome their financing problems (Shane and Cable 2002). Additionally, network ties are useful in mitigating the problem of information asymmetry faced by entrepreneurs when acquiring resources at the early stage of venture creation. Appropriate signals from the entrepreneur's social network are useful for potential investors to evaluate ideas, the entrepreneur's skills and capabilities and their long-term commitment to the venture (Jing *et al.* 2011).

## 7.5 DIFFERENT FINANCIAL SOURCES FOR NEW ENTREPRENEURS

New entrepreneurs seek financial investment from both internal and external sources. Traditionally financial decisions have concentrated on choices between personal investments (savings, friends/relatives), debt finance (bank loans and government guaranteed loans), equity finance (business angel and venture capital funds) or a mix of all three. While each option certainly has its pros and cons, a careful consideration of the capitalization configuration is essential to future success. The costs attached to some of these resources can be substantial and making repayments through retained earnings is often more a myth than a reality for most entrepreneurs. Alternative methods to raise finance, including bootstrapping (see Chapter 8) and crowd financing (see Box 7.1) have therefore become popular among early stage entrepreneurs.

Atherton (2012) provides two explanations for the capitalization structures of new ventures. First, a majority of firms suffer from under-capitalization at start-up and this not only limits venture growth prospects, but also makes ventures vulnerable to closure. Second, there is noticeable variation in the scale and nature of capitalization structures, and new entrepreneurs have a tendency to acquire 'bundles' of resources from a wide variety of sources. In practice, financing choices depend on multiple factors: the characteristics, preferences and aspirations of the

---

**BOX 7.1**

**Crowd financing** is an alternative financing method largely used in charities, but equally relevant in resource-poor new ventures to raise the capital required to fund projects/enterprise. Here large numbers of individuals network and pool small amounts of cash to support a worthy/interested cause by collective cooperation. This method of financing helps entrepreneurs to replace one large loan that demands higher returns with small amounts of donated money (or in some cases through selling small amounts of equity to investors). Although this is not an ideal financing option for all entrepreneurs, it gives some entrepreneurs, especially those who have a solid set of goals and principles but fail to access necessary finances, the opportunity to test their venturing ideas.

---

entrepreneur, capital requirements (depending on the type of the venture), venture growth potential, and the availability of collateral. Atherton (2012) highlights the 'subjectivized influences' that determine new venture financing patterns. For example, entrepreneurs employ different levels of risk-taking, which has implications for their willingness to take on debt. The stage of the business is also a decisive factor. For example, debt financing at the inception stage is riskier as repayment of loan instalments may not be possible due to limited cash flow. Equities can ease cash deficiencies, even though attracting equity funding is a difficult challenge for entrepreneurs without a strong capital base. Here the founder/team's ability to negotiate with funders and their 'financial literacy' in relation to resourcing the start-up is particularly valuable.

## 7.5.1 Debt finance

Debt finance includes loans provided by creditors including commercial banks, brokerage firms, credit unions and leasing companies as well as non-traditional lenders including family, friends, government and other businesses. Three forms of debt financing are available for entrepreneurs in their early stage of venture development: credit card or overdrafts from banks, asset-based finance (e.g. equipment based loans) and supplier credit (credit offered by suppliers for inventory and equipment; Baron 2012). Credit cards are particularly useful because they require no explanation to lenders and are easier to obtain than other external funds. Overdrafts are also useful as they allow a flexible approach to borrow an agreed limit when needed by the entrepreneur. In addition to its attractiveness as working capital, this flexibility allows entrepreneurs to use overdrafts to 'even out' any cash-flow changes (Storey and Greene 2010). According to Scott (2009), nearly 60 per cent of entrepreneurs use multiple credit card debt and overdraft facilities to fund approximately one third of their debt in their first year.

The main source of capital debt (in terms of the amount borrowed) for entrepreneurs is bank loans. Banks are extremely conservative in their lending for early-stage businesses and therefore acquiring start-up finance from banks is not an easy process for new entrepreneurs. Usually, entrepreneurs have to offer collateral or personal guarantees to secure loans, since banks regard new businesses as very risky given their high failure rates. Banks typically finance a smaller proportion of debt in the first year when entrepreneurs face potentially large adverse-selection and risk-shifting incentives (Huyghebaert *et al.* 2007). At this stage, by lending on a short-term basis, banks retain more control over the firm and its investment decisions. Taking on short-term debt is riskier for entrepreneurs as it demands a positive cash-flow in the short term to make the loan repayments. Banks increase the availability of credit to entrepreneurs, often offered as long-term debt, as the banking relationship develops (see Box 7.2). Long-term debt allows entrepreneurs to invest in projects that are of interest to them and have long-term prospects. Indeed, banks reward successful entrepreneurs with more credit at favourable repayment rates. Banks decide to grant a new loan, or offer an extension to an existing loan, based on the level of current earnings, changes in earnings over time and the entrepreneur's debts with other lenders (Huyghebaert and Van de Gucht 2007). Entrepreneurs in high-debt ventures, and those who are keen to access future debt finance, embark on projects that boost immediate profits to the detriment of projects with smaller initial earnings but larger future prospects. More positively, debt finance does not require entrepreneurs to give up any ownership in their business. However, it involves a financial obligation to return the capital together with an interest rate set by the bank that makes it an expensive funding option for most entrepreneurs (see Table 7.1 for a summary of debt and equity finance).

## BOX 7.2

It was about a year later – about a year on. I was always calling it, 'The business' – it wasn't like it was just me calling it, 'The business', but it was probably about a year later when I had too much work and I needed to take somebody on to assist with that work, and so I went to the bank and got £10,000 and I matched that. They could see I had work as I had proved I was kind of trading, and I matched that with about £6,000 from Merseyside Special Investment Fund at that time which opened up another door.

[Anna Heyes, *Active Profile*]

**Table 7.1** *Debt and equity finance: advantages and disadvantages*

| Funding type | Advantages | Disadvantages |
| --- | --- | --- |
| Debt finance | • Does not decrease/dilute the entrepreneur's equity position<br>• Entrepreneur is singularly accountable for successes/failure<br>• Entrepreneur is the sole recipient for all the ensuing profits<br>• Can enjoy the complete liberty to control the venture without any undue interference<br>• Autonomy<br>• As the interest repayed is tax-deductible, it shields part of the business income from taxes | • Potential cost of financial distress<br>• Agency costs arising between owners and financial creditors<br>• High-risk strategy as far as company growth is concerned<br>• Debt repayments can vary based on changes to interest rate<br>• Additional management time to manage the debt<br>• Failing to make repayments leading to firm liquidation<br>• Demanding pay-back schedule<br>• Risk of losing collateral |
| Equity finance | • Relatively large investments<br>• Fewer restrictions on repayments<br>• Often are 'hands on' investors who are willing to contribute experience, knowledge and contacts<br>• Equity providers are motivated by non-financial considerations<br>• Receive close monitoring<br>• Willing to take more risks | • Dilution of founder's share<br>• Potential loss of control |

## 7.5.2 Equity finance

Entrepreneurs can obtain equity finance through internal and external sources; the choice depends on resource requirements, market conditions and the stage in venture development. Internal equity, primarily in the form of entrepreneur contributions (owned or accessed through relatives and partners) and retained profits are widely used by entrepreneurs. External equity can originate from informal angel investment or via venture capital markets. Access to these funding sources is, however, quite limited for new ventures or provides only a partial solution to capital requirements in the early stages of venture development.

### 7.5.2.1 Internal equity (personal investment)

The most common source of new venture capital is the entrepreneur's personal finance. In additional to investing personal savings, entrepreneurs provide funding through credit cards, overdrafts and earnings from employment. Many entrepreneurs also turn to friends and family to raise the capital that they need to finance their businesses. GEM (2007) reported that personal finance on average represents over 60 per cent of the $65,000 start-up capital needed by the new entrepreneurs. According to Fraser (2009) personal savings are the most common source of internal finance (91 per cent of all internal sources) followed by loans and gifts from family and friends, credit cards and home mortgages. Investments by family and friends are less expensive, have flexible return policies and make fewer demands in terms of equity. Although there is rarely sufficient funding from these sources, they do provide the capital to set-up and run the venture in the short term. In the longer term, these forms of capital can act as a signalling mechanism to investors and lenders about the entrepreneur's commitment to the new venture and its future prospects (Han *et al.* 2009b). Investment by the owner forms a major component of a firm's collateral.

## 7.5.2.2 External equity

Entrepreneurs who have a viable business idea that involves high R&D (research and development) investment often regard external equity as the preferred form of finance. Ou and Haynes (2006) give examples of two other situations when start-up ventures seek equity finance: first, when they experience financial distress and finance from alternative sources is lacking. Uncertainty about a firm's future discourages regular lenders from granting a loan, and therefore equity would be the only viable alternative for working capital for some entrepreneurs. Second, when there is an imbalance between cash outflow from internal operations and cash inflow from regular financing sources. Here high-growth demands new products and services for new and existing markets. In this situation, equity capital is a useful resource to fill cash shortages for such expansion plans. Research also reveals that access to equity finance helps improve debt equity ratios that open the possibility of debt financing for expansion (Franck *et al.* 2010).

Despite its benefits of faster business growth and increased value of the business, equity finance can put pressure on entrepreneurs to make immediate post-entry profits and also involves sharing of management control with equity providers. It is important, therefore, that entrepreneurs maintain a balance between the costs of losing control of the venture with the prospects for faster business growth.

## 7.5.2.3 Business angels

Business angels are high net-worth private individuals who provide their own finance, time and expertise directly to new ventures with a view to financial gain (Giurca Vasilescu 2009). Although typical business angels are former or current entrepreneurs themselves, they are extremely difficult to identify because of the private and unreported nature of their investment activities (Mason and Harrison 1995). In the 2008/2009 period, business angels invested $19.2 billion in the US

(Sohl 2009) and £62.8 million in the UK (Mason and Harrison 2010). Interestingly, 45 per cent of all the US and over 69 per cent of the UK business angel investments were in early stage ventures. Mason (2009) provided four reasons why informal business angel finance is important for entrepreneurs. First, business angels are often motivated by non-financial considerations and are, therefore, willing to make more risky investments. Their investment decisions are largely based on personal preferences, which make them one of the few financing options available for entrepreneurs operating in the seed and start-up stages of venture creation. Second, business angels, for convenience, largely make investments locally, and this not only helps to address regional gaps in the availability of finance, it also helps entrepreneurs gain regional knowledge related to local markets. Third, business angels are typically 'hands on' investors who willingly contribute their experience, knowledge and contacts to the entrepreneur. Because business angels often come from an entrepreneurial background, they have high-levels of commitment to contribute to venture success. Finally, due to the policy commitment to expand angel investment activity, there are more opportunities for entrepreneurs to access angel investments. As existing investment from business angels is often a prerequisite for obtaining investments from venture capitalists (Madill *et al.* 2005), it is very important that more business angel investment is available for new entrepreneurs. However, the lack of information relating to business angels' existence hinders the scope and impact of this form of investment.

Past research has explained a wide variety of possible criteria that business angels use when evaluating opportunities (see Mason and Stark, 2004, for a review). These include both tangible measures (such as sales, profits, market place advantages, intellectual property rights) and intangible measures (such as skills, experience, characteristics of the entrepreneur and the quality of the management team). Additionally, entrepreneur qualities such as openness, honesty, integrity, business understanding and the ability to realistically value venture ideas can positively influence Angel decisions (Madill *et al.* 2005). Recently Maxwell *et al.* (2011) came up with a business angel decision-making behaviour model following the Canadian version of the reality TV show *Dragons' Den* (see Box 7.3). The two studies confirmed that business angels follow a non-compensatory decision-making heuristic to select a few from the set of opportunities looking for investment, and this method of opportunity identification is very common in business angel funding for start-ups.

### 7.5.2.4 Venture capital

Venture capital (VC) funding constitutes investment from institutional investors (including pure VC firms, corporate VC units of large industrial companies, investment banks and private equity firms) who are interested in gaining equity stakes in entrepreneurial ventures with strong growth potential (Colombo *et al.*

## BOX 7.3

First launched in Japan, *Dragons' Den*, a reality show that is now airing in countries across the globe, showcases the business angel investment and decision-making process for new entrepreneurial ventures. Here entrepreneurs pitch for investment in the Den to venture capitalists (called Dragons) willing to invest their money in exchange for equity from the venture, the amount of which is stipulated at the beginning of the discussion. Upon an agreed investment by an Angel, entrepreneurs get the opportunity to accept the offer, negotiate further or simply walk away (see more information on BBC *Dragons' Den* at www.bbc.co.uk/programmes/b006vq92).

Recent research evidence from the recordings of the interactions from *Dragons' Den* suggests that the business angels do not use a fully compensatory decision-making model in the first selection stage, and that they trade off speed for decision accuracy. One 'fatal flaw' from the objective criteria in this initial stage can result in rejecting a good candidate and thereby filtering them out from the decisions in the subsequent stages, which are largely subjective (see more details in Maxwell *et al.*, 2011).

2007). The stage of venture development, levels of risk, the entrepreneur's background, geographic location and exit opportunities affect venture capitalists' assessment of potential returns and motivation to invest (Van Auken 2002). As venture capitalists only support high-growth enterprises that need large amounts of investment, a very small proportion of entrepreneurs meet their funding criteria (Timmons and Spinelli 2004). VC funding therefore represents only a small percentage of total capital invested in entrepreneurial businesses. Moreover, due to high agency costs associated with due diligence, VC finance is an expensive solution for new entrepreneurs; only a limited number of VCs are involved in seed-stage funding. In general, venture capitalists expect a large share of ownership, although the share depends on the perceived growth potential of the venture. Additionally, in riskier investments, venture capitalists impose restrictions on the actions of entrepreneurs to protect their financial investment. High-risk/high-return opportunities offered by VC investment can be suitable for young innovative entrepreneurs, as traditional financing sources are unavailable, inadequate or inappropriate to fund risky business ideas. In this respect, VC funding is generally considered as the most appropriate source of external finance for high-tech ventures with secure IPR (Colombo *et al.* 2007). Due to their sectoral knowledge,

VC investors are in a stronger position to distinguish between 'good' and 'bad' investment opportunities than any other external investors.

The evaluation criteria for venture capitalists are largely related to the characteristics of the entrepreneur, their background and experience rather than market or product characteristics (Pintado et al. 2007). As there are information asymmetries between entrepreneurs and VC investors, they need to be embedded in local social networks to evaluate an investment opportunity efficiently (Ferrary 2010). Venture capitalists who are involved in first-round funding at the seed stage learn by collaboration through their involvement in the venture management. This reduces information asymmetries between investor and entrepreneur.

In addition to finance, venture capitalists provide entrepreneurs with additional resources through their experience, knowledge, social networks and enhanced image and market creditability (Hanlon and Saunders 2007). They add value to entrepreneurs' ideas by bringing investors and entrepreneurs together in an efficient manner and by making better investment decisions than entrepreneurs themselves. Also, VC investment essentially helps new ventures build reputation and achieve legitimacy. Large and Muegge (2008) point to the benefit of successful mentoring, which strengthens the entrepreneur's networks. The multifaceted forms of support that originate from venture capitalism also include moral support to build the investor base, and to review and help to formulate strategy.

## 7.6 FINANCE AND BUSINESS LIFECYCLE

Literature on capital structure theory acknowledges that entrepreneurial financing choices evolve with the changing characteristics of their venture. The structure of finance at later stages is dependent on the initial conditions and financing decisions made at start-up (Storey and Greene, 2010). Uncertainty and information asymmetries mean that entrepreneurs face difficulties in accessing finance during the start-up phase. At this stage, entrepreneurs largely rely on interpersonal networks and resource their businesses through various financial bootstrapping methods (see Chapter 8). Personal finance and finance acquired through family and friends is a significant proportion of the initial investment for most entrepreneurs. Personal finance can act as collateral to secure bank borrowings for the entrepreneur once the business begins to operate. Banks typically finance a smaller proportion of debt in the start-up year when firms face potentially large adverse-selection and risk-shifting incentives (Huyghebaert et al. 2007). Along with bank debt, entrepreneurs can also approach leasing companies and form research and development partnerships for product development.

As ventures mature, entrepreneurs generate more stable earnings, which help them to develop a record of accomplishment useful for future access to finance (Franck et al. 2010). Those who were fortunate to gain bank finance at early stages can develop an intense lending relationship with their banks, thus reducing information asymmetries between entrepreneurs and their banks. Consequently, banks will decrease credit terms and provide entrepreneurs with longer-term finance. This reduces the pressure on entrepreneurs enabling them to focus on more stable long-term income rather than riskier short-term earnings. Also, the availability of alternative financing sources – in particular internally generated cash – helps entrepreneurs focus on more innovative ideas that could be further funded by external equity. Additional capital required to fund high-risk projects and business expansion generally comes from business angels, VC funds, institutional investors and venture leasing companies (Nofsinger and Wang 2011). High-growth technology firms have a substantially higher probability of acquiring external equity at a relatively early stage of venture development. Changes in financing strategies along the venture lifecycle are depicted in Figure 7.1.

## 7.7 VARIATION IN FINANCING STRATEGIES FOR DIFFERENT ENTREPRENEURS

The lifecycle approach to business finance clearly indicates that smaller businesses do not have access to the same sources of finance as larger businesses. Firms utilize very different sources of finance depending on the stage of business development (Figure 7.1). Additionally, finance strategies for firms differ according to the type of entrepreneurial venture. The discussion that follows explains the financing strategies employed by entrepreneurs running social enterprises, high-technology ventures and family businesses (Figure 7.2).

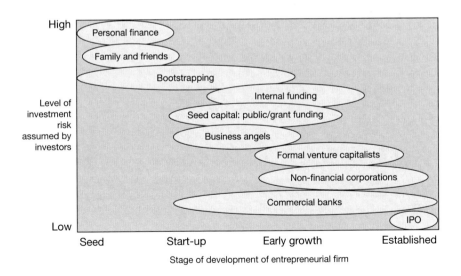

### Figure 7.1
*Change in financing strategies along the venture lifecycle*

**115**

### 7.7.1 Social entrepreneurs

Existing strategy typologies (see for example, Di Domenico *et al.* 2010, Moizer and Tracey 2010) highlight the different combinations of financial and non-financial resources that social entrepreneurs draw on. Financial resources come in the form of (a) earned income; (b) government and other contracts; and (c) philanthropic capital. Earned income includes generating financial revenue from services, programmes or products provided by social ventures themselves, or by their for-profit subsidiaries (at full, discounted or sliding-fee rates). These enterprises also create wealth through delivering mission-related services funded through government and other contracts. The non-distribution restriction limits the ability of social entrepreneurs to access the same capital markets as commercial entrepreneurs and their ability to pay commercial rates for human and other resources (Austin *et al.* 2006).

Restricted access to capital markets means that social entrepreneurs are often reliant on philanthropic funding in the form of grants, goods and in-kind donations from private individuals, third-party funding sources and membership fees. Philanthropic capital accounts for a considerable portion of the funding at start-up. The use of philanthropic capital raises a number of issues. First, the capacity to attract non-market sources of capital is tied to the social motives of the enterprise. Reliance on philanthropic funding can lead to what Teasdale (2010: 274) describes as 'coercive isomorphism' as social entrepreneurs tailor their processes, practices, objectives and goals to those prescribed by funding bodies. A corollary is that, because social entrepreneurs rarely recover the full cost of goods or services from consumers, funding bodies can become the most important clients. Hence, procuring resources can become the primary activity of social entrepreneurs (Austin *et al.* 2006). Second, limited access to capital markets means that it is essential for social entrepreneurs to engage with a wide range of stakeholders and develop substantial networks and partnerships if they are to leverage external resources (Austin *et al.* 2006, Khaire 2010, Moizer and Tracey 2010). Here the tensions between the social and economic imperatives of an enterprise become clear.

### 7.7.2 Family business finance

Entrepreneurs running family businesses follow a different strategies and financing structures from traditional entrepreneurs. The family-business literature provides both supply-side (ability to borrow) and demand-side (willingness to borrow) explanations for financing family businesses (Basu and Parker 2008). The supply-side explanation uses the idea of generational evolution in the family firm to argue that, given a smooth transition from one generation to the next, family firms have a better chance to access to debt financing. They have higher propensity to build long-term relationships with banks who consider them as less risky, profitable and more reliable. Arguably, these entrepreneurs have higher incentives to meet current and future obligations because failing to do so can damage the family name (Jones *et al.* 2013). Demand-side explanations on the other hand build on the premise that, irrespective of access opportunities, family-based entrepreneurs are reluctant to use external sources of capital as they dilute family control. Interestingly, Romano *et al.* (2001) highlight the importance of studying the behavioural dimensions such as the risk-taking, values and goals of family business owners. Although intergenerational differences can have an impact on the capital structure of family firms, they are in general in favour of internal, rather than external, sources of finance. Formal and informal external equity investment is therefore very limited as these entrepreneurs see financing their firms through these sources as a riskier option. Bank funding, on the other hand, can form a part of the funding equation for those family businesses that pursue expansion plans.

### 7.7.3 High-tech firms

High R&D costs, untested technology markets and long lead-time in commercializing new products make technology-based firms very high-risk investments (Mason and Harrison 1995). Entrepreneurs rarely have enough personal investment to fund expensive innovations. Access to external funds is problematic due to severe information asymmetries associated with new technologies. To overcome the problem of adverse selection finance, providers need a lengthy due-diligence process to access relevant information about the entrepreneur, the firm's scientific knowledge and intellectual property rights. Because large investments are required at an early stage, debt is not a suitable financing strategy for high-tech entrepreneurs. Short-term loans put unrealistic pressure on entrepreneurs to pay-off debts from internally generated cash. Empirical evidence shows that high-tech ventures have a significantly lower probability of being successful with long-term loan applications; the probability of being successful with loan applications decreases as the R&D intensity increases (Freel 2007). External equity investment is also a high risk for both entrepreneur and equity provider. The high risk-return characteristics of institutional investments, however, make VC funding sometimes the only suitable financing strategy for high-tech entrepreneurs (Van Auken 2002). VCs manage the risk of technology investments through close monitoring, personal involvement and through entering into legal and contractual agreements. Their sectoral specialization is particularly useful to overcome the information asymmetries between the entrepreneur and the VC investors and to highlight and support 'hidden values' of new technological innovations (Colombo *et al.* 2007). Research evidence suggests that, for the new entrepreneur, venture capitalists are an unlikely option since they are reluctant to finance technology-based companies at a very early stage (Bottazzi and Da Rin 2002) See Figure 7.2 for a summary of the debt and equity finance patterns of the firms discussed in this chapter.

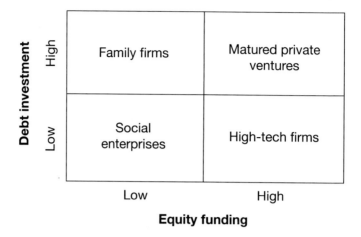

**Figure 7.2**
Debt and equity finance: type of venture

## 7.8 IS THERE A FUNDING GAP FOR ENTREPRENEURS?

It is widely accepted that entrepreneurs find it increasingly difficult to acquire external funding. Ways to improve the 'funding gap' has been a topic of national and international debate for some time. Funding gaps arise where businesses are unable to access finance that they could use productively (Cressy 2002, OECD 2009). There is a clearly recognized need to improve access to finance for new ventures on reasonable terms by banks and to set-up policies to ensure ventures with 'good growth prospects have access to appropriately structured risk capital at all stages of their development' (OECD 2006). While 'funding gaps' may be a global phenomenon, the theoretical justification is more controversial. Stiglitz and Weiss (1981) argue that small venture funding markets could be in a state of equilibrium yet still prevent access to finance for some ventures when banks *rationally* engage in processes of 'credit rationing'. According to Stiglitz and Weiss (1981), credit rationing occurs either when some receive credit while others do not, or there are identifiable groups in the population that are unable to obtain credit at any price. This asserts that asymmetric information and agency problems make it difficult for financial institutions to distinguish between 'good credit risks' and 'bad credit risks' (Han *et al.* 2009a). Therefore, finance providers are often unwilling to provide funding or put prohibitive restrictions on the type and amount of funding for small firms (Blumberg and Letterie 2008). These market failures create funding gaps for new ventures, particularly in technology-based sectors.

Indeed, despite an agreement that there is a shortage in the supply side of new venture financing, there is an unquestionable need to understand the interplay between supply and demand in the process of business creation and business growth (Han *et al.* 2009a). A review of public policies related to small firms confirms a common misconception that 'improving' the supply of finance will close the funding gap and thus solve the problem of small venture finance (Black and Strahan 2002, Rahman and Jianchao 2011). Recent research argues that this focus on funding supply is misguided for several reasons (Atherton 2012). There is a challenge to the common assumption that the 'funding gap' is a supply-side problem and demand for finance is out of the owner's control. Lam (2010) for example, alludes to the 'funding gap' being just as much a demand-side as a supply-side issue. Nascent, or start-up, new ventures enact their environment by actively managing demand as well as supply of finance to narrow the 'funding gap'. For example, this narrowing is done by creating the required start-up capital themselves, or relying on friends or family members to subsidize the venture. In other words, the 'funding gap' is not static or concrete, but it is dynamic and manageable in most cases (Lam 2010). This position is echoed by Harding (2002) who points out that it is the knowledge gap, rather than the funding gap, that needs to be addressed. Indeed, studies suggest that there are different banking and financial facilities (e.g. letters of credit, factoring, forfeiting – see Box 7.4) that business owners use to manage their financial needs without seeking external finance (bank loans, equity finance, etc.). Yet many business owners are not aware

## BOX 7.4

In issuing **letters of credit**, banks act as an uninterested party between customer and seller to assure payment to a seller for goods and/or services and therefore protecting the sellers from illegitimate customers. This is particularly useful for inexperienced entrepreneurs as payments authorized in the letter of credit are paid by the bank upon the delivery of the merchandise irrespective of any damages to the merchandise (which will be dealt with by the insurances).

**Factoring** releases the money tied up in customer invoices and help firms to prevent problems caused by late paying customers. This type of lending is important for firms to regulate their cash flows.

In international trading, **forfeiting** allows the exporter to receive immediate cash against its accounts receivable. Because the forfeiter takes on all the risks associated with the receivables (for a small return), like in factoring, forfeiting can make a direct contribution to the firm's immediate cash flow.

of their existence or relevance to their businesses. In other words, addressing this knowledge gap (the gap between availability of financial facilities for small firms and the level of the owner-manager's awareness) appears to be a realistic way of addressing financing needs without substantial government investment.

## 7.9 SUMMARY AND KEY LEARNING POINTS

In this chapter, we have examined the types of finance entrepreneurs can access to resource new ventures. Access to resources is one of the key ingredients that separates successful entrepreneurs from the unsuccessful. In most cases, business failure can be traced to a lack of finance, and many businesses are never started because of financial hardship. Using personal savings, assistance from family and friends and bootstrapping have become the best and sometimes the only ways in which a new entrepreneur can raise capital. Concerning external finance, most entrepreneurs do not have much flexibility in their choices. If it is a risky business with limited assets, it is impossible to get bank debt without putting up some collateral other than business assets (usually personal property). Many start-ups do not have high-growth potential and will never be candidates for equity finance from venture capitalists. Taken together the key learning points from this chapter are:

- For both nascent and early stage entrepreneurs finding seed and early stage funding is a difficult task.
- Entrepreneurs acquire very different forms of finance in different configurations; the choice of which is influenced by multiple factors including type of company, founder's aspirations, growth potential, market sector and the availability of collateral. Finance choice also depends on the stage of business development.
- Most start-ups are initially funded by the entrepreneur and family and friends. Bootstrap resources (including overdrafts and credit cards) also form a major part of the initial capital base of new ventures.
- As a venture matures and requires investments for growth, use of external finance increases with debt financing (mainly bank loans) and equity finance (business angels and venture capitalists) taking a role in providing finance for the firm.
- Entrepreneurs have to make a trade-off between paying interest and giving up some of their ownership when making a choice between debt or equity finance.
- Due to information asymmetry and the moral hazard problems, external financial providers are often unwilling to provide finance, or put prohibitive restrictions on the type and amount of finance for early entrepreneurial activities.

■ Financing-structure decisions for entrepreneurs vary based on the type of the venture they run. While early stage social enterprises are largely funded through informal bootstrap finance and philanthropic capital (with no or very limited bank loans or equity finance), high-growth businesses operating in high-tech industries often rely on equity finance (business angels and venture capitalists) for early stage finance. Entrepreneurs from family businesses often rely on debt finance to promote growth; external equity is an uncommon form of funding for family firms as access to these finances can result in family members losing control in their business.

## 7.10 DISCUSSION QUESTIONS

■ Why might financing strategies differ in early stages of a new venture from a more established venture?

■ What are the key principles that differentiate debt finance from equity finance?

■ An analysis of both the supply-side and demand-side issues related to financing behaviour of new venture suggests that there is no evidence for venture funding gap. Discuss this.

■ Why is business lifecycle important for understanding the financing behaviour of entrepreneurial ventures?

■ What are the key contextual characteristics that differentiate the financing patterns of different types of firms?

# Chapter 8

# Bootstrapping the start-up business

## 8.1 INTRODUCTION

Unless pursued in a perfect financial market, securing resources to exploit business opportunities is beyond the capabilities of most young entrepreneurs. In addition to facing disadvantage due to the liabilities of newness, these entrepreneurs often have limited potential for internal cash generation through realization of economies of scale. This puts pressure on the entrepreneur to enter into negotiations with traditional institutional sources such as banks. When they are inexperienced and lack a reputation in debt markets, external finance is difficult to access, expensive and often makes a negligible contribution to the early stage resource base of the entrepreneur. More specifically, financial investors are sceptical of new entrepreneurial ventures' potential for success due to substantial information asymmetries. High monitoring cost, moral hazards and associated mistrust are overheads for financers who make unfavourable investment decisions. As a mechanism to shield them from financial risks and to recover overheads, lenders often put additional constraints on lending terms, making external finance prohibitively expensive for the entrepreneur (Cassar 2004). This puts more pressure on the entrepreneur as expensive repayments further limit the cash-flows that are essential to set-up and run a successful new venture.

Given problems in securing market solutions to resource needs, there has been a push for entrepreneurs to seek resources by applying different kinds of financial bootstrapping methods. Bootstrapping promotes personal, intangible and opportunistic mechanisms to enhance entrepreneurs' ability to use and extract value from resources without necessarily gaining the ownership of the resource at hand. These methods collectively reduce the need for outside finance, improve cash flow and enable entrepreneurs to operate their businesses in a resourceful and creative manner. Bootstrapping has become a vital part of entrepreneurial finance, with as many as 80–95 per cent of entrepreneurs utilizing some form of bootstrapping in the early stages of business start-up (Bhide 1992, Harrison et al. 2004). The general assertion is that venture creators can use bootstrapping effectively to improve the chances for entrepreneurial success and provide opportunities for future growth if it is managed strategically.

In this chapter, we intend to demonstrate the use of bootstrapping as an alternative solution to traditional financing strategies. We first provide our working definition for bootstrapping and the theoretical position we take in explaining bootstrap behaviour by new entrepreneurs. We follow this with a discussion of different types of bootstrapping techniques entrepreneurs can consider when resourcing their ventures. Understanding how the entrepreneurs' financing preferences and the type of opportunities they are pursuing influence choices is important for those who wish to pursue a career in entrepreneurship. Also included in the discussion is a brief note about the gendered nature of bootstrapping and an explanation of how the preferences and the nature of bootstrapping vary over the course of the business lifecycle. Finally, we discuss how an entrepreneur might better position their venture for growth by adopting a range of bootstrapping behaviours.

## 8.2 LEARNING OBJECTIVES

- To analyse the importance of bootstrapping as an alternative resource strategy for those who face capital market imperfections.
- To describe different types of bootstrapping available for the entrepreneur to resource their ventures.
- To explain how the entrepreneur's motives and gender roles influence the bootstrap decision.
- To demonstrate bootstrapping as relevant to business lifecycle.
- To evaluate the potential of bootstrapping as a business growth strategy for the entrepreneur.

## 8.3 DEFINING THE CONCEPT AND THEORETICAL PERSPECTIVES

Financial bootstrapping has developed around the idea that resources not owned or controlled by the entrepreneur often play a key role in pursuing new opportunities for those who are resource-constrained. It essentially acknowledges resource acquisition that is either internally or externally generated and is often available at zero cost, or at least, below market price. Harrison *et al.* (2004: 308) define bootstrapping as a venture strategy that involves creative and economical means for 'marshalling and gaining control of resources'. They highlight two forms of bootstrapping strategy that operate in practice. The first form involves being resource 'rich' without recourse to bank finance or external equity finance. There are instances where entrepreneurs have no alternatives other than to resource the venture activities through borrowings from personal credit cards or cash generated by cross-subsidizing from other activities. The second form includes strategies that minimize the need for finance by securing resources at little or no cost. Such strategies largely refer to network advantages as social contacts often provide the entrepreneur access to free resources or resources accessed through subsidized rates (see Chapter 5 for a fuller discussion of entrepreneur networks).

The traditional view of bootstrapping coincides with a number of theoretical perspectives (see Figure 8.1). First, pecking order theory (Myers 1984) indicates that due to the existence of asymmetric information and monitoring costs, the higher risks associated with start-ups mean external financers demand higher returns on loans. Consequently, entrepreneurs are likely to resort to internal finance and will only raise external funds when retained earnings are depleted. Resource-constraint theory provides another interesting perspective to the idea of bootstrapping. It argues that entrepreneurial ventures may grow despite owning a limited resource base through more efficient use of limited resources at hand. For example, entrepreneurs can exploit available resource inputs more effectively by recombining them to make unique resources useful to build competitive advantage (Baker and Nelson 2005). Development of cash management skills and the use of network ties to gain access to resources are other typical examples within this context.

A third, and the most widely used, theoretical explanation for overcoming the inherent deficiencies of gaining access to formal finance and still running a successful venture is based on resource-dependency theory (Pfeffer and Salancik 1978). Resource dependency takes on the 'open systems' model to the problem and defines organizations as strategic agents that are strongly influenced by their external environment (Bretherton and Chaston 2005). As entrepreneurs do not possess all the resources they need, the environment in which their firm operates

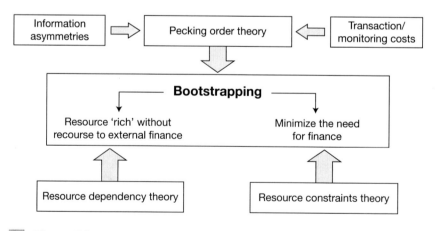

**Figure 8.1**
*Bootstrapping: a theoretical explanation*

is a very important resource base. Indeed, the extent to which an entrepreneur is dependent upon a given environment/social group can be determined by the organization's need for the resource controlled by that environment/social group. Therefore, the types of responses that organizations exhibit depend on the level and nature of dependencies they develop (Villanueva *et al.* 2012). As new ventures develop, dependencies will change, and therefore some alteration to the availability and desirability of the bootstrapping techniques is inevitable. This suggests that organizational theory also plays an important role in explaining the bootstrapping behaviour in new ventures (Ebben and Johnson 2006).

## 8.4 DIFFERENT TYPES OF BOOTSTRAPPING METHODS FOR THE ENTREPRENEUR

A number of models have emerged to explain the process of bootstrapping and the associated practices. Common to all these models is the view that entrepreneurs at inception are less likely to be funded through traditional sources and that capital minimization is a common practice. While the former rests on the notion that seeking alternative means to raise cash are important start-up and survival strategies, the latter recommend practices that minimize cash flow and business expenses, thereby opening up opportunities for exploring and expanding new ideas.

Work by Winborg and Landström (2001) has made a major contribution to our understanding of bootstrapping techniques (see Figure 8.2 for a summary). Their in-depth study using a sample of over 800 small businesses revealed the qualities of financial bootstrappers whose behaviour differed according to internal, social and quasi-market modes of resource acquisition patterns. These modes of bootstrapping generally fall into five groups (see Table 8.1).

The first group, 'owner-financed' bootstrapping includes methods the owner and his/her family and friends use to acquire necessary resources for the venture. These methods include using personal loans or own savings, cross-subsidizing through multiple assignments, using a private credit card for business expenses, withholding salary, and relatives working for the entrepreneur for free or below-market salary (see Box 8.1).

The second group, payment-related bootstrapping, is a combination of the practices associated with 'minimization of accounts receivable' and 'delaying payments'. These methods together provide cash-flow advantages to the entrepreneur through speeding up invoicing, using interest on overdue payments, negotiating longer terms with suppliers and practice leasing then making full payments during equipment purchase.

Customer-related bootstrapping (Group 3) includes practices such as obtaining advance payments, ceasing relations with late-paying customers and charging interest on overdue invoices. While all of these methods tend to improve cash

## BOX 8.1

With my computer recycling company I was quite convinced that there was a viable enterprise in it and started working on it. My daughter had just been born and my wife wasn't happy as she wanted me to go and get a job with somebody else, and I was convinced and I took on a supermarket free of charge, an old derelict supermarket in Toxteth – 5,000 square feet, and I filled it with computer equipment within weeks – just going out myself driving a van and picking stuff up and bringing it back, but those first six months were hard, and I just deferred any salary and ended up building up £20,000 worth of debt on credit cards – in the next year we got £40,000 worth of grants from the Liverpool City Council and I was able to pay that back and I said, 'never again' but I have done it again since, particularly the salary deferment because when things are tight or when you are trying to get over a hump, particularly with cash flow, but yes, all of the above salary deferment, credit cards, yes I've done them all.

[Paul, *Wigan Recycling*]

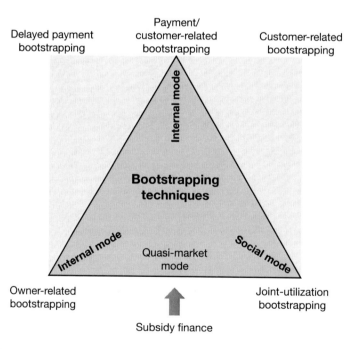

Figure 8.2
*Bootstrapping techniques*

flow from customers, some of these can have a negative long-term effect in terms of maintaining customer relationships.

These three methods are more internally oriented as they involve actively seeking means to improve internal cash flow either through introducing more discipline to entrepreneurial practices or through perseverance of the owner and his/her relatives.

The fourth group, 'joint-utilization bootstrapping', consists of a range of activities aimed at absorbing and borrowing resources at no/low financial cost from the entrepreneur's social networks. The presence of interpersonal relationships with resource owners is instrumental in gaining access to this socially oriented resource acquisition. Some of the most common methods of joint resource utilization include bartering, sharing or borrowing employees, premises, equipment and other assets. Methods to take advantage of economies of scale, such as coordinating purchases with others, working in partnerships and outsourcing are also useful means of resource sharing for this relationship-based entrepreneurship. The degree of trust between parties appears to explain the level of usage and impact of this method of bootstrapping.

**Table 8.1** *Bootstrapping: internal, social and quasi-market modes of resource acquisition*

| | | |
|---|---|---|
| • Internal mode of resource acquisition | • Owner-related financing and resources | • Use of manager's credit card<br>• Loan from relatives/friends<br>• Withholding manager's salary<br>• Assignments in other businesses<br>• Relatives working for non-market salary |
| | • Customer-related methods | • Cease business relations with late payers<br>• Lease equipment instead of buying<br>• Best conditions possible with suppliers<br>• Offer customers discounts if paying cash<br>• Choose customers who pay quickly |
| | • Payment-related methods | • Use routines for speeding up invoicing<br>• Use interest on overdue payment<br>• Delay payment to suppliers<br>• Delay payment of value-added tax<br>• Use routines in order to minimize stock |
| • Social mode of resource acquisition | • Joint-utilization of resources with other firms | • Borrow equipment from others<br>• Own equipment in common with others<br>• Coordinate purchases with others<br>• Share premises with others<br>• Share employees with others<br>• Practise bartering instead of buying/selling<br>• Raise capital from a factoring company |
| • Quasi-market mode of resource acquisition | • Subsidy finance | • Subsidy from local, regional and national support and funding bodies |

In addition to these four key bootstrapping methods, we have examples where subsidy finance or philanthropic capital from government and public organizations forms a major part of the resource formula for some entrepreneurs. This quasi-market mode of resource acquisition is particularly relevant for social entrepreneurs to discharge their social duties.

## 8.5 VARIATIONS IN THE USE OF BOOTSTRAPPING

While all these methods are useful for gaining access to resources, it seems fair to assume a significant variability in the extent to which entrepreneurs rely on financial bootstrapping. Recent research shows how the use of bootstrap strategies varies per entrepreneur preferences, motives and business lifecycle stage. The following discussion addresses these contingency perspectives on bootstrapping.

### 8.5.1 Entrepreneurs' financial motives and the use of bootstrapping

Winborg (2009) provides empirical evidence to suggest three groups of new business founders, differing in terms of their relative importance of motives for bootstrapping. The first group's – 'cost-reducing bootstrappers' – choice of techniques is governed by their desire to minimize costs during financial or non-financial transactions. By minimizing outgoings, these entrepreneurs operate their businesses with low-levels of resource demands. The second group, 'risk-reducing bootstrappers', have a preference for bootstrapping as it helps to reduce the risks of entering into contracts with formal financial providers. These entrepreneurs perceive their ventures to be risky and are more likely to pursue bootstrapping rather than more formal means of resourcing their ventures (Carter and Van Auken 2005). Empirical evidence suggests that both these groups of entrepreneurs consider bootstrapping as an effective resource acquisition strategy and therefore seek every opportunity to access bootstrap resources rather than using them as a 'last resort'. The third group, 'capital constrained bootstrappers', choose to utilize bootstrapping as a means of overcoming financial constraints, and therefore, for them, bootstrapping is very much a survival strategy.

### 8.5.2 Gendered nature of bootstrapping

It has been argued that obtaining external finance is much more difficult for female entrepreneurs than for male entrepreneurs. Traditionally, women's limited human capital and the general trend that they operate small, service-sector firms, with less focus on growth, are the main supply- and demand-side challenges for female-owned businesses. Since external finance is difficult and costly to obtain, bootstrapping is vital for female entrepreneurs. There is also some variation in the type of bootstrapping techniques used by male and female entrepreneurs. Brush *et al.* (2006) revealed that while bootstrapping is a common phenomenon among female owners, how they use the various techniques is based on the type and the stage of their business development. At the emergent stage of their businesses, female entrepreneurs minimize capital by reducing labour costs. As they progress, their emphasis changes to focus on minimizing capital by reducing operational costs. Jayawarna *et al.* (2012) also observed clear gender differences in the use of bootstrapping techniques. While men engaged in far more payment-related bootstrapping (customer and delay payment) activities than women, women made more use of joint-utilization and owner-related methods. Research evidence suggests that women have a significantly higher tendency to withhold salary, forgo income and subsidize the business with their personal credit cards than men (see Box 8.2).

According to Gupta *et al.* (2009), entrepreneurship is a 'gendered profession' (p. 409) and gender stereotypical differences place limitations on women's ability to accrue necessary resources for their businesses. Following this line of argument, Jayawarna *et al.* (2012) studied how men and women bootstrap their resources following stereotypical views that female entrepreneurs are more cautious, have less business competence, are less strategic, less interested in growth and adopt a more participative management style compared with male entrepreneurs. The study confirms the importance of bootstrapping to both male and female businesses, but the techniques have distinct gender-related patterns. Women in general have a higher tendency to use owner-related and joint-utilization methods, whereas men's bootstrapping practices are largely limited to payment-related techniques. This supports the broader view that individuals draw upon their own personal values, preferences and ambitions when choosing among alternative strategies (Carter *et al.* 1997). The results also provide strong support for the gendered nature of resource acquisition through payment-related methods; men make greater

## BOX 8.2

At the start, I charged ridiculous rates like £75 per day – stupid tiny amounts of money and got a few case studies of things that were working under my belt really. I think my first client was a photographer, something like that. I was working for one-man bands really and charging ridiculous fees. I also did some work for the previous company I had worked for and that subsidized the work that I was doing in the business.

[Anna Heyes, *Active Profile*]

**129**

use of payment-related methods than women. It is possible to argue that a risk-taking propensity, proactive thinking and perceived higher financial skills help men develop relationships with external parties, and these relationships are beneficial to negotiate payment-related resources with customers and suppliers. Similarly, behaviours associated with women entrepreneurs – including low risk-taking, limited commitment to growth, participative management and limited business skills – are linked with higher use of owner-related and joint-utilization methods by women.

The association between resource acquisition patterns, networking behaviour and generalized gender characteristics also confirms that there are clear structural barriers, which mean that women are disadvantaged when starting new businesses (Greene *et al.* 2001, Manolova *et al.* 2006). For example, negotiating competitively to acquire external finance, through brokers and bootstrapping supplier- and customer-related resources via weak ties, appears to require stereotypical masculine behaviour. Clearly, this presents problems if women are to acquire similar levels and types of resources as men. Concentration on strong ties means that female entrepreneurs will find it more difficult than men to obtain the resources necessary to grow their businesses (see Chapter 5 for a discussion of networking and resource acquisition).

### 8.5.3 Lifecycle approach to bootstrapping

Lifecycle research suggests that the financial structure followed by the entrepreneur should differ across the stages of organizational lifecycle, as different approaches are needed to finance the growth of the business at different stages (see Chapter 7 for more information). Within this hierarchical financial structure, it is argued that entrepreneurs will first seek funding through flexible internal sources, followed by bank financing (debt) and, finally, expensive equity capital financing (Cassar 2004). The administrative tasks of setting-up a business are diverse and entrepreneurs need to produce products/services cost-effectively to minimize financial burdens. Additionally, they have less formal organizational structures and therefore are resistant to formal contracts and relationships. Consequently, the use of informal, internal financing, such as bootstrapping, is more common among entrepreneurs in the emergent and early stages of business development. The purpose of bootstrapping at this stage is aimed towards minimizing expenses and meeting short-term cash-flow needs. As firms move from these early stages to stages of stability and growth (Chapter 10), resource constraints are likely to ease. Therefore, resource acquisition behaviour changes from an internal reactive approach to an external proactive approach, which minimizes the need for bootstrapping. During growth stages, entrepreneurs rely more on formal rules and procedures to ensure organizational and administrative efficiency, which makes formal financing a possibility for the entrepreneurs.

While entrepreneurs may use diverse sets of activities, lifecycle theories imply that the stage of the firm should affect the type of bootstrapping used in the same way as it affects the actual use of bootstrapping as a resourcing strategy across various stages of business development (see Figure 8.3). In other words, the type of bootstrapping used in different lifecycle phases should reflect differences in entrepreneurs' need for capital as suggested by organizational development theories. In terms of the type of bootstrapping utilized, the stage model suggests that the methods change as the business develops. Certain methods are more widely used at the beginning of the lifecycle with different approaches becoming important as the entrepreneur gains experience in capital markets and building relationships with stakeholders.

Ebben and Johnson (2006) use resource-dependence theory to explain why entrepreneurs use different types of bootstrapping at different stages of business; they also explain why certain bootstrapping methods are more prevalent than others. Their findings indicate that entrepreneurs who are forced to use boot-strapping methods at the early stages of start-up tend to adopt more attractive methods as they gain legitimacy and leverage. Resource-dependency theory is very relevant in explaining why entrepreneurs rely heavily on owner-related bootstrapping at the start and why this trend declines over time. As entrepreneurs pass the hurdle of information asymmetry, and establish close ties with investors, they are no longer keen to risk their personal wealth by making further financial

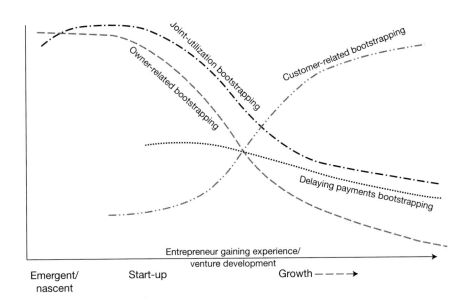

**Figure 8.3**
*Bootstrapping and business lifecycle*

investments. Resource-dependence theory also predicts that joint-utilization bootstrapping techniques should decrease over time. The entrepreneur's personal credibility and the firm's legitimacy are valuable resources for those operating in resource-poor environments. In the early stages, joint-utilization of resources acts as an effective way to obtain organizational legitimacy (through building relationships), which when developed could act as an effective way to access valuable resources from external parties as the business develops. Once the entrepreneur gains business credibility, they reduce their dependency on others for resource access purposes.

Significant increases in the use of customer-related bootstrapping techniques over time explain the importance of maintaining strong relationships with customers. Initially, limited customer relationships mean that imposing trading rules is not possible, and, instead, entrepreneurs should consider offering credit terms to improve sales and thereby increase working capital. With long-term customer relationships, entrepreneurs can replace credit terms with credit rules as these relationships help the firm to gain leverage to impose customer payment terms directed at enhancing cash-flow. Moreover, formal organization systems developed over time should lead to structured approaches to managing the customer base, which includes implementing systems that speed up billing and provide incentives for upfront or earlier customer payments (see Box 8.3). Unlike customer-related methods, explanation for the declining patter of payment-related methods is not straightforward; the negative effects of compromising on time and quality of supplier service for cost and cash-flow are a possible explanation for the limited acceptance of favourable payment arrangements with suppliers and customers as a firm matures.

## 8.6 BOOTSTRAPPING AS A GROWTH STRATEGY

Availability of resources continues to be the single largest predictor of entrepreneurial success and resource access though bootstrapping continues to contribute a major part in the resource formula for new entrepreneurs (Harrison *et al.* 2004). The main questions are:

- Does bootstrapping create value, or simply reduce costs?
- Is it practical to use bootstrapping as a substitute for more traditional sources of funding and other resources?

Thus far, research evidence attempting to check the relevance of bootstrapping as a firm performance indicator has been mixed at best. Accessing resources through bootstrapping is contrary to the teaching of the traditional resource-based view, which predicts firm performance comes from the availability of 'strategic resources'. Those who follow this view argue that while bootstrapping is a useful

**BOX 8.3**

We have moved on from our early suppliers. The thing with suppliers is there are a lot of agents who are middle men and they take a couple of per cent, and unless you can get the factories, you can't build a relationship and make them understand about good quality and what you expect from them, and so a lot of them we have moved away from and changed because other people will give us better prices – we now try to deal with the core factory that manufactures the product rather than those agents and buy bulk.

We've always been cash rich and have worked hard at chasing payments and things like that – we just run the business with common-sense. I think our systems contribute a lot in making that efficient because the systems we use invoice customers on the day which will then say you have 30 days to pay – it will then send reminders and issue a statement on the day saying we are now ready to collect money from you.

We went from a very labour intensive company to a systems base about six months before we moved here [to the warehouse]. When we imple-mented the system it enabled us, from one stock source, to sell across all of our channels and to know at any point in time what we had in stock. When an item was sold it would be deducted, the system creates an invoice, prints a dispatch note and addresses. It is able to tell us our daily sales, plot a graph and basically took out 90 per cent of the labour, which was just incredible.

[Ben Wilson, *Jazooli*]

strategy for entrepreneurs to improve their chances of success, strategic approaches to bootstrapping are not practised by most entrepreneurs. The practice is largely reactionary in nature; entrepreneurs who already have acquired external finance are less likely to consider bootstrapping (Myers 1984). Many entrepreneurs use bootstrapping as a short-term reactive financing strategy largely focusing on cost reduction. Therefore, it is reasonable to assume that relying on bootstrapping may constrain firms from growing as fast as might otherwise be the case. Ebben (2009) also found detrimental returns from some forms of bootstrapping. The negative effects from higher levels of customer- and payments-related bootstrapping on profitability are due to the breaking up of customer–supplier relationships due to the rules imposed for short-term cash flow advantages. Vanacker *et al.* (2011) provided at least five reasons that undermine the use of bootstrapping as a growth strategy for entrepreneurs:

1   As bootstrapped firms tend to be undercapitalized, the resources acquired through bootstrapping will be largely insufficient to finance growth.

2   Resources obtained through bootstrapping underestimate the venture's potential for future growth in the eyes of the stakeholders.

3   Managing bootstrapping activities takes time and limits the entrepreneur's ability to concentrate on more critical tasks such as developing new opportunities.

4   Obtaining access to cheap resources through social contacts may bring imperfect resources.

5   The opportunity costs of identifying resource-rich social contacts are high; some techniques, such as delay-payments to suppliers can damage relationships with network providers.

Cornwall (2010), using evidence from a number of case studies, however, provides three explanations to clarify some misinterpretations about the relevance of bootstrapping as a resourcing strategy. First bootstrapping should not be seen as the cheapest way to resource a venture, but as a creative way to access the full benefits from the limited resources available to new entrepreneurs. Second, evidence confirms that bootstrapping is not simply a survival strategy for new ventures, but it is a resourcing method for high-growth, high-potential ventures. Third, bootstrapping is also used as a resourcing strategy by businesses that make extensive use of debt and equity finance; it is not a choice between bootstrapping and gaining access to external funding through debt/equity.

Taken together the evidence suggests that entrepreneurs should use bootstrapping as a proactive strategy for preserving ownership and maintaining control of useful resources. At the emergent and start-up stages, entrepreneurs work in an environment characterized by resource constraints. It is possible to argue that, if the demand for resources exceeds availability, they need to be more efficient in the deployment of available resources. This causes entrepreneurs to develop management skills that help to exploit resource inputs from the external environment and effectively recombine those with the available internal resources (Smith and Smith 2000). This practice stimulates entrepreneurs to find more innovative ways to achieve growth in areas that resource-rich entrepreneurs would not necessarily consider. The general contention is that the use of bootstrap strategies is desirable as it helps entrepreneurs to focus on the efficient and more creative use of resources (Bhide 1992, Timmons 1999). This is particularly the case with women entrepreneurs as it signals to potential investors that they have the ability to generate internal funds, to control costs in creative ways and to gain access to other resources when access is limited. Effective execution of the start-up activities indirectly informs investors and other stakeholders that the entrepreneur has the potential to satisfy their growth expectations that come with their investments (Brush et al. 2006).

**134**

Interest in bootstrapping lies in the general agreement that there are benefits that go beyond its use as a creative means to access resources at the early stages of business start-up to greater opportunities for real growth. Jones *et al.* (2010a) adopt the concept of bricolage (see Chapter 9) to suggest that bootstrapping is a dynamic capability in new ventures. Bricolage helps flexible and innovative adaptation of acquired bootstrap resources through learning processes embedded in a firm's routines (see Chapter 9 for a full discussion of dynamic capabilities in new ventures). Following this line of argument, there is evidence that bootstrapping contributes directly to entrepreneurs' resourcing formula for value creation. There are examples that indicate that many successful companies, including Microsoft, Apple and Dell, relied on bootstrap finance and other resources when they started as small ventures, and this provided the foundation for achieving very high-growth (Tomory 2011; see Box 8.4). The environment created through bootstrap practices encourages entrepreneurs to make the most efficient use of their limited resource base. Bootstrapping not only introduces 'a discipline of leanness', which forces firms to spend and use resources wisely (Timmons 1999: 39), it also promotes rapid growth using 'capital raising ingenuity' (Brush *et al.* 2006). This practice of leveraging and stretching available resources provides an explanation for why some apparently undercapitalized ventures outperform ventures that are resource rich (Baker *et al.* 2000).

Bootstrapping strategies free new ventures from excessive debt and thereby take the pressure off entrepreneurs when seeking growth opportunities. Most importantly bootstrapping is a less risky option than external debt for nascent entrepreneurs, as they have limited experience of investing finance wisely when it is available. Bootstrapping helps nascent entrepreneurs learn financial and resource discipline and provides valuable lessons in how to run an efficient business (Bhide 1992). In the long run, bootstrapping can be the basis for acquiring other resources such as new equipment, premises, outside equity investment or venture capital, which can support the next stage of growth (Carter *et al.* 2003, Brush *et al.* 2006). Also resourcing through bootstrapping provides flexibility to the entrepreneur in terms of the approach to the business. As informal options are often readily available and access to these options is dependent on short-term needs, bootstrapping helps embed dynamic capabilities within the nascent firm (see Chapter 9). Increased flexibility of resources (rather than the restriction of external resource-providers) is particularly useful for nascent entrepreneurs who want to change the strategic direction of their ventures whenever they feel is necessary. Moreover, entrepreneurs who actively engage in bootstrapping are able to respond more effectively to their customers (Carter *et al.* 2003, Brush *et al.* 2006). Flexibility in acquiring resources is particularly helpful for dealing with unpredictable sales and acts as a survival strategy for firms in competitive markets (Bhide 1992, Baker *et al.* 2000).

## BOX 8.4

When Bill Gates and Paul Allen decided to form their own software company, **Microsoft**, they were determined to build it without outside financing and follow a 'bootstrapping' model. To avoid unnecessary overheads they moved into an inexpensive apartment and negotiated with MITS, the manufacturer of the Altair, for computer time and office space in their first years. Everything was funded through their savings from employment and 'late night poker games' (Gates *et al.* 1996, p. 19). Human resource has been a major challenge: they were understaffed and hired students on a part-time basis. Everybody worked over-long hours including the owners and were paid below industry averages.

Steve Wozniak and Steve Jobs raised $1,300 needed to get Apple started by selling Wosniak's scientific Hewlett-Packard calculator and Jobs's Volkswagen van. They were not only operating out of Jobs's parents' garage but received subsidized help from Jobs's family in the assembly line and in day-to-day business operations. Additionally, they relied on their network of friends who offered free service and financial assistance, which included a $5,000 loan received from a friend of Wozniak's father. Bills were largely paid by Wosniak's salary from his job at Hewlett-Packard. This bootstrapping model of financing at the inception stage helped Wozniak and Jobs to give a sound foundation for Apple, which eventually formed as **Apple Computer Inc**. in 1977 after venture capitalist Mike Markkula underwrote a bank loan of $250,000.

At the age of 18 Michael Dell converted his informal business of upgrading IBM PC-compatible computers into an entrepreneurial venture, **Dell Computer Corporation**, using his savings of $1,000. Hit by cash deficiencies, Dell have employed every measure to ensure minimum spending and cut unnecessary operating costs. Dell, together with an engineer whom he hired to design his first computer, worked long hours in his own bedroom until he hired a few employees and moved to a 1,000-square-foot office to start formal manufacturing operations. Rather than employing additional staff, the foundation team increased their work hours to save financial resources towards staff salaries.

Source: Tomory (2011)

It may very well be that the bootstrapping impact on firm performance and its inimitability is an idiosyncratic contingency. Following Ebben's (2009) research it is reasonable to suggest that bootstrapping only has a systematic impact on the bottom-line when it is embedded in the firm's strategic objectives and provides solutions for strategic problems. A properly aligned process for bootstrap resources represents a core capability and can become a form of organizational capital. Jones and Jayawarna (2010) suggest that networking activity has a strong mediating role on bootstrapping on the performance of start-up firms (see Chapter 5 for more details). The study was based on the argument that the decisions to use joint-utilization and payment-related methods (Winborg and Landström 2001) are strategic, while owner-related techniques are largely used in reaction to cash flow problems and have little impact on longer-term business outcomes. Joint-utilization techniques are particularly important for start-ups as they incur very limited costs. Techniques such as sharing staff can provide valuable human capital, and equipment or premises sharing can release other capital to invest in resources essential for business development (Carter and Van Auken 2005).

## 8.7 BOOTSTRAPPING IN SOCIAL VENTURES

In the current economic climate, financial capital, albeit important, is used by only a small proportion of social enterprises. Non-monetary, alternative sources of funding have become a major resourcing strategy for social enterprises. A study by Jayawarna and Jones (2012) explored the role of bootstrapping in gaining access to non-monetary resources for social enterprises during recession. Access to skilled voluntary labour (volunteer-based bootstrapping), competent, committed and ethical leadership (leadership-associated bootstrapping), and accumulation of social capital (relationship-oriented bootstrapping) has a critical role in this process (see Figure 8.4).

Relationships may affect access, sharing and mobilization of bootstrap resources in the early stages of a social enterprise in multiple ways (Jayawarna and Jones 2012). Results indicate that relationship formation is one of the most useful mechanisms for social enterprises to accumulate and exploit social capital as well as brokering structural holes with key stakeholders. Social enterprises tend to establish close relationships with those who have a strong control over key bootstrap resources to overcome strategic and institutional weaknesses. A key finding is that relationship-based bootstrapping is as important to social enterprises as it is to traditional enterprises (Guo and Acar 2005, Meyskens et al. 2010a, Meyskens et al. 2010b, Moizer and Tracey 2010). Findings provide strong support for the resource-dependency model as social enterprises cannot generate sufficient resources internally and therefore largely depend on their task environment for additional inputs. Voluntary labour also forms a key alternative human resource for social entrepreneurs. There are instances where the entire management team serve wholly in a voluntary capacity and receive no financial compensation, beyond expenses, for their work.

Volunteerism as a bootstrap resource is not normally found in conventional enterprises, although, in social enterprises, it raises important organizational

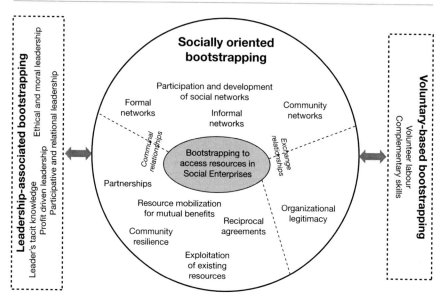

**Figure 8.4**
*Non-monetary forms of resourcing in social enterprises*

questions about addressing skill shortages and extra resource demands for voluntary management to gain full benefits of this resource (Guo and Acar 2005). Research by Jayawarna and Jones (2012) also provides empirical evidence for the role of community leadership in accessing and utilizing bootstrap resources. The study identifies the importance of leaders who encourage staff and other stakeholders to develop their own capabilities to access resources. More particularly, the research provided explanations as to how social and ethical values of leaders can promote collaborative relationships and generate change by combining indigenous commitment based on friendship and solidarity. Experience, skills and competence of leaders are also enabling mechanisms to realize resource needs in the form of credibility, reputation and firm references.

## 8.8 SUMMARY AND KEY LEARNING POINTS

It is commonly reported that new businesses have difficulty in accessing finance and other resources. Such businesses can engage in 'bootstrapping' activities as a way of compensating for this lack of resource capacity. Defined as a creative means to overcome resource constraints when entrepreneurs launch and grow their successful venture, bootstrapping covers a variety of strategies and techniques for entrepreneurs who are either at the early stages of setting up a small business or running high-growth, high-potential ventures. Techniques such as using the parental home as a base (as in *Jazooli*), subsidizing from other activities (as in *Active Profile*), salary deferment and use of credit cards (as in *Wigan Recycling*), and bartering and sharing equipment are some of the bootstrap activities that are worth pursuing for entrepreneurs when considering starting a new business. Although entrepreneurial finance has been widely studied, the use of bootstrapping as an alternative resourcing strategy has attracted much less interest from academic researchers. While the limited available literature largely agrees with the ideas put forward by Winborg and Landström (2001), new research evidence points to the importance of considering the business lifecycle, entrepreneurial motives and gender in explaining the usage of different bootstrapping methods. Taken together the key learning points from this chapter are:

- Bootstrapping is a key organizational capability, which influences the ability of new firms to respond to their resource needs in a more efficient and cost-effective way. It is focused on enhancing cash flow and minimizing outgoing and maximizing income.
- The literature largely agrees that there are four different types of bootstrapping techniques for entrepreneurs to resource their ventures: owner-related, payment-related, customer-related and joint-utilization methods.
- Research categorizes bootstrapping into either internally or externally oriented activities. While internal activities aim at maximizing outcomes from the limited available resources, external methods of bootstrapping often target the securing of external sources of resources through sharing or jointly utilizing with other businesses or individuals.
- While the use of owner-related and joint-utilization techniques declines as the venture matures, which fits with theories of entrepreneurial risk-taking, use of payment-related techniques tends to increase over time, which coincides with theories of resource dependency (Pfeffer and Salancik 1978) and organizational learning (Argyris 1992).
- In addition to the direct benefit of gaining access to additional resources, bootstrapping can indirectly benefit entrepreneurs through (1) encouraging efficient use of resources; (2) overcoming the problem of information asymmetries; (3) introducing discipline to resource use; and (4) enabling flexible work delivery.
- Examples of the use of bootstrapping techniques can be found in ventures of all types and sizes, operating at different stages of venture development.

## 8.9 DISCUSSION QUESTIONS

- What are the key reasons that influence new entrepreneurs to seek bootstrap resources to set up and run a new venture?

- How do a resource-based view of the firm, resource-dependency theory and resource-constraints theory help to explain the need for bootstrapping in new ventures?

- What might be the potential techniques of bootstrapping that a nascent entrepreneur can bring to their business? How might they access these resources and what are the short- and long-term benefits (and challenges) of using bootstrap resources in the new venture?

- How does the business lifecycle help to understand the dynamic and practical nature of bootstrap behaviour by different entrepreneurs?

- Why is it challenging to define a generic set of bootstrap techniques that an entrepreneur might use to start a new business? (Use gender, business sector, business age and entrepreneur character, preferences and motivations in your discussion.)

## 8.10 FURTHER READING

Cornwall, J. (2010) *Bootstrapping*, Upper Saddle River, NJ: Prentice Hall.

Winborg, J. and Landström, H. (2001) 'Financial bootstrapping in small businesses. Examining small business managers' resource acquisition behaviours', *Journal of Business Venturing*, 16, 235–254.

Villanueva, J., Van de Ven, A. H. and Sapienza, H. J. (2012) 'Resource mobilization in entrepreneurial firms', *Journal of Business Venturing*, 27(1), 19–30.

# Chapter 9

# Dynamic capabilities in entrepreneurial ventures

## 9.1 INTRODUCTION

Penrose (1959) proposes that it is the way resources are applied to new problems and opportunities, rather than the resources themselves, that influences a firm's ability to grow. From her perspective, it is the entrepreneur's *applied* judgment and intuition that have the potential to generate higher profits and growth compared with rivals faced with similar resources. However, it is important to recognize, as we have argued elsewhere (see for example Chapters 2 and 5), that entrepreneurship is not necessarily an individual endeavour. In essence, entrepreneurship is a collective creative process where those working within the firm help to deploy the resources available in a way that is superior to what can be achieved by an individual (Foss *et al.* 2008). In their conceptual paper, Zahra *et al.* (2006: 918) define such activity as dynamic capabilities: 'the abilities to reconfigure a firm's resources and routines in the manner envisioned and deemed appropriate by its principal decision makers'. They go on to argue that we know relatively little about dynamic capabilities in new firms, but they are likely to be different from those in larger firms given the resource constraints under which they operate. Another important consideration is that at the start of a new venture, the influence of the principal decision-maker(s) is probably at its most apparent. As Baron *et al.* (1999) identify in their study of 76 firms in Silicon Valley the 'logics of organizing' adopted in the early stages of venture creation have a long-term effect on the intensity and structures of bureaucracy within the firm. This means that, unless entrepreneurs embed dynamic capabilities in the firm's blueprint at the outset, path dependencies will make it difficult to do so later without significant effort.

In this chapter, we note the theoretical antecedents of the dynamic-capabilities approach within the resource-based view (RBV) of the firm, and we give an overview of dynamic capabilities, reviewing some relevant theoretical and empirical contributions made to the subject. By drawing insights from these studies, we consider the types of routines that might provide new ventures with the capacity to develop and renew their competencies that will support dynamic capabilities.

We highlight that resource deficiencies provide a particular challenge for new enterprises. Here, we discuss how the concept of bricolage, the art of making do with resources at hand or discarded by others (Baker *et al.* 2003), can provide insight into the process of renewal and change. We also discuss the important role of learning processes that link the availability and adoption of resources to new configurations of routines and capabilities within the firm. So, we provide direct links to other chapters that reflect on the types of resources necessary to build a new venture, but explore more how firms respond to changes in the environment, and the key role of 'principal decision-makers' in defining the trajectory of the firm.

## 9.2 LEARNING OBJECTIVES

- To explain the concept of dynamic capabilities.
- To define the nature of dynamic capabilities in new ventures.
- To identify how bricolage can provide a creative way of managing and innovating, despite resource deficiencies.
- To analyse the role of entrepreneurial action in focusing the trajectory of dynamic capabilities in new ventures.

## 9.3 FROM RESOURCES TO DYNAMIC CAPABILITIES

In Chapters 2, 5, 6, 7 and 8 we explored the types of resources that are necessary to start a new firm, and how an entrepreneur might augment those resources through such processes as bootstrapping and developing appropriate networks, as well as through gaining experience. The RBV suggests that competitive advantage depends on the unique combination of resources available in the firm that entrepreneurs use to generate profit (Barney 1991; Figure 9.1). In their study, Lichtenstein and Brush (2001) identify what they describe as 'salient resources' for entrepreneurial ventures, which include financial capital, organizational systems/structures, management know-how, technology, physical resources, leadership, culture and 'informal systems'. They go on to argue that, in new ventures, organizational resources evolve over a period of weeks, months and years. They suggest, as part of the development process, and in order to become established or self-sustaining, 'a series of resource acquisitions and combinations might be necessary' (Lichtenstein and Brush 2001: 41). Interestingly though, in their longitudinal analysis of three firms, they found intangible resources (knowledge, expertise, relationships, sales/service delivery and decision-making) to be more salient than tangible resources (such as equipment and financial capital).

Despite the RBV's intuitive appeal, (a firm with better resources is more competitive) it has been criticized as being too static and tautological. Those firms with high-quality resources deliver higher profits; profitable firms tend to have access to superior resources. Some have argued that resources provide a particular set of asset positions that an entrepreneur and his or her strategic team can deploy creatively in order to (re)configure opportunities. So, rather than being objective entities as described in resource-dependence theory (Pfeffer and Salancik 1978), their worth is dependent on how they are used. For example, Lockett *et al.* (2009: 13) argue that:

> the role of the manager in the RBV is akin to that of a card player. The player is provided with a dealt hand of cards, the value of each card is determined *ex ante* by the rules of the game. Success depends on the relative skill with which that hand . . . is played in competition against rivals.

This means that resources alone are not the source of value, but it is how entrepreneurs use them that matters. This is a point made quite clearly by Penrose (1959), as noted above in the introduction; resources are benign and need to be applied, which allows those with greater capacity or skill, or perhaps even with some 'blind luck' (Storey 2011), to be able to get more from fewer resources. This also means that we cannot judge or measure intangible resources such as knowledge and capabilities as a proxy for potential success. The capacity to perform depends on how entrepreneurs both apply and reconfigure their available resources in response to contingencies, such as changing markets, or other crises. Indeed, the potential of the firm also depends on how effectively the venture's principal decision-makers can manage and change existing resources to match those contingencies.

As we saw in Chapter 5, where there is potential for collaboration (networking), this can potentially increase the amount of available resources quite substantially,

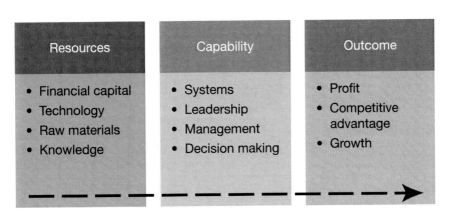

**Figure 9.1**
*From resources to rents*

providing the entrepreneur with the possibility to create new combinations of resources. Here prior experience and knowledge of particular markets, or technical expertise and 'inside knowledge' provide an advantage; there are a number of studies that show how such experience is invaluable in navigating successfully the complex terrain of specific markets (Lockett *et al.* 2009). Resources matter, but managers must attend to the relevance, availability and deployment of such resources, and they will need strategies and processes to do so. For venture owners to overcome the limitations and path-dependency of existing resources they need to be alert and develop systems and mechanisms that are more dynamic; these can then be a route to renew and redeploy such resources. The ability to reconfigure resources in order to respond to environmental challenges has been termed 'dynamic capabilities' (Teece *et al.* 1997, Eisenhardt and Martin 2000, Zollo and Winter 2002). This dynamic-capabilities view of competitive advantages focuses more clearly on the history of resource development and organization processes, which researchers have argued are fundamental to success (Teece *et al.* 1997).

In their original conceptualization of 'dynamic capabilities', Teece and his colleagues presented a view of competitive advantage that meant any strategy analysis must be sensitive to the actual situation of each firm and consider five key aspects:

1 Selecting and committing to a particular product portfolio means committing to developing path-dependent competencies.
2 Such entry decisions also depend on existing competencies and capabilities of the entrants.
3 There are possibilities for organizations to expand when significant overlap exists between the core capabilities possessed within the firm and those needed in the market.
4 Therefore, such diversification must build on existing competencies.
5 This means that specialization should focus on competencies not products, supported by the use of internal processes for their deployment and evolution.

It is this unique combination of competencies and routines in a firm, they argue, that makes success difficult to replicate. Therefore, it is not possible to just copy a template of success and deploy it any market. From this perspective, Teece *et al.* (1997) present core competencies as resident in, and a function of, organizational processes. They argue that processes represent a firm's ability to respond to a changing business environment creating those 'dynamic capabilities' essential for success. Organizations confronted with changing markets or changing technologies must develop new capabilities to avoid the problem of 'core rigidities', where significant investment in past successes creates routines and path dependencies that become inflexible when dealing with changing contexts (Leonard-

Barton 1995). In short, 'dynamic capabilities' refer to the ability to create innovative responses to changing business environments and other crises.

## 9.4 ROUTINES THAT SUPPORT CHANGE

If it is important for new venture owners to learn how to respond to changing contexts (Breslin and Jones 2012), as proposed in the dynamic-capabilities view, this raises the question: what are the types of processes in new firms that we can consider as 'dynamic'? Eisenhardt and Martin (2000: 1107) suggest that, while much of the strategy literature is 'vague' on the nature of dynamic capabilities, there are a number of specific examples of routines that support change from other areas and they provide some insight. These include:

- product development routines;
- strategic decision-making routines;
- resource-allocation routines;
- and routines related to the acquisition and release of resources.

Zahra *et al.* (2006), on the other hand, make a distinction between substantive capabilities and dynamic capabilities. The former, they argue, are routines that contribute to the operational effectiveness and efficiency of the venture, while the latter provide the ability to renew such substantive capabilities. They comment:

> The challenge for new and established firms is to create – to a degree sufficient to meet the challenges of their environment – a systematic openness to upgrading and revising their substantive capabilities, through a variety of learning modes.
>
> (Zahra *et al.* 2006: 945)

In other words, they are higher order capabilities, but it can be difficult to distinguish between those capabilities that provide incremental learning and those that create dramatic shifts in a firm's trajectory (Easterby-Smith *et al.* 2009). In this regard, according to Bowman and Ambrosini (2003), dynamic capabilities have four main processes: reconfiguration, leveraging, learning and creative integration (see Table 9.1). Leveraging, which refers to the replication of processes or systems in another business unit, is unlikely to be relevant in the context of a new venture. Reconfiguration involves the transformation of assets and resources; learning allows tasks to be performed more effectively as a result of previous experimentation; and creative integration refers to the firm's ability to combine assets and resources that leads to new resource configurations (Ambrosini and Bowman 2009). Teece *et al.* (1997: 1319), in their contribution to the debate, list three fundamental types of dynamic capabilities:

the capacity (1) to sense and shape opportunities and threats, (2) to seize opportunities, and (3) to maintain competitiveness through enhancing, protecting and, when necessary, reconfiguring the business enterprise's intangible and tangible assets.

Like Bowman and Ambrosini (2003), Zollo and Winter (2002) specifically note the significance of learning mechanisms that are deliberately enacted to continually build experience and to change existing routines and practices. Indeed, Easterby-Smith and Prieto (2008: 245), in their conceptual paper, also propose that learning processes are 'a common theme underlying both dynamic capabilities and knowledge management'. Furthermore, they note that learning processes have an integrative and moderating influence that leads to the creative use of resources in dynamic firms.

Taken together, then, there is significant agreement that dynamic capabilities, 'as the capacity to effect change', are routines and processes that depend on managerial cognition and intangible knowledge to make a difference to the trajectory and capability of the firm (Easterby-Smith *et al.* 2009: S4). In that sense, dynamic capabilities are likely to take a variety of forms and probably involve a number of different functions such as marketing, product development or process development. Despite this, there is some agreement among scholars that dynamic capabilities are 'higher level capabilities which provide opportunities for knowledge gathering and sharing, continual updating of operational processes, interaction with the environment, and decision-making evaluations' (Easterby-Smith *et al.* 2009: S7). Several scholars have made the link between dynamic capabilities and learning processes, although the distinction between radical and incremental change is unclear. We discuss the issue and relevance of learning routines further in Section 9.6, and a fuller discussion of entrepreneurial learning is included in

**Table 9.1** Dynamic capabilities in new firms

| Dynamic capability | Types of process |
|---|---|
| Reconfiguration | Reallocation of resources |
| | Restructuring |
| | Recruitment |
| | Bootstrapping |
| Learning | Experimentation |
| | Improvisation |
| | Quality management and improvement |
| | Customer relations management |
| | New product development |
| | R&D |
| | Market analysis |
| Integration | Embedding of new routines, or systems of production |

Chapter 3. However, it is also worth injecting a note of caution at this point. Successful outcomes of resource (re)configuration are not assured. The dynamic capabilities that lead to resource reconfigurations can just as easily destroy the routines and processes that provided competitive advantage in the first place (Ambrosini and Bowman 2009).

## 9.5 DYNAMIC CAPABILITIES IN NEW VENTURES

The small numbers of studies that have examined the entrepreneurial start-up process in detail provide some consensus on those 'dynamic' factors that are most important (Gatewood *et al.* 1995, Carter *et al.* 1996, Reynolds and White 1997). Drawing on the work of Reynolds and White (1997), Newbert's (2005) study of 817 US nascent entrepreneurs using the panel study of entrepreneurial dynamics (PSED) combines gestation activities (including prepared business plan, developed model, hired employees, etc.) with six measures of market dynamism. A number of control variables are also incorporated and these include race, gender, education, marital status and sector. Factors that were significant for all nascent entrepreneurs were: developing a model, purchasing materials, investing own money, committing full-time, hiring employees and engaging in promotional efforts (Newbert 2005: 67). There were, however, interesting variations for high-tech entrepreneurs: development of models and purchasing materials were statistically significant with the likelihood of starting a business. Based on these results, Newbert (2005: 74) claims that a 'dynamic capabilities perspective provides a theoretical perspective by which to understand the process of new firm formation'. Other studies have also measured resource availability and integration in order to assess the relevance of dynamic capabilities. Wu's (2007) study of Taiwanese high-tech firms also confirmed that resource availability and their integration and reconfiguration were central to enhanced performance. A study of 'trans-generational value creation' in family firms also indicates that dynamic capabilities are the link between knowledge resources and entrepreneurial performance (Chirico and Nordqvist 2010).

In a case study approach, Macpherson *et al.* (2004) identify dynamic capabilities as a key antecedent to innovation and growth in a new, small and rapidly growing, technology-based entrepreneurial firm. The case demonstrates how building effective business networks helped to expand a firm's resource capacity (see Chapter 5), allowing it to respond flexibly to customers' needs and to exploit opportunities quickly by mobilizing external assets. In *PPE Co.* (the case company – see Box 9.1) new suppliers were identified through searches for companies with the capacity to provide innovative products and materials. Thus, initial weak ties (Granovetter 1973) provided a 'loosely-coupled network' and the directors obtained access to critical resources that existed outside the firm's boundaries (Dyer and Singh 1998). Routines of collaboration and problem solving within this network enabled the development of new products and solutions to technical problems for the main customer. In this instance, the dynamic capability was the effective coordination and integration of companies in its supply chain with existing processes at *PPE Co.* This allowed the firm to respond quickly to their main customer and supply technologically robust solutions (Macpherson *et al.* 2004). *PPE Co.* essentially borrowed and shared resources in order to respond to a major new market opportunity. This bootstrapping of resources is discussed in detail in Chapter 8, but there is also a discussion below in Section 9.7, where we explore further the role of bootstrapping as a dynamic capability.

These studies suggest that in resource-scarce firms (and almost all new firms are in this category) a key competitive capability involves accessing the necessary knowledge and information to enact the entrepreneur's (or firm's strategic team) goals (Shane 2000). Thus, a dynamic-capabilities approach places more emphasis on activities and processes rather than the possession of resources (Ambrosini and Bowman 2009). In resource-rich established firms, dynamic capabilities are important to preserve their competitive endowments (Barney 1991, Bowman and Ambrosini 2003, Teece 2007). In new and emerging firms, such capabilities can bring value to otherwise worthless resources and assist in the growth of the firm despite resource scarcity (Baker and Nelson 2005). This means that a key aspect of dynamic capacity is the way that venture owners learn to cope with changing

## BOX 9.1

At *PPE Co.*, early in the development of the firm, they won a single source supply contract for their main customer. However, within the contract was a requirement to provide continuous improvement and innovation of products to meet the customer's changing requirements. This focus on value engineering and innovation meant that the firm's technical and creative resources were overloaded. In order to overcome this limitation they engaged in collaboration with the suppliers they managed as part of the contract. The directors established a number of close relationships and mutual trust grew through the exchange of ideas and knowledge with benefits for both parties. The network they created allowed the businesses to be able to share development time, costs, resources and expertise. In overcoming one particular problematic equipment failure, the directors noted that expertise from three firms was incorporated into the design, with each company benefiting from the improved finished product. This firm overcame its resource scarcity by seeking external expertise and support from a number of sources, including suppliers.

market conditions and operational or strategic crises (Breslin and Jones 2012). According to Ambrosini and Bowman (2009), aspects that are critical to dynamic capabilities are thus learning how to use existing resources creatively.

## 9.6 DYNAMIC CAPABILITIES AND LEARNING PROCESSES

Many have argued, and it is discussed in Chapter 3, that learning is central to entrepreneurial activity, particularly in relationship to opportunity creation. Zahra et al. (2006) also suggest that learning processes are central to the development and application of dynamic capabilities, while Bowman and Ambrosini (2003) propose that learning is a dynamic capability. However, because most new firms lack their own resources, they are particularly dependent on external knowledge including feedback from customers and suppliers (Gibb 1997, Pittaway et al. 2004), and advice and support from business and personal networks (see Chapter 5) in order to learn. It is through these interactions, as discussed in Chapter 3, that they have the opportunity to engage in activities and discussions through which they can reflect on and adapt their existing activities. However, if they are to sustain developments and enhance substantive capabilities with the firm, owners need to integrate their learning into a firm's routines.

Jones and Macpherson (2006), for example, in their case study of three manufacturing firms, stress that if venture owners are to effectively embed and share their learning within the firm, they must create effective communication structures and repeatable routines. There are similar findings by Lans et al. (2008). In their study of 25 small horticulture businesses in the Netherlands, they distinguish between internal and external factors that promote learning. Formal internal communications included team meetings and clear communication lines. Informal communications included opportunities to obtain and provide feedback, trust and attention to cultural differences. External interactions had four elements: traders/buyers, consumers, suppliers and 'experts' (Lans et al. 2008: 6–7). In summary, the authors suggest that there are four features crucial to the entrepreneurial learning environment: support and guidance, task characteristics (division of labour), internal communication and external interaction. This means that there are specific individual and organizational mechanisms through which firms can evolve, and through which entrepreneurs can adapt their firms to respond to change in their environments (Breslin and Jones 2012).

Zahra et al. (2006) identify four learning modes that they link to the utilization of dynamic capabilities within entrepreneurial firms (improvisation, trial-and-error, experimentation and imitation). They also note that in the early years of formation firms are likely to engage in the first two, improvisation and trial-and-error (experiential) learning (see Chapter 3 for a discussion of experiential learning). Baker et al. (2003) support this idea and note that improvisation occurs at the point of both design and execution. Firms adopting improvisational learning routines are more likely to reconfigure 'resources at hand' in the actual act of problem solving, which delivers unplanned (potentially beneficial) organizational outcomes (Miner *et al.* 2001). This is also because new firms are unlikely to have the slack resources that allow prior planning to create a solution. Therefore, by using resources that they can redirect or borrow, improvisation and trial-and-error learning occurs unsystematically and coterminously with problem solving. It seems likely that new firms will use these types of learning early in their formation in order to overcome resource scarcity, to deal with specific problems, as well as to create or respond to new opportunities. As they grow, however, they are more likely to develop structured learning routines, such as R&D, new product development, quality management systems and to engage in more formal experimentation (Baker *et al.* 2003). Zahra and colleagues (2006) suggest that imitation is not affected by age, since it can occur at any point in venture development. For example, venture owners will imitate norms within a sector, in response to accreditation bodies' requirements, based on prior experience within an industry sector, or in order to comply with existing regulation. Each of these learning modes requires a change to substantive capabilities, but improvisation and trial-and-error learning seem to be particularly important in the early stages of venture formation. See Table 9.2 for a description of learning modes and associated activities.

Although learning routines, as dynamic capabilities, tend to support renewal, there is a central tension: the balance between exploration of new learning and the exploitation of past learning (March 1991). As firms age they begin to adopt specific processes, equipment and norms such that they become restricted by their path dependencies (David 1985). Learning processes can facilitate a renewal of existing routines at the collective level, only if an entrepreneur or others within the venture share their individual learning and it is institutionalized into new systems and routines (Crossan *et al.* 1999, Jones and Macpherson 2006). This

**Table 9.2** Learning modes and activities

| Learning mode | Types of activity |
| --- | --- |
| Improvisation and trial-and-error learning | Problem solving<br>Responding to crisis<br>Making do<br>Experiences |
| Experimentation | R&D processes<br>Market testing |
| Imitation | Quality management and assurance<br>Continuous improvement techniques<br>Regulation compliance |

## BOX 9.2

When starting out, the technical director of *PPE Co.* knew what he wanted to achieve in designing a new protection suit, but he did not have the technical materials expertise to do so. To begin with, he contacted a variety of suppliers and experimented with a range of material swatches they sent him, working out through trial and error what might work. Over time, he became aware of the properties of different technical materials. He was then able to stipulate the hydrophilic properties of certain types of fibres and to become more specific in his requirements. At the same time, he was experimenting with different ways of 'welding' the materials together to create flexible, but strong, material joins. He developed a unique process for joining the material from which he was then able to create other products such as bespoke containment tenting and different types of suits. In other words, he embedded his trial-and-error learning within a manufacturing process that provided a new and unique scalable revenue stream.

means that, while improvisation may lead to a new configuration of resources, this learning has to be embedded if long-run benefits are to be realized. In terms of a dynamic-capabilities perspective, systems and routines provide organizational learning and allow integration of learning into new routines (Popper and Lipshitz 2000), and thus the renewal of existing capabilities. However, existing systems and routines can also actually block progress, since learning may require a radical shift from existing practices if the entrepreneur is to sustain the firm's development trajectory (see Box 9.2 above).

In summary, because new firms are generally short of resources from which to generate new products and processes, routines that support improvisation and experiential learning are likely to be the most common modes of supporting dynamic capabilities and renew existing capabilities in new ventures. However, when entrepreneurs embed successful innovation in the firm, tensions between exploration and exploitation are likely to make improvisation less likely as firms age and grow. This is because the institutionalization of learning creates path dependencies and rigidities (David 1985, Leonard-Barton 1995). Moreover, as noted earlier, it is worth considering that improvisation and trial-and-error learning can disrupt the resource configurations that created favourable outcomes in the first place (Ambrosini and Bowman 2009). Thus, the creative aspect of learning can have negative effects on capabilities, particularly if such learning is not embedded and exploited effectively (Jones and Macpherson 2006).

## 9.7 BOOTSTRAPPING AND BRICOLAGE: ENTREPRENEURS ACTING RESOURCEFULLY

All of the foregoing discussion suggests that the role of agency is important in understanding dynamic capabilities, since reconfiguration is driven by internal endogenous action as much as it is by exogenous shocks (Newey and Zahra 2009). This is most acutely evident in new ventures where the influence of the venture owners (the principal decision-makers) is pervasive. A field study by Miner *et al.* (2001), on the other hand, indicated that improvisational competencies flowed from organizational routines rather than residing with specific individuals. As Sullivan-Taylor and Branicki (2011: 5577) have recently found, it is important to consider that 'organizational resilience', the ability to bounce back and cope with change or shocks in the environment, is likely to depend on 'key strengths and capabilities already possessed by SMEs'. Baker and Nelson (2005: 232) suggest that the resources available to new firms are idiosyncratic, as is the ability of the firm's principal decision-makers to be able to make use of such resources. Therefore, they argue, there are three important implications for entrepreneurs engaged in business start-up:

1   All new firms are unique in their 'idiosyncratic' relationship with the resource environment.
2   There are substantial variations in the ability of such firms to survive even if they have access to 'ostensibly similar resource environments'.
3   Entrepreneurial firms can use resources that are worthless to one organization and make them extremely valuable, if they are combined with existing internal knowledge and skills.

In this view, there are clear links with Sarasvathy's (2001, 2008) articulation of effectuation (discussed in Chapter 2) in which entrepreneurs use the means at their disposal, combined with their ability and characteristics, to shape and exploit contingencies. However, one of the challenges faced by entrepreneurs when enacting responses to changing environmental conditions is significant resource constraints (Brush 2008).

Obtaining and developing adequate resources remains a key issue for any entrepreneur, but this is especially difficult for new entrepreneurs, and even harder in technology-based new firms that require higher capital investment, and generally longer lead times to get the product to market (Deeds *et al.* 1999). As noted in Chapter 8, bootstrapping refers to methods by which entrepreneurs access financial capital, but they can also 'bootstrap' other important resources (such as knowledge and information, materials and expertise) that are lacking for most new business ventures (Carter and Van Auken 2005; Winborg 2009). All organizations depend on external resources including human, material, information, knowledge, and finance (Hannan and Freeman 1977). This is accentuated in the case of start-up businesses that are highly resource deficient compared with their longer established rivals (Baker and Nelson 2005, Katila and Shane 2005, Rouse and Jayawarna 2011). Indeed, Davidsson *et al.* (2006) have demonstrated that low survival rates of new businesses can be attributed to their lack of resources.

It is possible, and probably essential, for new venture owners to try to establish access to both functional and technical expertise that might be missing from their firm's human capital portfolio (Smith *et al.* 2005). A systematic review of knowledge resources in small firms identifies a range of ways in which particular types of human and social capital can help promote growth (Macpherson and Holt 2007). In particular, by drawing on the experience available from existing business relationships, prior employment, customer and supplier networks and non-executive directors, new owners can gain access to scarce tangible and 'intangible' resources. These can include technological and managerial skills, information and knowledge (Deeds *et al.* 1999, Boussouara and Deakins 1999, 2000, Lichtenstein and Brush 2001, Baker *et al.* 2003, Bruni and Verona 2009), and social networks can also provide access or the sharing of tangible assets such as labour, office space and equipment (Jenssen and Koenig 2002). Networks are thus a 'means at hand' through which entrepreneurs can access a variety of resources that are either surplus to requirements or discarded by other firms (Baker *et al.* 2003). In other words, those firms that can bootstrap knowledge, equipment and financial resources may be able to respond more effectively to problems so that they can create opportunities. In short, increasing resource availability, or bootstrapping, is an essential precursor to problem solving, particularly when a firm's existing assets are in short supply.

The next step is to apply those new resources creatively. Baker and Nelson (2005) take a view that entrepreneurs often use physical, social and institutional resources that more established firms disregard. Drawing on work by Lévi-Strauss (1967), Baker and Nelson (2005) adopt the concept of bricolage (introduced in Chapter 2) to suggest that entrepreneurs redefine these resources by enacting alternative practices and routines. Bricolage is, 'making do by applying combinations of resources at hand to new problems and opportunities', and this helps to conceptualize the flexible and innovative adaptation of entrepreneurs using all available resources (Baker and Nelson 2005: 333), and the concept of bricolage fits very well with entrepreneurial activity. In their study, they note that bricolage relies on scavenging resources (bootstrapping) in order to extract use from goods that others do not value, or do not intend to use. Importantly, entrepreneurs who target this activity at a particular problem (selective bricolage) are more likely to be successful. In other words, while bricolage may provide a way of recombining and reconfiguring resources, entrepreneurs still have to integrate the solution into the firm's existing routines if it is to provide long-term benefits. Baker and Nelson (2005) contrast this with 'parallel bricoleurs' who flit between projects depending on customer expectations and obligations. While such entrepreneurs take pride in being able to fashion something from nothing, they rarely generate substantial gains from their projects. Notwithstanding the differences between these types of bricolage, they both rely on improvisation, or trial-and-error learning, in order to create and test solutions; in so doing, resource combinations are broken down and/or reconfigured. In that sense, bricolage helps firms to explore new opportunities that might otherwise be too expensive to investigate by means that are used in more traditional and resource-rich enterprises, such as formal research and development (Miner *et al.* 2001, Baker and Nelson 2005). This articulation of bricolage resonates with the dynamic-capabilities literature above.

By overcoming resource scarcity, Baker *et al.* (2003) and Baker and Nelson (2005) argue that entrepreneurs are essentially refusing to accept the resource limitations imposed by their constrained environment. They go on to suggest that resources available do not restrict such entrepreneurs' understanding of opportunities. A number of researchers have applied this perspective in a variety of contexts and they find validity in this theoretical approach. For example, Desa (2012) found that social enterprises were able to mobilize resources in a variety of institutional conditions. The study examined 220 social technology enterprises in 45 countries and concluded that bricolage is an important factor in enterprise resilience that helps social enterprises navigate a variety of resource and institutional conditions. Stritar (2012) introduces the concept of 'resource hijacking' to describe resources that were bootstrapped and used in a novel way (bricolage) to provide a new product. In this study, they use the example of SKYPE to highlight how the firm appropriated and used technology infrastructure, marketing, content and management resources for business, so that the actual capital costs of set-up and expansion were very low. Their argument is that, in this internet venture, entrepreneurs looked beyond resources 'at hand' and actually designed their services to use others' resources. Embedding this process in the firm at the outset provides a dynamic solution to overcome resource limitations.

These studies suggest that resources and opportunities are not an objective restriction, but are (re)constructed through entrepreneurial ingenuity. If crises impact on entrepreneurial learning trajectories (Cope 2005), and entrepreneurs creatively use resources to solve these crises (Baker and Nelson 2005), it seems logical that we need to understand better the routines and activity through which this learning is then realized at the firm level (Jones and Macpherson 2006, Jones *et al.* 2010b). Here the distinction noted above between parallel and selective bricolage is crucial. The latter connotes an activity where the entrepreneur engages in tackling and learning from a particular problem. If it is to be effective, bricolage requires the entrepreneur to integrate learning outcomes into existing routines and to embed that learning in long-term activities. Entrepreneurial learning (Chapter 3) thus provides the dynamic capabilities to allow the firm to evolve in response to changing contexts (Breslin and Jones 2012).

**154**

We have represented this argument in Figure 9.2. Entrepreneurs can bolster their limited resource base through bootstrapping. This need not be just financial resources, but could be material or knowledge (in the form of expertise), which can be applied to solve problems, or to improvise solutions. In this way, learning routines, such as improvisation and trial-and-error learning, potentially provide dynamic capabilities that support a reconfiguration of existing resource configurations and capabilities. Once embedded in the firm this creates a new resource base from which the next round of learning can occur. As such, learning routines that support the sharing and institutionalization of new routines from *selective bricolage* are likely to develop a revised resource base through which entrepreneurial firms deliver new products and services. However, resource reconfigurations over time, and with growing success, become path dependencies that make future innovations more challenging. It seems, as Zahra *et al.* (2006) argue, that at this point more structured learning routines, such as experimentation, will be necessary to purposefully challenge the status quo.

In summary, in new ventures, the concept of bootstrapping suggests the new entrepreneurs creatively engage with others to borrow, share or appropriate resources. The concept of bricolage suggests that nascent entrepreneurs deploy and integrate resources in novel ways. Thus, bootstrapping and bricolage are potentially key dynamic capabilities that provide opportunities for new firms to

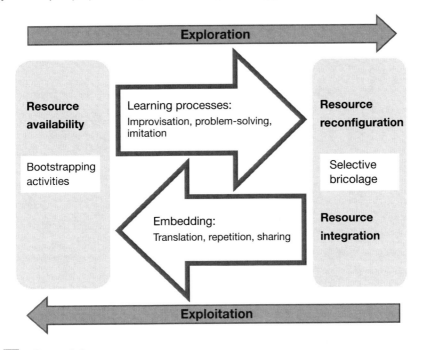

**Figure 9.2**
*Dynamic capabilities in start-up businesses*

enhance the value of external resources by extending and integrating such resources with the firm's limited internal resource base. However, the distinction between parallel and selective bricolage seems crucial. The former is a habituated process of making-do and a modus operandi for some entrepreneurs. The latter is a way of targeting particular problems or opportunities such that entrepreneurs can generate long-run rents from the solutions they create by embedding the outcomes in new processes and routines. As indicated above, this view is consistent with conceptualizations of dynamic capabilities, which concentrate on the integration and reconfiguration of internal and external resources in response to environmental change (Teece *et al.* 1997, Wu 2007). New resource configurations potentially provide increased rents, but, over time, they may also become liabilities.

## 9.8 SUMMARY AND KEY LEARNING POINTS

At the outset, new ventures are likely to operate with constrained resources. In order to develop, entrepreneurs will need to both enhance and reconfigure their resource base. The activities that this involves are likely to depend on the way entrepreneurs and the principal decision-makers can improvise and skilfully make use of their limited resources and perhaps borrow or use resources discarded by others. The owner's founding 'blueprint' has a long-term effect on the administrative systems of the firm, so entrepreneurs need to adopt dynamic capabilities at the outset. Although research in the area is scarce, we can consider the types of activities that we might define as dynamic capabilities, the types of routines that allow a firm to sense and respond to the market changes and crises in order to reconfigure their assets for long-term survival and growth. If firms are to make best use of available resources they need to be alert to changes in the market context, and aware of what resource might be available within the firm and its network. This is a very human ability, since it relies on the agency of the principal decision-makers. New venture owners must be able to deftly adopt and adapt routines that allow the firm to respond and institutionalize learning gained as they engage in improvisation to cope with problems and opportunities that they encounter. Thus, the concepts of bootstrapping and bricolage highlight the agency with which entrepreneurs can target their activities to gain access to scarce resources and create new resource combinations. This exemplifies a Penrosian view of how firms create idiosyncratic solutions within similar resource and market constraints in order to create potential.

In summary, the following key points are worth consideration:

■ Every new firm's owner(s) have a unique resource base. In order to survive in the long term they will need to make the best use of this resource base, but they will also need to renew and reconfigure it in response to crises and changing market conditions.

- Renewal and reconfiguration require dynamic capabilities, higher-level routines that provide access to, and reconfiguration and integration of, new resources. The entrepreneur needs to embed these dynamic capabilities at the inception of the firm.
- Changing existing substantive capabilities inevitably involves learning, which in new ventures is most likely to involve improvisation and trial-and-error processes, although imitation is also a learning routine that can support change.
- Given that resources are likely to be scarce at the outset, the concept of bootstrapping highlights how new venture owners can be creative in sourcing necessary finance, material, information and knowledge, by getting access to and adopting or borrowing resources unused by others to create their solutions.
- Improvisation and experiential learning routines can be transitory, but the concept of selective bricolage highlights the importance of embedding and integrating new processes to generate long-term profits and growth.

## 9.9 DISCUSSION QUESTIONS

- How does a dynamic-capabilities view differ from a resource-based view of the firm?
- What are the key principles of a dynamic-capabilities view?
- Why might dynamic capabilities differ in a new firm from those of a larger, more established firm?
- Why is learning important for understanding the role of dynamic capabilities in firms?
- Why is bootstrapping an important aspect of dynamic capabilities in new ventures?
- How do the concepts of bricolage and improvisation help us to consider the types of dynamic capabilities a new firm might need to develop?

## 9.10 FURTHER READING

Teece, D. (2007) Explicating Dynamic Capabilities: The Nature and Microfoundations of (Sustainable) Enterprise Performance, *Strategic Management Journal*, 28(13): 1319–1350.

Zahra, S. A., Sapienza, H., and Davidsson, P. (2006) Enterpreneurship and Dynamic Capabilities: A Review, Model and Research Agenda, *Journal of Management Studies*, 43(4): 917–955.

# Chapter 10

# Growing new businesses

## 10.1 INTRODUCTION

Understanding why some new firms grow quickly while the majority remain small and relatively insignificant is a key issue in entrepreneurship (Brush *et al.* 2009). Some theories of firm growth focus on key transition points, or stages, where particular resources and structures are required to develop the firm and to continue on a growth trajectory. While these theories have face validity, some have questioned the evidence that supports these models. In particular, there are significant criticisms that the underlying constructs lack any consensus and that the empirical confirmation of such models is inconclusive at best (Levie and Lichtenstein 2010). Rather than providing a useful tool to analyse particular transition states of firms, some argue such models provide little explanatory power (Phelps *et al.* 2007). Other authors suggest that firms, and particularly newer firms, are unstable, are constantly facing crises in their practice, and that they frequently have to learn to do new things (Macpherson 2005). Whatever perspective we take on the nature of growth, for new firms it is clear that change is essential to deal with new challenges that a growth trajectory will create. The faster that growth, the faster the need to adapt to new circumstances and to deal with the crises this creates (Nicholls-Nixon 2005).

These crises, or tipping points, provide opportunities, if firms can embed and share learning across the firm (Jones *et al.* 2010b). A crisis-based view of growth, rather than suggesting that entrepreneurs solve crises at distinct stages, proposes that this is a day-to-day challenge for owners and their senior team; it is an on-going accomplishment (Macpherson 2005, Herbane 2010). Such a dynamic view of growth recognizes that activities, resources and strategies are constantly evolving (Phelps *et al.* 2007, Levie and Lichtenstein 2010), and that the current configuration represents the best efforts of the entrepreneur to match organizational capabilities to the market and customer demands. If entrepreneurs are to realize their opportunities over the long term, it is important that they embed learning in organizational routines to ensure that they can exploit tangible and intangible assets over the long term. So, it is not just resource appropriation that defines innovative capacity to grow, but resource integration and application (Cohen and Levinthal 1990). In this chapter, we briefly review the legacy of business growth models, before exploring a more dynamic view of growth and suggesting that growth involves continuous adaptation; crises are likely to recur and intensify during periods of growth.

## 10.2 LEARNING OBJECTIVES

■   To analyse the contribution of traditional stage models of growth.
■   To describe a more nuanced understanding of the processes that support growth.
■   To explain an understanding of growth as a dynamic learning process.
■   To identify the importance of institutionalizing learning in order to realize growth potential of a new venture.

## 10.3 STAGES OF GROWTH AND LINEAR GROWTH TRAJECTORIES

As we have discussed in several other chapters, the link between management competencies and growth is a legacy of Penrose's (1959) seminal text *The Theory of the Growth of the Firm* (Pitelis 2002). For Penrose, growth is closely related to the processes through which entrepreneurs obtain and use knowledge. If this is the case, then, a shortfall in suitable resources and/or managerial competencies that will undermine a new firm's ability to grow (Goffee and Scase 1995). Phase models, normally representing a number of sequential periods through which a firm will develop, also highlight the role of knowledge resources in managing organizational growth (for example, Greiner 1972, Churchill and Lewis 1983, Scott and Bruce 1987). Notwithstanding the variation in conceptualization, stage models generally discuss the accumulation of organizational resources and capabilities *in relation to the age and size of the firm*. In essence, such models highlight the difficulties a growing firm is likely to encounter at a particular point in its growth curve, and suggest what solution will be necessary to move on to the next phase of its development. Primarily what these models suggest is that growth involves a predictable sequence of events. Continued evolution is dependent on the way human capabilities can create appropriate systems and processes to exploit opportunities (Chandler 1977).

These models identify specific resource dependencies – physical, financial and human – that entrepreneurs will need to deal with, at particular points, if firms are to grow successfully. A review of growth theories by Levie and Lichtenstein (2010) identified 104 different stage models in academic literature published between 1962 and 2006. They note that these models continue to proliferate, and that the number of phases or stages of growth vary between three and six. Such models propose that each firm goes through identifiable points where transition is necessary in order to reach 'the next level' (Phelps *et al.* 2007). Consequently, at each stage of development firms will have to face and resolve similar problems. For example, Churchill and Lewis (1983: 42) note that 'issues of people, planning and systems gradually increase in importance as the company progresses from slow initial growth'. Burns (1996) defines four stages as existence, survival, success and take-off. During each of these phases, different strategies, management approaches and structures, and marketing, accounting and finance models are necessary to sustain each phase of development. Stage or linear models thus imply that firms grow in a predictable way and that entrepreneurs will be able to diagnose a particular resource or systems deficiency at a specific stage in their development cycle and apply the appropriate solution.

Levie and Lichtenstein (2010) note that, while none of the models has gained theoretical primacy, perhaps the most influential model is the five-phase model of firm evolution and revolution provided by Greiner (1972). In this model, Greiner (1972) argues that the organizational systems that support the growth of the firm will eventually limit expansion. In order to continue growing, entrepreneurs will have to implement new organizational systems. Greiner's linear model proposes organizational structures will go through phases of change as the firm ages and grows, and that new coordination mechanisms will be essential to do so:

> each evolutionary period is characterized by the dominant *management style* used to achieve growth, while each revolutionary period is characterized by the dominant *management problem* that must be solved before growth can continue.
>
> (Greiner 1972, p. 40, original italics)

The crisis stages and their solutions are included in Table 10.1. Greiner's main point is that while the firm is growing successfully this legitimates the dominant management approach at that time and the institutionalization of particular procedures, processes and rules. When this approach begins to fail, as it inevitably will, then a new organizational paradigm will be essential. Entrepreneurs will need to 'revolutionize' existing systems to enter the next phase of growth. The length of time between evolutionary and revolutionary stages will depend on growth rate within the industry. In order to grow, Greiner argues that these new systems will inevitably fail and cause problems in the future, and so on. Greiner updated his original model in 1998. He now proposes that the revolutionary phases may not be clean breaks; legacy systems may overlap between periods of evolution. He also alludes to the role of consultants in the later phases of evolution who provide new ideas, new knowledge resources, to facilitate the organizational

**Table 10.1** *Greiner's growth phases and their crises*

| Growth phase | Crisis |
| --- | --- |
| **Creativity**<br>(implementing the new idea) | **Leadership**<br>(the firm grows beyond the leadership capacity to manage informally) |
| **Direction**<br>(the professionalization of management systems) | **Autonomy**<br>(the systems become too complex for the capacity of the owner to manage) |
| **Delegation**<br>(the responsibility for systems is devolved to middle managers) | **Control**<br>(as the firm grows overview systems are required to monitor activity) |
| **Coordination**<br>(systems are designed to incentivise and manage performance in different business units | **Bureaucracy**<br>(the proliferation of systems stifles adaptability and responsiveness) |
| **Collaboration**<br>(restructuring and development of a culture and systems to support cross functional and project work) | **Internal growth**<br>(limited internal capacity of the firm to achieve higher growth) |
| **Alliances**<br>(engagement with consultants, alliances, mergers, networks and outsourcing) | [Greiner does not identify a crisis for this stage of growth.] |

revolution, since solutions to the crises involved in the latter stages of growth may lie outside of the organization (Greiner 1998).

Stage models conceptualize management transitions as requiring access to specific knowledge resources that will solve predictable crises; resource saliency will change depending on which crisis is being managed. In addition, stage models recognize that path-dependent experience limits the repertoire of managerial and entrepreneurial resources and can create barriers for change: '[h]olding onto old strategies and old ways ill serves a company that is entering the growth stages and can even be fatal' (Churchill and Lewis 1983: 44–48). If management knowledge resources are fundamental to restructuring for growth, entrepreneurs in the early stages of firm inception are particularly vulnerable and may not be able to achieve transitions due to limited resources (Goffee and Scase 1995). However, in later stages they are also vulnerable as investments in past practices create organizational rigidities (David 1985, Leonard-Barton 1995). There is no clear agreement in these models about the types of stages and resources necessary to manage growth. However, what is common to these phase models is that they identify the importance of watershed moments where management must alter their approach during transition periods, but that they will need additional resources in order to do so (Bessant *et al.* 2005). Table 10.2 compares two models and their transition points.

**Table 10.2** Growth stage models and processes

| Churchill and Lewis (1983) | | Scott and Bruce (1987) | |
| --- | --- | --- | --- |
| **Stage** | Key challenges and activities | **Growth** | Key challenges and activities |
| **Existence** | Owner manages everything and relies on close contacts for help | **Inception** | Obtaining customers and demand placed on time and finances |
| **Survival** | Simple organization with key challenge of managing cash flow – costs and revenues | **Survival** | Balancing budgets and managing increasing complexity |
| **Success** | Firm is managing cash flow and becomes more professional with established delegated management functions and appropriate systems | **Growth** | Securing necessary resources, dealing with threats from competition, developing product portfolio |
| **Take off** | Push for growth requires further access to finance and the ability to delegate and manage an increasingly complex organization | **Expansion** | Securing finance for growth and maintaining internal control. Maintaining market awareness |
| **Maturity** | Owner has accumulated the financial, human, system and business resources necessary to trade effectively. Requires strategic abilities to look for future opportunities and threats | **Maturity** | Managing expenses and productivity. Sustaining relevance of product portfolio |

Stage theories exemplify Penrose's (1959) argument that increases in knowledge resources and managerial capacity are essential for managing growth. Greiner's (1972) model, for example, has three essential similarities to Penrose's theory. They both suggest that:

1 Systems of organizing are essential for the application of resources to achieve growth.

2 Entrepreneurial or managerial capabilities are fundamental resources that define the systems implemented.

3 Innovation to structures and systems is required to both renew the organizational resources and to make best use of them.

While Greiner and other 'stage models' acknowledge that managerial competence and knowledge are important for enacting suitable organizational systems, they do not explore how these knowledge resources are acquired or altered during the stages of revolution. What is also not clear is how managers are convinced of the need to innovate and change, or how they might identify and incorporate new knowledge (see Box 10.1).

**BOX 10.1**

Tony was a packaging manufacturer (Pack Co.) who provided packaging solutions for large corporate clients and small businesses. He set up the firm and was quickly successful in establishing a reputation for cost-effective products, and he grew the business quickly. He outgrew his premises, but was lucky when he heard a local competitor with larger premises was going out of business. He managed to buy out the failing firm and transferred his operations. However, as the business expanded he ran into further trouble. He quickly exceeded the storage capacity of his new premises and, although he knew about just-in-time production scheduling, he commented: 'I know the theory, but I have never done it and that would be really scary. It could be a real mess.' He struggled on and chose to cut his overheads to offset extra costs of material and product storage, by making some staff redundant. He also had some legacy human resource issues, since he had hired new staff on different contracts from his old staff which was causing friction. Rather than replace his retiring salesman, he also took this job on as well as managing the company. Despite growth in employment and turnover, his gross value added per employee reduced. At one point he commented:

> Short-term, it's like we're in a hell of a lot of trouble. We've oversold and we can't get the stuff out and we've got staff problems, production planning, we've got maintenance planning, distribution planning, storage and all of those are almighty great problems really.

Tony was unable to recover from the multiple human resource, production and operational crises he faced and went out of business six months later.

## 10.4 CRITICAL REFLECTIONS ON STAGE MODELS

One of the key underpinning theoretical assumptions is that stage models are generally applicable to all growing firms. However, Levie and Lichtenstein (2010), in an extensive review of 104 stage models, could not find a common template. Perhaps more concerning is the fact that when these theories have been tested (Tushman *et al.* 1986, Birch 1987, Birch *et al.* 1995), supporting evidence was very weak and did not validate stage model theories of growth. Perhaps particularly telling for understanding new ventures and their growth trajectories, McCann (1991) noted in his study of 100 high-tech firms that there was no predictable pattern of growth. More importantly, perhaps, he also suggested that such new ventures were able to make a number of choices at several different points in their development that influenced their growth trajectories. While stages of growth or transition points might be evident through large-scale analyses of such theories, they do not provide support for a general model (Levie and Lichtenstein 2010).

The Scott and Bruce (1987) model, which was initially developed through empirical research in the USA in the 1970s, can only reflect the environmental influences that were present when the study was conducted. Even if the model were valid at that time, it would only be relevant in similar contexts. So, for example, structures of social capital are more formal in the German economic context than they are in the UK or USA, and this will influence engagement with external knowledge resources in order to manage transitions (Spence and Schmidpeter 2003). In China, the concept of *Guanxi* is important for appropriating resources and establishing firm legitimacy, but is not appropriate for understanding growth in other contexts. In the USA, Renski (2009) notes significant differences in growth trajectories depending on locations of firms in rural, suburban and urban environments, due to differences in market and resource opportunities. However, different types of new firm enjoy more growth potential (high-tech firms in particular) due to knowledge spill-overs from clustering (Maine *et al.* 2010), or from an urban environment if they are service rather than manufacturing firms (Raspe and Oort 2011). In other words, context is a significant factor that influences growth trajectories.

Levie and Lichtenstein (2010) recognize that stage models have significant face validity, and that most entrepreneurs can easily identify with the problems or crises they highlight, and indeed the solutions. Stage models are still included in almost every entrepreneurship textbook since they provide a helpful way of describing the challenges of developing a growing firm (Burns 2007). However, despite their intuitive appeal, their underpinning assumptions that firm growth is sequential, predictable and universal are being increasingly scrutinized (Bessant *et al.* 2005). Emerging theoretical directions in entrepreneurial development attend to issues of ecology and focus primarily on how individual entrepreneurs make sense of the environment in which they are located (Di Gregorio and Shane 2003, Sarasvathy 2001, Dutta and Crossan 2005, Kitila and Shane 2005, Breslin 2008, Sarasvathy 2008). These authors recognize that analysis of entrepreneurial activity has to appreciate the uneven distribution in society of knowledge and information (Shane 2000), of reputation and ties to potential investors (Di Gregorio and Shane 2003), and of market conditions (Kitila and Shane 2005). They argue that a condition of the entrepreneurial experience is the uneven access to resources and the fluidity of markets and potential opportunities creating different environments over time. Perhaps what is most striking about the entrepreneurial experience is a search for, and recognition of, how entrepreneurs can reconfigure assets to make the most of particular circumstances (Schumpeter 1934).

**164**

Taken together, this means that the process of firm evolution is dependent very much on responses to changing contexts, and that simple generalizations of stages of growth are likely to miss the dynamic and unpredictable nature of managing a growing firm (Breslin 2008).

## 10.5 MAKING SENSE OF CRISIS IN CONTEXT

Given the unpredictable nature of the economic environment and the uneven availability of resources, we should generalize on growth phases and resource salience with great care. A study in China of 238 new high-tech firms, for example, found that the uneven availability of resources influenced the growth strategies adopted and achieved by these firms (Chen *et al.* 2009). This theme is taken up by Lichtenstein *et al.* (2006) who argue that, although emergence or growth may be punctuated by significant events (such as crises noted by Greiner), the way entrepreneurs make sense of those events is crucial in determining the actions they take to resolve them. In this regard, rather than rational opportunity analysis, a firm's emergence is dependent on how sense is made out of specific contexts and the process by which responses are institutionalized to inform collective action and organizational identity (Lichtenstein *et al.* 2006). As Aldrich (1999: 40) notes, organizations are influenced by many forces, including:

> the competencies carried by experienced members, accumulated under-
> standings within a work group, competitive and cooperative pressures
> from a population, and normative and regulatory obligations from a
> community and society.

He argues these forces control responses to uncertain situations, and thus social norms and influential agents in effect construct the opportunities and trajectory of a firm's evolution. This means that firm growth is a contextually sensitive process, rather than a predictable sequence of emergence events (Breslin 2008) – see Figure 10.1.

Dodge *et al.* (1994) argue that, while crises act as focal points for action during transition, they do not occur in a predictable sequence. They suggest that crises occur and reoccur over time, are dependent on the state of the market and can be both internal and external. Herbane (2010) takes a crisis management perspective to small businesses and argues that, when managing crises, both soft and hard systems interact with the internal and external environment in unpredictable ways to cause 'interruptions'. In dealing with these interruptions, the entrepreneur has limited resources and their responses are personalized, continuous and focused around a limited set of threats. Managing growth from a crisis perspective must recognize the dynamic, personal and active nature of practical coping (Cope 2010). Moreover, in order to grow it is likely that a new

**Figure 10.1**
Growth in contexts

firm will have to resolve recurring and concurrent crises, across the full range of organizational activities, rather than dealing with discrete problems and particular points in the growth trajectory (Macpherson 2005).

Growth is not linear, but can be punctuated by growth spurts, plateaus or even regression depending on a number of factors such as fluctuations in the market, the skill of the management in dealing with crises and the availability of financial and other resources (Brush *et al.* 2009). If we take a more contextually sensitive approach to firm evolution, exactly what resources or capabilities are required for growth may be dependent on the specific challenges the firm's management is having to negotiate: 'growth and survival are inextricably linked to channelling organizational perceptions of the task environment' (Dodge *et al.* 1994: 131). To put it another way, while crises occur during a firm's growth, their nature and solution is dependent on the context, the available experience embedded in organizational systems that sustain current activity and on relationships that provide access to alternative experience through business or social networks (see Chapter 5). Moreover, given that the environment is constantly in flux and unpredictable, this means understanding the processes that support a dynamic view of growth (see also Chapter 9) might be a more fruitful undertaking rather than identifying stages of transition.

## 10.6 MANAGING GROWTH DYNAMICALLY

What is clear from the review of stage models, and the empirical evidence, is that firms do operate in periods of relative stability. They also go through periods of flux when the operating systems and structures are incrementally or significantly revised (Levie and Lichtenstein 2010). What is also clear is that these transitions are not predictable. Nevertheless, what may be common in all of the growth models is that they identify significant transition points, or crises and crisis management, as a function of managing growth (Macpherson 2005, Phelps *et al.* 2007). Dodge *et al.* (1994) suggest seven core crises that exist regardless of stage: customer networks, competition, leadership, financial management, organizational structures, organizational systems and human resources. They argue that managers perceive particular problems and then embed problem solutions in the firm, which guides future decisions. In a similar vein, Phelps *et al.* (2007) identify six key routines, or practices, that influence the trajectory of a growing firm:

1  people management (a focus on delegation, leadership, recruitment and training);
2  strategy (the need to develop a more focused approach or alternative strategy);
3  formalized systems (crucial to shift from informal approaches to data collection and knowledge acquisition to implementation of formal systems);
4  new market entry (the need to identify new customers and new areas through the modification of existing products and/or introduction of new products);
5  obtaining finance (accessing external finance is central to effective growth in all ventures);
6  operational improvement (understanding process capabilities and best practices for such operations as sales, marketing, production, etc.).

They argue that, at some point, and in no particular order, firms will approach a crisis, or 'tipping point' in one or all of these key knowledge areas. They will have to address flaws in their current template of operations in order to continue to grow. Which part of their operations and how they adopt a solution will be dependent on context. In that regard, they will require access to and need to integrate new knowledge into their routines and develop new practices to overcome their difficulties. Drawing on the work of Cohen and Levinthal (1990), they argue that solutions will depend on the 'absorptive capacity' of the firm: the ability to access, recognize and integrate the appropriate knowledge to provide solutions.

For example, an owner's previous experience in supply-chain management in a large manufacturing firm might be useful in searching for a solution when overcoming supply shortages or in developing lean manufacturing protocols to improve efficiency and reduce costs in their own firm. In doing so, they may access expertise from their business network, or from relationships they had developed previously. Levie and Lichtenstein (2010) make similar arguments in their recent critique of the stages models of growth. In proposing a 'dynamic states' model, they recognize that firms do go through transition points, but argue that the current 'state' of the firm represents management's attempts to provide the most efficient and effective organizational solutions to meet the challenges faced in the market and customer expectations – *at that time*. Since dynamic states (aim to) reflect an optimal relationship between the firm's business model and its environment, and since both sides of the equation can technically change *ad infinitem*, there can be any number of dynamic states in an organization's existence. Each solution can develop continually into any number of 'states' rather than go through a predictable sequence of stages, depending on how dynamic the context is in which the firm operates (see Box 10.2).

Solutions, or developing appropriate 'states', will require access to salient resources such as knowledge. In addressing this issue of resource saliency, Lichtenstein and Brush (2001) conducted a study of three growing high-technology firms. They found that while traditional growth models concentrated on systems and financial capital to explain growth potential, in fact it is was social and

## BOX 10.2

When he was setting up his fitness business Jerry (*Fit Co.*) spent some time establishing a clientele as a personal trainer, developing a network and reputation. However, he recognized that his business lacked the capacity to expand since he was the only fitness instructor, and he did not have the time or resources to take the business to the next level. He was managing to survive, but he could not find a way to grow the business. He knew he lacked both the financial and business experience to convince the banks to lend him money, and he did not have time to spend searching for premises or developing the business because all his time was spent running classes. He contacted an old school friend whom he thought might be interested in investing in the business. Together they created a business plan and bought a gym in the local area that had been struggling for some time. With the new partner able to take care of the financial, infrastructure and marketing side of the business, Jerry was able to concentrate on the operational side, the delivery of classes and the hiring of instructors. His previous reputation and networks helped to establish a regular clientele quickly enough to ensure regular turnover. By solving his crisis, Jerry was able to grow the business, but his solution depended very much on the local network, extra resources and business acumen of his business partner and his own reputation.

organizational capital that was most salient to the firms in their study. Intangible resources, Lichtenstein and Brush argue, suggest the importance of business relationships, alliances and tacit knowledge that help owner-managers strengthen their firm's position. Such intangibles provide access to scarce 'soft' resources, including skills, information and knowledge. In addition, they note how *what entrepreneurs consider salient will depend on experience and access to alternative conceptions of a particular crisis*. This again reinforces the view that there are a range of responses available to any crisis; the actual response is dependent on how entrepreneurs, or key agents within the firm, perceive problems in their environment (Child 1972). In another study involving three growing high-tech firms, Macpherson (2005) found that, while entrepreneurs faced crises of organization (such as collaboration, coordination, control and leadership), these were repeated issues that needed on-going attention, and were never resolved, as suggested by Greiner. While managing such crises required skill, an adept application of knowledge and the development and integration of new systems of organization, the crises were concurrent, rather than sequential, and (re)occurred in no particular order.

Crises, then, are not necessarily specific moments that occur within a particular linear trajectory of growth, but they do provide a focal activity against which sensemaking emerges over time. Success or failure, and subsequent growth, may be influenced by which resources the entrepreneur can gain access to at a particular point in the firm's development, but they will also depend on the entrepreneur's

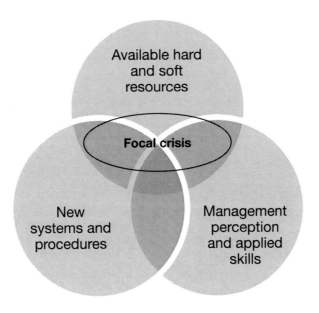

**Figure 10.2**
Dealing with crises during growth

experience, skill and adoption of systems that can provide organizations with the ability to explore and adapt, and break out of, existing path dependencies (see Figure 10.2). This also suggests that we need to look beyond individual entrepreneurs when considering growth processes. Entrepreneurs who are in search of growth need to reflect on the support and constraints of their unique internal and external environment (Dutta and Crossan 2005). Growth, then, is a challenging and unpredictable journey that intensifies the challenges for entrepreneurs to establish appropriate systems to manage their business.

## 10.7 MANAGING GROWTH THROUGH RESILIENCE

In order to explain the unpredictability of the solutions and trajectories, some scholars have turned to reconceptualizing the nature of the underpinning assumptions of growth models. One of these, as alluded to above, is to distinguish the difference between a practice-based and a resource-based perspective of knowledge. In the resource-based view (RBV), knowledge is an entity that entrepreneurs 'find' and 'apply' to resolve a crisis. A practice-based view of knowledge considers it an emergent capacity that is evident in action. Knowledge is a relational construction, which evolves and is made 'real' during application, in context.

From this perspective what may sustain growth is the capacity to get things done when current structures, systems and capabilities start to fail (Nicholls-Nixon 2005), and organizations will have different capacities and motivations to learn new ways of coping (Spicer and Sadler-Smith 2006). For example, recent research on new high-tech firms in the USA found that the financial competence of the firms' founders was a significant factor in managing successfully and coping with strategic growth (Brinckmann et al. 2011). The corollary of this is that managing growing firms may be less about creating a template for growth than it is about creating an infrastructure and culture that enable self-organized change to occur (Baron et al. 1999, Lichtenstein 2000). Thus, a perspective that examines growth as practical coping may be useful, particularly if it provides an understanding of the processes that support growth, rather than trying to predict growth patterns. From this perspective, solutions to crises are likely to be idiosyncratic rather than prescriptive responses to predictable crises; 'stage of growth' will be less important than understanding the specific contexts that shape the possibility for developing solutions.

Taking a view of knowledge as a practical accomplishment, or knowing, means that entrepreneurial strategies for growth will require owners to make sense of and deal with particular problems as they arise (Dutta and Crossan 2005) rather than to apply prescriptive solutions. Crises might provide the impetus to reconsider the effectiveness of existing activities or the effectiveness of existing systems (Cope 2003, 2005), but the acknowledgement that entrepreneurs act in response to their perceptions of the challenges faced suggests a more dynamic and evolutionary understanding of managing growth (Breslin 2008). It directs our attention to both processes and context, and this view of knowledge indicates that transition through such crises will depend on the meaning construction and sensemaking and strategic choices of key individuals (Child 1972, Weick 1995). This complicates the unit of analysis, and we would need to consider the search for, and recognition and exploitation of, opportunity as a dynamic process rather than simply the acquisition and exploitation of pre-existing knowledge or other resources (Nicholls-Nixon 2005).

The concept of resilience can help to explore the nature of this relationship (see Figure 10.3). Lengnick-Hall and Beck (2005) define 'resilience capacity' as a combination of cognitive, behavioural and contextual factors. They suggest that an organization develops its ability to cope with crises based on how key actors deploy these three properties. So the ability to interpret ambiguous and uncertain situations creatively (cognitive resilience) helps to conceive, develop and deploy both existing and unconventional activities or processes (behavioural resilience) in order to take advantage of, or develop, new relationships and resources (contextual resilience). However, resilience 'involves more than simply knowing how to regroup during a crisis and keep going; it also means being able to come away from the event with an even greater capacity to prevent and contain future errors' (Weick *et al.* 2002: 14). In other words, managing crises and sustaining the firm's development requires the capability to innovate and adapt to rapid, turbulent changes in markets and technologies, but also to sustain the firm once the crisis has been resolved. In order to do so, and particularly in a new firm, it is unlikely that the necessary competencies and other resources will be immediately 'at hand'. This means that the entrepreneur may have to engage in improvisation (using existing unused and discarded resources and capacity) and to develop and use social capital available through their networks in order to benefit from resources and expertise outside of the firm.

Solving crises and learning are therefore activities that provide seminal moments within a firm's operational trajectory, and solving such crises is likely to require the entrepreneur to engage purposefully in the search for a solution. Furthermore, the crisis-induced learning processes in small firms are likely to resemble more closely real-time learning for adaptation and innovation. Such intra-crisis learning (Moynihan 2008) takes place during the crisis episode (rather than between several episodes) and is suggested to be problematized by both the time constraints and the contextual ambiguities placed on those involved (Deverell 2009). In other words, solutions may be short term and reactive, rather than result in learning and knowledge being embedded in the firm, as is suggested by such concepts as absorptive capacity (Cohen and Levinthal 1990). However, the argument put forward by Baker and Nelson (2005), and discussed in Chapter 9, seems pertinent here. Such improvised solutions through bricolage might provide short-term relief from the current crisis, but if entrepreneurs are to gain long-term benefits through

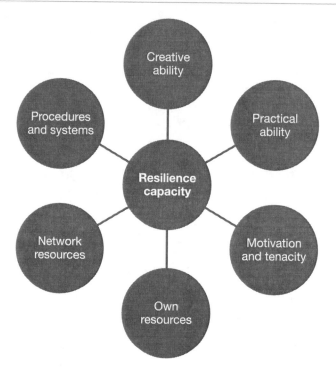

**Figure 10.3**
Resilience capacity

their solutions to crises then they will have to embed them within the firm in order to capitalize on their efforts.

If existing resources within the firm are inadequate to manage a given problem, then reorganization and embedding of new practices will be necessary. Some entrepreneurs will be more capable than others of gaining access to new ideas and absorbing new knowledge in order to manage transformations (Bessant *et al.* 2005). However, access to knowledge resources is not enough. Firms and individuals are partly dependent on their ability to draw on knowledge through their links to appropriate social and business networks (Cohen and Levinthal 1990, Aldrich 1999). So, for example, Bretherton and Chaston (2005) argue that resource-dependent firms (such as new firms) that can leverage their relational and structural ties achieve better access to scarce resources and capabilities, and it is these firms that 'over-perform' in comparison with others. Moreover, as noted by Zhang *et al.* (2006) in their study of 26 SMEs, some entrepreneurs have the ability to reflect on practical problems contemporaneously, to learn while working. They argue that this capacity enables firms to modify their existing practices appropriately and to develop continually. Those firms that are also open to learning and have systems and cultures that can support collective learning are more likely

**BOX 10.3**

David was aware that the reputation of his business (*Fume Co.*) was suffering through inconsistent quality of his products. As a fume cupboard manufacturer, he also knew that in such a specialized and regulated industry, he had to maintain that reputation if he was to survive: 'It's all word of mouth you know and if people talk about you in a negative way it will kill the business.' He set about reorganizing the quality systems and ensuring that his products met the needs of his customers: 'so we started having brainstorming sessions when we came up against a problem, because we have all worked in other places we can use that to help solve our problems.' The solutions were proposed by his staff and were then captured for future projects in systematic records: 'I make sure now that every one of our engineers uses the same sequence for their documentation. So one could pick up the contract off someone else and know exactly where everything is.' This standard process improved consistency. In generating ideas for continuing improvement he says that he reflects on his management education and that can stimulate him into action.

> Every so often if I think that something needs a shot in the arm, I read through my university notes and think, what about doing that? And it's surprising that you can always improve.

He was able to turn around the firm and grow the order book based on a reputation for quality, consistency and customer service.

to be successful in managing transitions when faced with specific challenges (Lumpkin and Lichtenstein 2005) – see Box 10.3.

This perspective on managing growth acknowledges that managers of small firms and entrepreneurs are likely to have their own quirky approach to running a business and that they will manage crises with their own perspectives on business concepts such as strategy, marketing and operations (Perks 2006). These will not necessarily accord with existing management theory (Storey 1994), and they are more likely to be improvised solutions that have been developed to cope with a multitude of challenges across a whole range of issues. The robustness of these solutions will depend on the skills that new firms have available, the resources they can deploy, and the specific, and largely unique, contexts and challenges they face. Growth will depend on the resilience new firms have to cope practically with the current crisis, and the solutions will only ever be a temporary fix until the next crisis has to be (re)solved.

## 10.8 SUMMARY AND KEY LEARNING POINTS

Burns (2007), in reviewing selected growth models in his textbook, notes that despite significant criticisms of the models, they do highlight a process of growth that incorporates three linked elements: growth, crisis and consolidation. Perhaps, then, the usefulness of such models is not in providing a predictable sequence of events that can guide entrepreneurs, but in highlighting that entrepreneurship is a dynamic process, and one that inevitably involves points of disequilibrium and crisis management in order to survive. Such models might provide heuristics with which to make sense of experiences, but the reality may be less predictable. With that in mind, it is important to consider emerging research and conceptualization of growth as managing 'dynamic states' and continual crisis. Here the view is that growth trajectories are not predictable, but involve entrepreneurs reacting purposefully to particular contexts and crises by implementing their solutions. Crises provide the opportunity for a firm to look forward (Herbane 2010), but the effectiveness of the solution will depend on access to appropriate resources and the ability to envision and enact solutions creatively. Essential to this transition is the application of human resources in order to (re)structure the firm appropriately to create new opportunities.

In a dynamic-states view, growth trajectories:

- are idiosyncratic and influenced by context-dependent environmental and organizational challenges;
- require the skill of the venture's key actors in developing appropriate solutions;
- depend on access to, and integration of, the necessary resources, including knowledge;
- are temporary, since the current 'state' is only a provisional solution to the current problems faced by the firm.

Thus, continued growth of new firms will be dependent on the resilience capacity to manage crises dynamically and to develop practical solutions.

## 10.9 DISCUSSION QUESTIONS

- What are the main principles of stage or phase models of growth?
- What are the main criticisms of the stage or phase models of growth?
- How does a 'dynamic states' or crisis-based view of transition points differ from stage-based models?
- What are the key elements of resilience, and how do they help to understand the dynamic and practical nature of growth?
- What are the implications of knowledge as practical activity, rather than a fixed resource, in understanding how new firms cope with growth?

**174**

## 10.10 FURTHER READING

Levie, J., and Lichtenstein, B. B. (2010) 'A Terminal Assessment of Stages Theory: Introducing a Dynamic States Approach to Entrepreneurship', *Entrepreneurship: Theory and Practice*, 34(2), 317–350.

Phelps, R., Adams, R., and Bessant, J. (2007) 'Life Cycles of Growing Organizations: A Review with Implications for Knowledge and Learning', *International Journal of Management Reviews*, 9(1), 1–30.

# Chapter 11

# New businesses and economic development

## 11.1 INTRODUCTION

For the governments of developed countries such as the UK, the US, France and Germany, as well as developing countries such as Brazil, China and India, entrepreneurship is seen as a 'magic bullet' by which to promote economic growth. Consequently, most governments have been concerned with encouraging entrepreneurship both directly and indirectly. The UK has initiated a number of schemes to support those engaged in business start-up. For example, Jayawarna *et al.* (2011) discuss how the 'New Entrepreneur Scholarship' helped those from disadvantaged areas establish new businesses. Whereas the US, which has a strong political aversion to direct support, promotes entrepreneurship indirectly through government funding of major projects concerned with expenditure on defence and space exploration. Such funding has certainly helped provide support for many of the high-technology businesses that are associated with Silicon Valley (Castells 2000).

The purpose of this book is to concentrate on the crucial early stages of entrepreneurship: identifying an opportunity, starting the business and ensuring that is it still operating after 12 months. Clearly, we believe that the principles on which we base this book, entrepreneurial learning, bootstrapping and bricolage, mean that businesses will have the potential to survive and grow in the longer term. However, as we are primarily concerned with the shorter-term survival of new firms, we intend to focus on government policies that encourage, promote and support early stage entrepreneurship. We acknowledge that there is not a clear distinction between policies aimed at nascent entrepreneurs and those policies designed to support more established SMEs. A dynamic small-firm sector depends on an inflow of viable new businesses. Equally, there will be a greater incentive for potential entrepreneurs to start a business if they can see that there is a thriving small-firm sector. Nevertheless, in this chapter, we are primarily concerned with the links between the creation of new businesses and the likely impact on economic development.

There is a considerable debate about the contribution of new firms to economic growth. As we discuss below, much of this debate was prompted by David Birch's work, which suggested that new firms were responsible for most of the growth in jobs. Despite extensive criticism, Birch's basic proposition that entrepreneurial firms lead to the creation of new jobs has proved to be extremely seductive to politicians and policy-makers. This debate is important because it is fundamental to questions about whether or not governments should provide publically financed support for entrepreneurs and SMEs (Shane 2009, Storey 2011). To provide greater clarity on the debate about the extent to which new firms are responsible for job creation and, therefore, the extent to which governments should support entrepreneurial activity, we draw on three bodies of evidence. First, the OECD (Organization for Economic Co-operation and Development) suggests there are six determinants of entrepreneurship that are the basis of public policy initiatives. The GEM (Global Entrepreneurship Monitor) studies also focus on policy initiative at three different levels of economic activity: factor-driven (less developed countries), efficiency-driven (rapidly developing countries) and innovation-driven (the most highly development countries). Finally, the World Bank concentrates on links between entrepreneurship and economic development by examining the 'barriers to doing business' in more than 180 countries.

In this chapter, we examine the findings from these three organizations to try to establish the links between entrepreneurship and economic development. We also investigate the extent to which governments can implement the appropriate policies to stimulate productive entrepreneurship.

## 11.2 LEARNING OBJECTIVES

- To explain the evolution of policies related to entrepreneurship over the last 40 years.
- To identify differences between various international contexts of entrepreneurship – with particular emphasis on policies designed to promote new business creation.
- To explain the role of higher education institutions (HEIs) in promoting enterprise and business start-up.
- To identify differences between the prescriptions offered by the OECD, GEM and the World Bank for promoting business start-up.

## 11.3 POLICY INITIATIVES 1970–2011

Post-war 'industrial policy' in the UK concentrated on those larger organizations that typified 'modern' economies. Gradually, during the 1960s and 1970s there was recognition that the successful post-war economies of Germany and Japan had thriving small business sectors (Jones and Tang 1998). In the late 1960s, the

Labour Prime Minister Harold Wilson commissioned a report on the state of the small firm sector in the UK. Publication of the Bolton Report (1971) stimulated much greater interest in small firms and entrepreneurship from both academics and policy makers. Later in the 1970s Birch (1979) published his influential work on the role of small firms in generating new jobs in the US. Birch claimed that 3 per cent of small firms were responsible for creating 70 per cent of the net new jobs in the US economy across all sectors. Such firms, described as 'gazelles', were growing at 20 per cent or more a year and had at least $100,000 in annual sales (Birch 1979). In subsequent years, Birch's (1979) study has been widely criticized for a number of methodological and analytical failings (Storey 1994: 163). Nevertheless, the work of Bolton and Birch had major implications for both policy-makers and for the academic community (for evaluations of UK policy see Bennett 2008, Huggins and Williams 2009).

In the late 1980s, the Economic and Social Research Council (ESRC) launched a small business research project, which helped legitimize the study of entrepreneurship and small business in the UK. As pointed out by Storey (1994) this initiative was a direct political response to David Birch's work in the US. The initiative led to the creation of three small-firm research centres at Kingston Polytechnic (now University), the University of Cambridge and the University of Sussex. More than 10,000 small firms participated in the research between 1989 and 1992 and the results were contained in three edited books (Atkinson and Storey 1993, Curran and Storey 1993, Hughes and Storey 1994). In addition, David Storey (1994), the programme coordinator, provided his own influential interpretation of the research findings. Storey (1994) argued that government intervention should be restricted to creating the appropriate macroeconomic conditions in which small firms could thrive. In essence, this meant low inflation, low interest rates, economic growth and high aggregate demand (Storey 1994: 513). At one level, such arguments are not contentious, but at the same time, not all those operating within the academic small-business community have accepted David Storey's prescriptions. For example, the work of Allan Gibb was a direct challenge to the 'free market' policies espoused by Storey. As we have stated earlier, we underpin this book with a 'Gibbsian' view of the world in which there is an important role for both policy-makers and academics in promoting the success of entrepreneurial businesses.

The economic historian, Walt Rostow (1960) suggested that countries go through five stages of economic growth: traditional society, preconditions for takeoff, takeoff, drive to maturity and mass consumption. Michael Porter (1998) updated Rostow's work by identifying three stages of economic development: factor-driven, investment-driven and innovation-driven. As discussed below, it is widely accepted that there is a U-shaped relationship between entrepreneurial activity and economic growth (Wennekers et al. 2005). Entrepreneurship declines during the transition from a factor-driven to efficiency-driven economy and then increases during the innovation-driven phase. Although there are high levels of entrepreneurship (or self-employment) at the factor-driven stage, it tends to be low value and makes little real contribution to economic development. During the innovation-driven phase, there is a switch from 'necessity' entrepreneurship to 'opportunity' entrepreneurship (Block and Sandner 2009). This is characterized by Wennekers *et al.* (2005) as the difference between unproductive (necessity) entrepreneurship and productive (opportunity) entrepreneurship. Therefore, one of the key issues that policy makers must address is how to discourage unproductive (necessity) entrepreneurship while encouraging productive (opportunity) entre-preneurship.

Bridge (2010) examines both the nature of policy initiatives and their impact on economic performance. Although the primary focus is UK policy, Bridge (2010: 34) asserts that policy recipes adopted by most countries are created from a set of common components:

- finance programmes (loans and grants);
- premises such as incubators and hatcheries;
- advice and mentoring programmes;
- business training, usually associated with preparing a business plan;
- marketing programmes, including support for exporting;
- management development programmes;
- support for innovation and R&D;
- start-up support programmes;
- awareness raising (advertising);
- programmes for specific sectors (digital for example);
- the government desire to be seen to be doing something.

Bridge (2010) suggests that there are very few useful evaluations of policies designed to create new businesses and create employment. However, studies that have rigorously assessed the impact of government policies indicate that they have had 'little or no impact' on relative levels of entrepreneurship. As we will demonstrate below, data available from sources such as the OECD, the GEM studies and the World Bank are largely contradictory. This appears to confirm that the links between government policy, entrepreneurship and economic growth are complex and are poorly understood. Or, as Bridge (2010) claims, they are based on inappropriate models of entrepreneurship. We will return to this issue at the end of this chapter.

## 11.4 INITIATIVES TO PROMOTE ENTREPRENEURSHIP

The OECD established an Entrepreneurship Indicators Programme (EIP) in 2006 to build an internationally comparable database related to entrepreneurship.

The following year, Eurostat joined with the OECD to create an OECD-Eurostat EIP based on standard definitions as a basis for the collection of empirical data (OECD 2009). Definitions were based on a combination of 'available empirical indicators' and 'conceptual contributions' from key figures in the field of entrepreneurship, such as Richard Cantillon, Adam Smith, Jean Baptiste Say, Alfred Marshall, Joseph Schumpeter, Israel Kirzner and Frank Knight (Chapter 2):

■ **Entrepreneurs** are those persons (business owners) who seek to generate value through the creation or expansion of economic activity by identifying and exploiting new products, processes or markets.
■ **Entrepreneurial activity** is enterprising human action in pursuit of the generation of value through the creation of expansion of economic activity by identifying and exploiting new products, processes or markets.

The OECD also developed a framework that indicates six determinants of entrepreneurship (Figure 11.1). These determinants influence entrepreneurial performance such as the number of firms and jobs created, which directly affects economic growth and poverty reduction. As we have discussed, the underlying philosophy of this book is that nascent entrepreneurs should make the best of the resources that they have without the need to seek external funding from banks, venture capitalists or business angels. In Chapters 2 and 8 we suggest that there are a number of ways to describe this approach: effectuation, bricolage and, the term we use most widely, bootstrapping. Therefore, our view is that access to formal finance is not an important factor to the majority of start-up businesses. Similarly, while R&D investment may be crucial to a small number of high-technology start-ups, technology diffusion or technological cooperation between firms is unlikely to be directly relevant to the vast majority of new businesses. We also believe that issues concerning regulation will not concern the majority of nascent entrepreneurs as long as there are not too many barriers related to actually setting up a new business. The other three factors, entrepreneurial capabilities, entrepreneurial culture and market conditions, illustrated in Figure 11.1, are certainly directly relevant to those actively engaged in business start-up.

### Entrepreneurial capabilities

Entrepreneurial capabilities refer to the education and training that is available to those who are considering setting up their own businesses. The OECD places particular emphasis on the numbers participating in tertiary education and proportions of the population with training in business start-up. Focusing on the development of entrepreneurial capabilities among younger people has become increasingly important for most countries. For example, in the last 10 years, UK universities have placed much more emphasis on enterprise education designed to develop and enhance the skills of students. US institutions such as Babson College

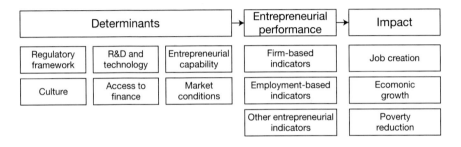

**Figure 11.1**
*OECD determinants of entrepreneurship*

have long been at the forefront of promoting education for entrepreneurs. In Chapters 3 and 4 we discuss the main mechanisms for helping students 'learn' to become enterprising.

## Entrepreneurial culture

Culture focuses attention on perceptions of entrepreneurship or self-employment as a real alternative to conventional employment (or unemployment). In other words, the extent to which, within a particular population, there is a positive image of entrepreneurs and entrepreneurship. An entrepreneurial culture can be enhanced or restricted by institutional factors such as laws relating to the legality of private enterprise as well as by informal norms and attitudes that encourage or discourage entrepreneurship. For example, in state-regulated economies such as the USSR and China, private enterprise was illegal until reforms at the end of the twentieth century and the beginning of the twenty-first century (Rogers 2006, Jiangyong and Zhigang 2010). During the 1980s, the first government of Margaret Thatcher instigated a number of political initiatives that were explicitly designed to create an entrepreneurial culture within the UK. These initiatives included paying an 'enterprise allowance' to those willing to set-up their own businesses and attempts to remove the stigma of failure by reducing the penalties for bankruptcy (Storey *et al.* 2007).

## Market conditions

The OECD concentrates on indicators such as competition law, policy indicators and import and export burdens on small firms. While we acknowledge that such macro-level factors are important in promoting entrepreneurship, we believe that more general market conditions will have a greater impact on promoting new business creation. The availability of business opportunities is likely to have much more positive impact on the propensity of individuals to start their own business than policies designed to 'stimulate' greater levels of competiveness within an economy. For example, UK data indicate that the likelihood of starting a business is twice as great in the southeast of England as it is in the northwest (100 start-ups per 10,000 head of population compared with 50 start-ups per 10,000). It is widely acknowledged that there are far more business opportunities within the southeast, which have very little to do with variations in access to finance, variations in the regulatory framework or knowledge creation and diffusion.

### Knowledge creation and diffusion

This factor includes a number of technology-based indicators such as 'business R&D intensity', firms with 'new to market innovations', firms 'collaborating on innovation' and 'turnover from e-commerce'. As indicated above, our view is that most of these measures have very little direct impact on the majority of new businesses. However, we do acknowledge that 'knowledge creation and diffusion' are central to the creation of a healthy and growing small-firm sector. In fact, knowledge creation and diffusion are central to the idea of effective entrepreneurial learning, the principle on which this book is based. So, as we discuss in Chapter 3, establishing thriving entrepreneurial communities by the creation of incubators such as *Innospace* is an extremely effective mechanism for promoting entrepreneurial learning.

### Regulatory framework

We seriously doubt whether either 'top statutory personal income tax rate' or 'top statutory corporate income tax rate' are likely to be important factors in decisions about whether or not an individual decides to become an entrepreneur. Although, in the longer-term, personal and corporate tax rates may influence where a successful entrepreneur resides or locates their main business activities. Other factors such as 'ease of doing business' and 'barriers to entrepreneurship' will be much more significant in terms of influencing potential entrepreneurs. For example, a number of European countries have extremely onerous and time-consuming regulations for those who want to establish a new business. As we discuss in Section 11.6, the World Bank uses four measures of entry barriers: start-up costs, number of procedures required to establish a business, number of days required to start a business and the difficulty of hiring/redundancy.

### Access to finance

Ease of access to loans, business angel networks, venture capital investments and share of high-technology sectors in total venture capital are the main indicators of access to finance. However, it is widely acknowledged (see Chapter 7) that only a very small proportion of new entrepreneurs seek external finance. Therefore, we suggest that, in fact, access to finance is not a major barrier to the majority of new businesses. In fact, it is our contention that 'learning' to manage without the need for loans or equity is likely to have a positive influence on the longer-term success of most start-up ventures.

## 11.5 THE GEM STUDIES

The GEM (global entrepreneurship monitor) carried out its thirteenth survey in 2011 (see www.gemconsortium.org for more information; Kelly *et al.* 2012) and is responsible for comparing entrepreneurial activity in an increasing number of companies (54 in 2011). Although the survey-based data are based on rather limited samples, GEM nevertheless provides a very interesting way of comparing entrepreneurial activity in a variety of countries. The survey examines entrepreneurial activity at two levels, which combine to give an overall index (TEA):

- **Nascent entrepreneurs** – those individuals who are actively committing resources to start their own businesses. Payment of a wage for more than three months (including the owner) is regarded as the birth of the firm.
- **New business ownership** – those who have established businesses that have paid salaries for more than 3 months, but less than 42 months.

Total entrepreneurial activity (TEA) is the total of nascent entrepreneurs and new business owners in any country.

Figure 11.2 illustrates the entrepreneurial process in which those potential entrepreneurs with the appropriate skills take the step into nascent entrepreneurship. Once the business is trading, the entrepreneur is then classified as a 'new business owner' for 3.5 years. Many businesses will fail during this stage and some entrepreneurs will, with the benefit of experience they have gained from failure, begin new businesses.

The overarching ethos of the GEM approach is illustrated in Figure 11.3. Porter's (1998) idea about three distinct phases of economic development are fundamental to the GEM model (Figure 11.3). The three boxes – basic requirements, efficiency enhancers and entrepreneurship and innovation summarize the influences on entrepreneurship at the three levels of economic development.

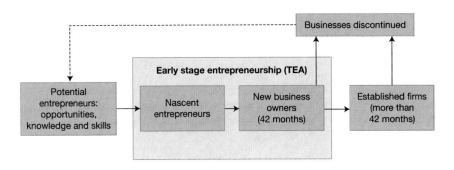

**Figure 11.2**
*The entrepreneurial process*

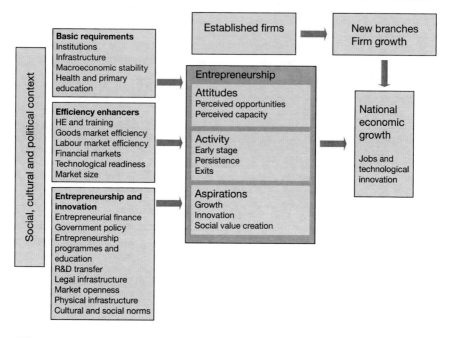

**Figure 11.3**
Entrepreneurship and economic growth

Factor-driven countries (least developed) include Algeria, Morocco and Saudi Arabia; efficiency-driven economies include the rapidly developing so-called BRICS, Brazil, Russia, India, China and South Africa; the innovation-driven economies include France, Germany, the US and the UK (see Appendices A, B and C). As we discuss below, according to the GEM studies, the requirements associated with entrepreneurship are very different at the various stages of development. Whatever the economic stage of development, entrepreneurs are influenced by prevailing attitudes, activities and aspirations that, in turn, influence national economic growth (Figure 11.3). Consequently, countries can be at the same stage of economic development, but have very different levels of entrepreneurship (Table 11.1).

**Basic factor requirements**

■ **Institutions** – including property rights, an effective legal system, regulations, start-up costs, savings and wealth creation, taxation.

■ **Infrastructure** – mechanisms by which trade can take place – in other words, functioning markets.

■ **Macroeconomic stability** – low levels of inflation promote trade, savings and investment that are important to support new and growing businesses.

**Table 11.1** *Variations in total entrepreneurial activity (TEA)*

| Stage of economic development | High TEA (%) | Low TEA (%) |
|---|---|---|
| Factor-driven | Ghana 33.9 | Saudi Arabia 9.4 |
| Efficiency-driven | China 24.6 | Russia 4.9 |
| Innovation-driven | US 12.3 | Denmark 4.6 |

■ **Health and primary education** – the population must be healthy and have reasonable levels of education.

Factor-driven economies require the creation of several basic institutional factors if entrepreneurship is to contribute to real economic development. Potential entrepreneurs are unlikely to risk starting a (legal) business unless they can access appropriate resources and know that the legal system will be able to offer them protection. Most entrepreneurial opportunities tend to be associated with subsistence agriculture – 'necessity' entrepreneurship. If entrepreneurs are to become more productive then it is essential that there is a functioning market whereby they can trade their produce for cash, which they can reinvest in the business.

### Efficiency enhancers

■ **Higher education and training** – there is a need for courses and programmes to provide higher-level scientific, technical and managerial skills.
■ **Goods and market efficiency** – needs effective supply chains (national and international) and appropriate retail outlets.
■ **Labour market efficiency** – the labour market must have high levels of mobility (from rural to urban) as well as the appropriate skills and motivation.
■ **Financial markets** – the availability of loans and credit for individuals and for businesses.
■ **Technological readiness** – individuals and businesses must have the knowledge and skills to exploit existing technologies.
■ **Market size** – high levels of efficiency depend on economies of scale in markets; hence the rapid development of Brazil, Russia, India, China and South Africa (BRICS).

Efficiency-driven economies need access to large domestic and, if possible, international markets. The rapid growth of China during the twenty-first century provides the best illustration of how an initial focus on exports helped stimulate demand in the home market as Chinese consumers had increasing levels of disposal income and ready access to consumer goods. A highly mobile labour force was also important as the population moved to the larger, rapidly developing, cities in the south of China. The transition from factor-driven to efficiency-driven economy presents opportunities for small manufacturing firms to enter the supply chain and the emergence of entrepreneurial opportunities to offer professional services.

## Innovation and entrepreneurship

- **Entrepreneurial finance** – obtainable from a variety of sources including banks, business angels and venture capitalists.
- **Government policy** – providing support for nascent entrepreneurs and growing businesses (information etc.).
- **Entrepreneurship programmes and education** – encouraging entrepreneurial activity via primary, secondary and tertiary education.
- **R&D transfer** – appropriate mechanisms to transfer knowledge from universities to the private sector.
- **Legal infrastructure** – an effective system of intellectual property rights including patents, copyrights and trademarks.
- **Market openness** – the effective operation of markets ensures that efficient companies survive and inefficient companies fail.
- **Physical infrastructure** – a developed economy needs high-quality infra-structure including roads, rail, airports and communication technologies (broadband).
- **Cultural and social norms** – these must be supportive of innovation and entrepreneurship.

Innovation-driven economies are associated with higher levels of commitment to the creation of new technologies via investment in R&D (research and develop-ment). There is also a more rigorous approach to the protection of intellectual property to encourage universities, businesses and individuals to invest in idea creation. Policy makers generally place a considerable amount of attention on technology-based new firms as these are seen to be the drivers of continued economic success. While innovation-driven economies have higher levels of 'opportunity' entrepreneurship, there is still a substantial amount of necessity entrepreneurship as developed economies increasingly suffer from high levels of unemployment. Of the 22 countries classified as innovation-driven, the US has the highest rate of new business formation as measured on TEA with a figure of 12.3 per cent. This compares with figures of 7.3 per cent for the UK, 5.7 per cent for France, 5.6 per cent for Germany and 5.2 per cent for Japan. Examples of countries from the three levels of economic activity are provided in the appendices. With regards to the efficiency-driven economies, China (24.0 per cent) and Peru (22.9 per cent) have the highest TEA scores. Russia has the lowest TEA for this group of countries (4.6 per cent). There are even greater variations among the factor-driven economies, which range from a TEA of 33.9 per cent for Ghana to 9.4 per cent for Saudi Arabia. However, as we discuss below, high rates of entrepreneurship are not linked to economic development for low-wage countries in which 'subsistence' entrepreneurship is largely necessity-based.

According to GEM figures for 2011 (Table 11.2), efficiency-driven economies have a higher average TEA figure (14.1 per cent) than the average figures for either innovation-driven (6.9 per cent) or factor-driven economies (13.4 per cent). However, it is important to bear in mind the distinction between opportunity-based entrepreneurship and necessity-based entrepreneurship. Necessity-driven entrepreneurship refers to those who resort to business start-up because they have no alternatives for paid employment. In general, necessity-based entrepreneurship is unlikely to have a significant economic impact as it acts as a substitute for low-wage or subsistence employment. In contrast, opportunity-based entrepreneurship describes those individuals who start new businesses because they identify genuine opportunities that will help improve their incomes and their independence. Therefore, in general, we would expect factor-based economies to have higher rates of necessity entrepreneurship than efficiency or innovation-based economies. As illustrated in Appendix C, 50 per cent of TEA in Uganda is necessity-based and only 34 per cent of TEA is opportunity-based. Other factor-based economies such as Pakistan, Iran and Ghana also have very high levels of necessity-based entrepreneurship. However, two countries in this group have very low-levels of necessity entrepreneurship: Saudi Arabia (10.0 per cent) and Guatemala (15.0 per cent).

Some efficiency-driven economies (see Appendix B), such as China (40.6 per cent), South Africa (34.8 per cent) and Brazil (30.7 per cent), have levels of necessity entrepreneurship that are very similar to those of the factor-based economies. There are also some countries in this group that have levels of opportunity-based entrepreneurship that are higher than the scores for most innovation-driven economies. For example, Malaysia (71.8 per cent) and Thailand (66.8 per cent) have extremely high rates of opportunity-based entrepreneurship. Nevertheless, in general, innovation-driven economies do have lower levels of necessity entrepreneurship than the majority of factor-driven and efficiency-driven economies, although it is important to point out that one innovation-driven economy, South Korea, has very high levels of necessity-based entrepreneurship (41.5 per cent; see Appendix A). Consequently, it is impossible to claim that the GEM data provide conclusive evidence that necessity-based entrepreneurship is concentrated in factor-driven economies and declines in efficiency-driven and innovation-driven economies. Clearly, there are other factors than the stage of economic development that influence the TEA scores, as well as the balance between necessity-based and opportunity-based entrepreneurship. Some of these factors will be discussed in the next section.

**187**

**Table 11.2** *Average TEA for three levels of economic activity*

| | Nascent entrepreneurial activity (%) | New firm activity (%) | Total entrepreneurial activity (%) |
|---|---|---|---|
| Factor-driven | 9.2 | 4.8 | 13.4 |
| Efficiency-driven | 8.4 | 5.9 | 14.1 |
| Innovation-driven | 4.0 | 3.0 | 6.9 |

The GEM studies also provide some interesting data on variations based on both age and gender. Based on five age groups (18–24; 25–34; 35–44; 45–54; 55–65) the proportions remain largely similar across the three levels of economic activity. Those in the 25–34 age group have the highest levels of entrepreneurial activity and they are followed by the 35–44, 45–54, 18–24 and 55–65 groups. The only significant variation is in the US where entrepreneurs in the 35–44 age group have higher levels of start-up than the 25–34 group. This may indicate the higher proportion of technology-based start-ups in the US that demand more extensive resources than other new businesses. Across all three levels of economic activity, men are more likely than women to set-up their own businesses. Among the innovation-driven economies, Germany almost has equal numbers of male/female early stage entrepreneurs. In the UK there are much greater differences based on gender, with women only providing 40 per cent of early stage entrepreneurship. There are also substantial variations between efficiency-driven economies with Peru, Brazil, Mexico and Jamaica all having very high proportions of female entrepreneurs compared with Romania, Turkey and Macedonia.

In summary, according to the GEM studies, there is a progression in the types of economic activity from factor-driven to efficiency-driven and eventually innovation-driven economies. This progression is summarized in Figure 11.4. It is also anticipated that higher levels of economic development will be associated with a move to a much greater focus on opportunity-based entrepreneurship, with declining levels of necessity-based entrepreneurship. While innovation-driven economies do tend to have higher levels of opportunity-based entrepreneurship, as discussed above, there is little difference between the two forms of entrepreneurship in the efficiency-driven and factor-driven economies (see Appendices B and C).

## 11.6 FACTORS INFLUENCING NEW FIRM FORMATION

In addition to the two organizations already discussed (OECD and GEM) the World Bank also examines the extent to which entrepreneurship contributes to economic development. The World Bank's *Doing Business Project* was launched in

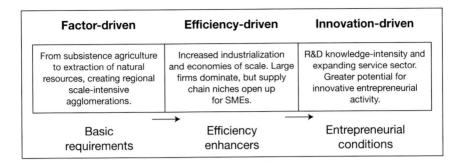

| Factor-driven | Efficiency-driven | Innovation-driven |
|---|---|---|
| From subsistence agriculture to extraction of natural resources, creating regional scale-intensive agglomerations. | Increased industrialization and economies of scale. Large firms dominate, but supply chain niches open up for SMEs. | R&D knowledge-intensity and expanding service sector. Greater potential for innovative entrepreneurial activity. |
| Basic requirements | Efficiency enhancers | Entrepreneurial conditions |

**Figure 11.4**
*Economic groups and entrepreneurship*

2002 to examine how business regulation impacts on small- and medium-sized companies. The most recent *Doing Business Project* (World Bank 2012) includes measures of regulation and their enforcement across 183 economies. The *Doing Business* index is constructed from 10 measures of business activity: starting a business, construction permits, registering property, getting credit, protecting investors, paying taxes, trading across borders, enforcing contracts, resolving insolvency and getting electricity. Based on these 10 measures, the top 10 and the bottom 10 countries for ease of doing business are shown in Table 11.3.

In this book, we are concerned about the factors that influence business start-up rather than broader influences on the economy indicated by the 'ease of doing business' measures. Therefore, in the remainder of this section we concentrate on

**Table 11.3** *Ease of doing business*

| Top 10 countries | | Bottom 10 countries | |
|---|---|---|---|
| Country | Ease of doing business | Country | Ease of doing business |
| Singapore | 1 | Haiti | 174 |
| Hong Kong | 2 | Benin | 175 |
| New Zealand | 3 | Guinea-Bissau | 176 |
| United States | 4 | Venezuela | 177 |
| Denmark | 5 | Dem. Congo Republic | 178 |
| Norway | 6 | Guinea | 179 |
| UK | 7 | Eritrea | 180 |
| South Korea | 8 | Congo Republic | 181 |
| Iceland | 9 | Cen. African Republic | 182 |
| Ireland | 10 | Chad | 183 |

**189**

World Bank measures for starting a business. The World Bank uses four factors to calculate barriers to business entry:

1 start-up costs including fees for legal and professional services;
2 number of procedures required to incorporate a business;
3 the number of days required to start a business;
4 employment rigidity including the difficulty of hiring/redundancy.

There have been a number of publications that have analysed the results of the *Doing Business* survey and they can be found on the *Doing Business* website (www.doingbusiness.org). For example, Klapper *et al.* (2009) found that the barriers to starting a business (above) were significantly and negatively related to both entry rate (business start-up) and density (number of small businesses). Quite simply, more procedures required to start a new business lead to lower new business entry rates. There was also an inverse relationship between political risk/instability and business start-up. Those countries that suffer from poor governance and/or political instability have the lowest rates of business start-up. This is largely confirmed by data in Table 11.4, which compares the 10 countries where it is easiest to start a business with the 10 where is it most difficult. Certainly the majority of the bottom 10 countries are typified by conflict and poor, unstable government. Most of the top 10 countries are stable with little internal conflict, although it is surprising that Rwanda, for example, appears in the top 10 countries in which it is easiest to start a business. Interestingly, firm formation was consistently higher in countries with smaller informal sectors. This indicates that, in economies with high entry barriers, entrepreneurs are much more likely to

**Table 11.4** *Ease of starting a business*

| Top 10 countries | | Bottom 10 countries | |
|---|---|---|---|
| Country | Starting a business | Country | Starting a business |
| New Zealand | 1 | Togo | 174 |
| Australia | 2 | Congo Republic | 175 |
| Canada | 3 | Iraq | 176 |
| Singapore | 4 | West Bank/Gaza | 177 |
| Hong Kong | 5 | Equatorial Guinea | 178 |
| Macedonia | 6 | Djibouti | 179 |
| Georgia | 7 | Haiti | 180 |
| Rwanda | 8 | Guinea | 181 |
| Belarus | 9 | Eritrea | 182 |
| Armenia | 10 | Chad | 183 |

operate in the informal (black) economy than they are to establish legitimate businesses (this issue is discussed in more detail below).

Table 11.5 compares leading innovation-driven economies with the major efficiency-driven and factor-driven economies based on the ease of starting a business. The UK and the US have the most favourable environments for business start-ups compared with the very low ratings of Germany and Japan. With the exception of South Africa, all of the so-called BRICS (Brazil, Russia, India, China and South Africa) have relatively low scores for ease of business start-up. This suggests that entrepreneurship is not a major factor in promoting the shift from factor-driven to efficiency-driven economies. It is also noticeable that, with the exception of Jamaica, all of the factor-driven economies are ranked low in terms of the ease of starting a business. We will discuss the various contradictions highlighted by the World Bank survey in the next section.

In a recent World Bank working paper, Klapper and Love (2010) discuss the impact of the 2008 financial crisis on new firm formation. The authors begin by stressing that there is an inverse relationship between the entry of new firms and the size of the informal sector (measured as a percentage of GDP). This could explain why the World Bank's 'ease of doing business' measures have little correlation with the levels of entrepreneurship. Particularly, in factor-driven economies the majority of 'necessity' entrepreneurs will be operating in the black economy. In the period 2002 to 2008, business entry rates increased from 3 per cent to 4.5 per cent in high-income countries. Following onset of the 2008 financial crisis, entry density of new firms began to decline in the high and upper-middle income countries. In the UK, for example, registered firms declined from 449,700 in 2007 to 373,400 in 2008 and 330,100 in 2009. Lower income countries

**Table 11.5** *Ease of starting a business based on stage of economic development*

| Innovation-driven | | Efficiency-driven | | Factor-driven | |
|---|---|---|---|---|---|
| *Country* | *Ease of starting a business* | *Country* | *Ease of starting a business* | *Country* | *Ease of starting a business* |
| US | 13 | South Africa | 35 | Jamaica | 23 |
| UK | 19 | Mexico | 53 | Bangladesh | 86 |
| South Korea | 24 | Thailand | 78 | Pakistan | 90 |
| France | 25 | Russia | 111 | Vietnam | 103 |
| Spain | 44 | Brazil | 120 | Iran | 144 |
| Italy | 77 | Argentina | 146 | Venezuela | 147 |
| Germany | 98 | China | 151 | Algeria | 153 |
| Japan | 107 | India | 166 | Guatemala | 165 |

suffered a delayed response to the crisis and new firm entries began to decline in 2009 (see Klapper and Love 2010). The authors go on to say that high-income economies saw a more rapid decline in new business formation because that is where the financial crisis originated. Furthermore, the crisis adversely affected operation of the financial markets that led to the 'credit crunch' and credit rationing for small firms. In lower-income countries, start-up companies, as well as established small firms, are less reliant on commercial funding and therefore were not so adversely affected by the financial crisis.

## 11.7 THE ECONOMIC CONTRIBUTION OF NEW BUSINESSES

In a special issue of the journal *Small Business Economics*, Acs and Szerb (2007) examined links between entrepreneurship, economic growth and public policy. They pointed out that there is empirical evidence that demonstrates entrepreneurial activity varies according to the stage of economic development. In particular, the data suggest that there is a U-shaped curve linking the level of economic development and the rate of entrepreneurship (Acs and Szerb 2007: 109). Entrepreneurship appears to have a positive effect on developed economies and a negative effect on the economies of developing countries. Wennekers *et al.* (2005) used GEM data to examine links between nascent entrepreneurship and the level of economic development. They were particularly concerned to establish whether there was empirical evidence for a U-shaped relationship between entrepreneurship and economic development (Figure 11.5). Essentially, the hypothesis is that as a country's economy begins to grow (moving from factor-driven to efficiency-driven for example), the rate of business start-up will decline. One of the key reasons for declining levels of self-employment (entrepreneurship) during the shift to higher levels of economic activity is that employment moves from agriculture to large-scale manufacturing (efficiency-driven). Those engaged in poorly paid agricultural self-employment find they have more opportunities for waged employment; marginal entrepreneurs become employees, thereby increasing their income. The shift from efficiency-driven to innovation-driven leads to increases in entrepreneurial activity. At this stage, technological innovation is an important driver of economic activity in a number of key clusters such as biotechnology and ICT (Porter *et al.* 2000). It is also important that there are generally high levels of cooperation between government, business and universities in a process described by Etzkowitz and Leydesdorff (2000) as the 'triple helix' (see Chapter 3). Innovation-driven economies are typified by a declining employment in manu-facturing while there is an increase in service-sector activity and a commensurate rise in what has been called the 'creative class' (Florida 2002). As economic activity increases, higher levels of per capita income create niche markets for entrepreneurial businesses (see Acs *et al.* 1994).

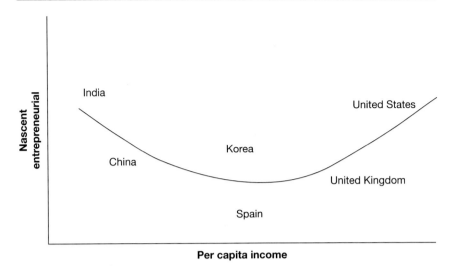

**Figure 11.5**
*U-shaped entrepreneurship curve*

Based on 36 countries that participated in the 2002 GEM study, the authors confirm that there is indeed a U-shaped relationship between entrepreneurship and economic development. Figure 11.5 provides a simple illustration of the results by showing the location of six countries. As well as identifying variations in the levels of entrepreneurial activity, Wennekers *et al.* (2005) also indicate that there are significant changes in the relationship between necessity- and opportunity-based entrepreneurship. In less developed nations (factor-driven economies) at least 50 per cent of entrepreneurial activity is necessity-based. This drops to less than 20 per cent in the most advanced economies based on the most recent GEM data. One of the main conclusions drawn from this study is that entrepreneurship is not an effective mechanism for promoting economic development in low-income countries. Instead, governments should encourage foreign direct investment (FDI), develop the physical infrastructure, promote education, create access to capital markets and ensure the macro-economic conditions are stable. In high-income countries government should encourage opportunity-based entrepreneurship by fostering expenditure on research and development (R&D), improve incentives for self-employment, stimulate entrepreneurship education, enhance intellectual property rights and stimulate a healthy venture capital market (Wennekers *et al.* 2005: 306).

Stel *et al.* (2007) use data related to rates of entrepreneurship from 39 countries participating in the GEM studies and data from the World Bank's 'doing business' survey to examine the impact of regulation on business start-up. According to Stel *et al.* (2007) governments have three main policy options related to the support of new and established small firms:

**193**

1  lower the entry barriers to new firm foundation (time taken to register business for example);
2  reduce the burdens of those operating small firms (hiring and firing employees, access to credit);
3  use public funds to provide information, training and advice to those engaged in business start-up.

It was not possible to obtain cross-country data on the provision of public support and therefore Stel *et al.* (2007) only examined entry barriers and regulatory burdens. The study revealed a number of interesting and important facts about the relationship between regulation and business start-up. First, the impact of regulation on entrepreneurship rates was found to be 'limited' with 'minimum capital requirement' as the only obstacle to start-up. Second, labour market 'rigidity' did have a negative relationship with entrepreneurship rates; higher levels of labour market regulation mean lower rates of business start-up. If, for example, job security is low (less regulation) then there may be more incentive to start a business. Third, not surprisingly, countries with high rates of nascent entrepreneurship had more 'young' businesses (up to 42 months). Less obviously, 'necessity-based' nascent entrepreneurs were more likely to establish businesses than those with an opportunity-based motive. As the authors point out, this may be because necessity-based entrepreneurs have fewer alternative employment opportunities and, therefore, are 'forced' into starting a business. Fourth, however, there were links between GDP growth and the rates of opportunity and necessity entrepreneurship. Growth in GDP had a positive influence on rates of opportunity-based entrepreneurship, but no impact on necessity entrepreneurship, as this group is not influenced by market demand. In addition, increased participation in tertiary education had a positive impact on opportunity entrepreneurship, but no influence on necessity entrepreneurship. Those with experience of higher education are more likely to start new businesses. Finally, the data suggest that neither taxation levels nor bankruptcy regulations influence business start-up rates. In summary, Stel *et al.* (2007: 183) conclude: 'the study finds no significant impact on nascent or young business formation of administrative considerations such as the time, cost, or the number of procedures needed to start a business.'

## 11.8 DO NEW BUSINESSES CREATE NEW JOBS?

Finally, we return to the crucial question concerning the extent to which new firms are responsible for the majority of new jobs. Anyadike-Danes *et al.* (2011) suggest that David Birch's (1979, 1987) work on the links between entrepreneurship and job creation led to a long-standing and acrimonious debate. Despite the fact that there have been many attempts to replicate Birch's (1987) finding there is still no consensus about the links between entrepreneurial activity and job creation. In response, Anyadike-Danes *et al.* (2011) draw on a database covering the period 1998–2010 created by the Office for National Statistics (ONS) in the UK. The Business Structure Database (BSD) relies on VAT (value added tax) and PAYE (pay as you earn), which provide the basis for firm-level longitudinal data. The BSD contains five million firm-level records detailing number of employees, turnover, sector and location. Using this database, Anyadike-Danes *et al.* were able to construct job creation and destruction metrics based on entries, exits and survivals.

UK private sector employment increased from 17.3 million to 18.6 million (7.6 per cent) and the number of firms increased by 250,000 (20 per cent) between 1998 and 2010. As we can see from Table 11.6, the stock of firms in the UK grew by a ratio of 1.2 in this 12-year period. However, all of that growth was concentrated in the smallest two size-bands – and most of that growth was in firms with just one employee. There was a negative relationship between firm size and reduction in the number of firms in the size-band (see ratios in Table 11.6). For example, the table demonstrates that firms employing 250+ were responsible for the largest proportionate decline with a ratio of 0.64 (compared with a ratio of 0.97 for size-band 3). In summary, the stock of firms increased in the 12-year period (1998–2010) meaning that 'birth-rate' exceeded 'death-rate' by an average of 19,200 firms per year. Importantly, we stress again, the majority of that growth is within the very smallest size-band. An important issue for policy-makers is the fact that there was a substantial decline in the number of small (10–49) and medium-sized (50–249) enterprises. What this appears to indicate is that start-up businesses appear very unlikely to grow into successful and viable SMEs.

Anyadike-Danes *et al.* (2011) then go on to deal with the issue raised by Birch: the extent to which entrepreneurship leads to job creation. As illustrated in Table 11.7, the number of private sector employees in the UK grew by 1.38 million between 1998 and 2010. As suggested above, employment growth was

**Table 11.6** Firm stock by size-band

| Employee size-band | 1998 (000s) | 2010 (000s) | 2010/1998 ratio |
|---|---|---|---|
| 1 | 447.5 | 775.5 | 1.73 |
| 2 | 254.7 | 270.8 | 1.06 |
| 3 | 122.2 | 118.5 | 0.97 |
| 4 | 86.8 | 74.5 | 0.85 |
| 5–9 | 181.5 | 149.8 | 0.83 |
| 10–24 | 115.8 | 89.0 | 0.77 |
| 25–49 | 33.1 | 24.3 | 0.73 |
| 50–249 | 25.5 | 17.6 | 0.69 |
| 250+ | 6.6 | 4.6 | 0.64 |
| **All** | **1,273.6** | **1,523.7** | **1.20** |

concentrated in the smallest (micro) firms. Very significantly, medium-sized firms (50–249) and large firms (250+) both suffered decreases in the numbers employed within those size-bands. The most noticeable and important trend is that firms in size-band 1 increased their share of total employment from 3.4 per cent in 1998 to 10.0 per cent in 2010. The authors conclude that very small firms create the majority of new jobs in the UK. Although the number of jobs created by start-ups declined in the recession of 2009 and 2010 compared with the earlier period (1998 to 2008) they were still responsible for the majority of new jobs (71 per cent).

A number of policy implications flow from the study carried out by Anyadike-Danes et al. (2011). First, the data are unambiguous – very small firms create the majority of jobs within the UK economy. It should also be noted that these firms are responsible for large numbers of job losses, which lead to considerable amounts of 'churn' in private sector employment. Interestingly, firms in the smallest size-band appear to be quite resilient, as their contribution to new jobs remained high during the post-2008 recession. As the authors point out: 'That is perhaps remarkable but clearly points to an underlying entrepreneurial process in a time of economic adversity which has been successful in exploiting business opportunities in domestic and international market places' (Anyadike-Danes et al. 2011: 17). The second major implication of this study is that most new firms simply do not grow; there is very little evidence of start-up businesses becoming 'gazelles'. We believe that this is an extremely important issue that needs to be addressed at the very early stages of entrepreneurial careers. Building a viable business rather than simply becoming self-employed (or undertaking 'necessity entrepreneurship') means that nascent entrepreneurs need the skills and competence to establish the appropriate foundations. It is our contention that understanding the nature of bootstrapping, bricolage and dynamic learning helps create the right conditions for longer-term business growth.

**Table 11.7** Employment by size-band

| Employee size-band | 1998 (emp. 000s) | 2010 (emp. 000s) | 2010/1998 ratio |
|---|---|---|---|
| 1 | 582.4 | 1,869.1 | 3.12 |
| 2 | 581.4 | 1,068.0 | 1.84 |
| 3 | 393.0 | 660.5 | 1.68 |
| 4 | 368.3 | 505.4 | 1.37 |
| 5–9 | 1,246.2 | 1,531.8 | 1.23 |
| 10–24 | 1,756.6 | 1,857.9 | 1.06 |
| 25–49 | 1,156.6 | 1,250.1 | 1.08 |
| 50–249 | 2,707.3 | 2,469.5 | 0.91 |
| 250+ | 8,504.3 | 7,401.4 | 0.87 |
| **All** | **17,296.1** | **18,613.8** | **1.08** |

## 11.9 SUMMARY AND KEY LEARNING POINTS

Naudé (2011) suggests that the priority for factor-driven economies is the need to establish the basic institutional arrangements associated with property rights, rule of law and the minimization of start-up costs. At the efficiency-driven stage, the state should adopt a more interventionist approach to encourage development of domestic technological capabilities. In addition, provision of financial support can strengthen the entrepreneurial base as achieved by Korea and Singapore. Finally, innovation-driven economies must focus on innovation and the development of new technologies as well as improving competitiveness through the entry of new entrepreneurial firms. However, Naudé (2011: 329) does acknowledge that the design of entrepreneurial policies relative to the stage of economic development 'is still a relatively unchartered area'.

One of the key outcomes of this overview of the policy literature is that there are substantial variations in the links between nascent entrepreneurship and the stage of economic development. Consequently, there are no simple and straightforward conclusions that can be drawn about the relationship between government support, nascent entrepreneurship and economic development. In fact, data provided by the three institutions discussed above (OECD, GEM and the World Bank) are often contradictory. For example, Wennekers et al. (2005) claim that their empirical data confirm that there is a U-shaped relationship between entrepreneurship and economic growth. In contrast, the GEM data suggest that 'total entrepreneurial activity' (TEA) is, in fact, highest for efficiency-driven economies and then undergoes a substantial decline for innovation-driven economies. However, as we have discussed in Section 11.5, there is probably too much variation in TEA for the GEM data to provide any useful insight into links between entrepreneurship and economic development.

It does seem clear that there are very few links between the nature of the regulatory environment and the levels of business start-up (Wennekers et al. 2005). Certainly, evidence from the BRICS is that low ratings for the 'ease of doing' business do not seem to hinder economic development. Equally, the US and the UK are in the top 20 countries for 'ease of starting a business', but this does not seem to have translated into high levels of economic performance compared with Germany, which is rated 98/183 for ease of starting a business. The one issue that does seem clear, at least as far as the UK is concerned, is that there is indeed support for Birch's hypothesis that new firms are responsible for the majority of new jobs. Unfortunately, for the UK, very few new firms develop into rapidly growing 'gazelles' that have the potential for a stronger impact on longer-term economic growth.

We now return to what Bridge (2010) describes as his alternative approach to enterprise policy, which rejects ideas associated with 'standard economic theory'. What this means is that individuals are assumed to make rational economic choices about engaging in business start-up based on risk assessments of the expected returns from entrepreneurship. In contrast, Bridge claims that social factors are much more important than economic factors in terms of influencing whether or not individuals engage in entrepreneurship. He also suggests that the population can be divided into three distinct groups: (1) an active group of entrepreneurs, (2) a group who will never consider entrepreneurship, and (3) those who could be encouraged to become entrepreneurial (Figure 11.6). The model's key assumption is that an individual's decision to become an entrepreneur is primarily influenced by, what we describe in Chapter 5 as, their close ties (family, friends and other influential people such as teachers). Conventional factors designed to promote entrepreneurship, including various enterprise support agencies, training, finance and reductions in 'red-tape', are unlikely to change attitudes to entrepreneurship. Bridge's model certainly goes some way in explaining the discrepancies we have discussed in relationship to the OECD, GEM and World Bank data. It also helps explain why there are substantial regional variations in the levels of entrepreneurship. As we discuss above, start-up rates are twice as high in the southeast of the UK compared with the northwest. According to Bridge, areas that have high levels of entrepreneurship will continue to have high start-up rates while the reverse will be true for areas with low levels of entrepreneurship.

We largely agree with Bridge's assertion that social influences are important in terms of encouraging individuals to consider entrepreneurship. Our view is that, in addition to family and friends higher education has an increasingly important role to play in promoting entrepreneurship to younger people (see Chapter 3). As a result of participating in enterprise-related courses at university or by belonging to societies, such as the Liverpool Enterprise Network, students are exposed to lecturers and guest speakers who are enthusiastic about entrepreneurship (Pittaway et al. 2011). Lourenço et al. (2012) evaluated the extent to which exposure to enterprise-related courses influenced students' attitudes and behaviours. The study was informed by Ajzen's theory of planned behaviour (Figure 11.7), which suggests that behaviours are influenced by intentions which, in turn, are influenced by three sets of beliefs: behavioural, normative and control. The study indicates that

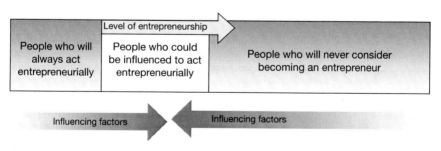

**Figure 11.6**
*Levels of entrepreneurship*

students' perceptions of benefits are a major driver of intentions to exploit their classroom learning. It also suggests that introducing less complex techniques is important in terms of raising students' perceptions of the benefits of learning about entrepreneurship. This finding extends the theory of planned behaviour by clarifying the role of perceived ease-of-use as a significant driver of the learning processes, although perceived 'ease-of-use' did not in itself predict intentions to exploit learning. In other words, potential student entrepreneurs will not acquire knowledge unless they perceive that it has real benefits in terms of helping them start their own businesses (see Lourenço *et al.* 2012). The positive influence of education on entrepreneurship is confirmed by an extensive study of more than 10,000 individuals in Europe and the USA (Block *et al.* 2013). Such studies support Ajzen's (1991) theory that attitudes (perception of benefits) are a strong influence on behavioural intentions. Hence, when students perceive there are real benefits to learning about entrepreneurship they are more likely to have intentions to exploit their learning.

Key learning points are:

- It is important to understand how the work of Birch in the US and the Bolton Commission in the UK stimulated greater interest from policy-makers in the links between entrepreneurship and economic development.
- One of the key factors in promoting economic development is to encourage a switch from necessity-based entrepreneurship to opportunity-based entrepreneurship.
- The OECD, GEM and the World Bank offer different prescriptions for promoting entrepreneurship – it is important to understand the extent to which the policies these institutions promote make a difference to entrepreneurial activity.

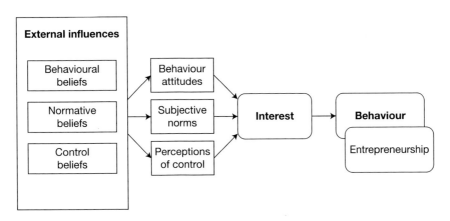

**Figure 11.7**
*Theory of planned behaviour*

- Governments are very keen to promote the importance of entrepreneurship and most see an important role for universities in encouraging business start-up and growth.

## 11.10 DISCUSSION QUESTIONS

- To what extent is access to finance a real barrier to business start-up?
- How does the level of entrepreneurship vary according to the three stages of economic development (factor, efficiency and innovation)?
- To what extent does necessity-based entrepreneurship decline with higher levels of economic development?
- What is the most important factor in stimulating greater levels of new business creation?
- Why does Bridge reject 'standard economic theory' as a basis for explaining improvements in the level of entrepreneurship?
- How does the theory of planned behaviour contribute to our understanding of the effectiveness of policies designed to promote entrepreneurship?

## 11.11 FURTHER READING

Bridge, S. (2010) *Rethinking Enterprise Policy: Can Failure Trigger New Understanding?* Basingstoke, UK: Palgrave Macmillan, 2010.

## 11.12 APPENDICES

### Appendix A *Innovation-driven economies*

| Country | Nascent (%) | New firms (%) | TEA (%) | Necessity (% TEA) | Opportunity (% TEA) |
|---|---|---|---|---|---|
| US | 8.3 | 4.3 | 12.3 | 21.2 | 58.9 |
| Netherlands | 4.3 | 4.1 | 8.2 | 9.1 | 62.3 |
| South Korea | 2.9 | 4.1 | 7.8 | 41.5 | 36.2 |
| UK | 4.7 | 2.6 | 7.3 | 17.2 | 46.3 |
| Finland | 3.0 | 3.3 | 6.3 | 18.3 | 59.4 |
| Spain | 3.3 | 2.5 | 5.8 | 25.9 | 39.3 |
| France | 4.1 | 1.7 | 5.7 | 14.8 | 70.7 |
| Germany | 3.4 | 2.4 | 5.6 | 18.6 | 54.9 |
| Japan | 3.3 | 2.0 | 5.2 | 24.9 | 63.5 |
| Denmark | 3.1 | 1.6 | 4.6 | 7.1 | 64.0 |

### Appendix B  Efficiency-driven economies

| Country | Nascent (%) | New firms (%) | TEA (%) | Necessity (% TEA) | Opportunity (% TEA) |
|---|---|---|---|---|---|
| China | 10.1 | 14.2 | 24.0 | 40.6 | 29.0 |
| Peru | 17.9 | 5.4 | 22.9 | 22.4 | 52.0 |
| Colombia | 15.2 | 6.7 | 21.4 | 25.1 | 30.1 |
| Argentina | 11.8 | 9.2 | 20.8 | 33.1 | 44.7 |
| Thailand | 8.3 | 12.2 | 19.5 | 18.9 | 66.8 |
| Brazil | 4.1 | 11.0 | 14.9 | 30.7 | 45.2 |
| South Africa | 5.2 | 4.0 | 9.1 | 34.8 | 39.3 |
| Hungary | 4.8 | 1.6 | 6.3 | 31.0 | 29.2 |
| Malaysia | 2.5 | 2.5 | 4.9 | 10.2 | 71.8 |
| Russia | 2.4 | 2.3 | 4.6 | 26.9 | 41.9 |

### Appendix C  Factor-driven economies

| Country | Nascent (%) | New firms (%) | TEA (%) | Necessity (% TEA) | Opportunity (% TEA) |
|---|---|---|---|---|---|
| Ghana | 10.7 | 24.6 | 33.9 | 37.0 | 35.0 |
| Zambia | 17.3 | 17.1 | 32.6 | 32.0 | 41.0 |
| Uganda | 10.6 | 22.0 | 31.3 | 50.0 | 34.0 |
| Guatemala | 8.3 | 8.4 | 16.3 | 15.0 | 28.0 |
| Venezuela | 13.1 | 2.6 | 15.4 | 28.5 | 43.4 |
| Iran | 4.8 | 7.8 | 12.4 | 38.0 | 39.0 |
| Jamaica | 5.5 | 5.1 | 10.5 | 33.0 | 39.8 |
| West Bank/Gaza | 7.9 | 2.6 | 10.4 | 32.0 | 33.0 |
| Algeria | 5.3 | 4.0 | 9.3 | 36.5 | 45.4 |
| Pakistan | 7.5 | 1.7 | 9.1 | 46.9 | 24.7 |
| Saudi Arabia | 5.9 | 3.5 | 9.4 | 10.0 | 75.0 |

# Chapter 12

# Conclusions: creating dynamic learning businesses

## 12.1 INTRODUCTION

In this book we have focused, for the most part, on the first 12 months of operation as we regard this as the crucial period in the life of an entrepreneurial business. As discussed in the previous chapter, the majority of new entrepreneurs do not get beyond the self-employment stage. We acknowledge that there is an important role for entrepreneurs who operate as sole-traders whether they are offering craft-based services (hairdressing/plumbing) or are providing a more technical service such as web design. However, it is our view that establishing a business according to the principles outlined in this book provides a sound basis for future growth – as outlined in Chapter 10. Successful entrepreneurship is not only important to those individuals who start their own businesses, it is the focus of policy-makers and politicians in mature, innovation-based economies including the UK and the US, efficiency-driven economies (the BRICS) and factor-driven economies such as Ghana, Zambia and Venezuela. Of course, one of the problems for less-developed countries is to shift from unproductive necessity-based entrepreneurship to the higher productivity of opportunity-based entrepreneurship (Valliere and Peterson 2009). Such a shift is heavily reliant on developing countries making real efforts to improve educational levels among the population, as demonstrated by highly successful economies such as South Korea or China. As illustrated in Figure 9.2, entrepreneurial resources are the starting point for understanding effective new venture creation. Knowledge or, more formally, human capital is the most important of the resources that any entrepreneur can mobilize.

In addition to knowledge, Aldrich and Yang (2012) point out the importance of three dispositions: routines, habits and heuristics. Rather than being fixed psychological attributes these dispositions are outcomes of learned behaviour. Such learning can come from many sources including family (see *Jazooli* case), friends, role-models or even from lecturers providing courses dealing with business start-up. Potential entrepreneurs will also take the opportunity to learn from a wide-range of experiences, which are part of our development during the early stages of the human life course (Jayawarna *et al.* 2007b). Learning can come from part-time work during school or university when there are many opportunities to observe the real-life management of small businesses (newsagents, restaurants, bars, retail outlets etc.). Learning can also come from our experiences as consumers when the provision of inadequate offerings from existing companies could help us imagine a business opportunity. Equally important, exposure provides opportunities to see the routines that underpin any successful business in action.

In the remainder of this chapter, we intend to summarize briefly the main factors that we believe contribute to dynamic entrepreneurial learning capabilities. It is our belief that these factors will lead the creation of new business ventures that have real potential for future growth and, hopefully, meaningful employment creation.

## 12.2 LEARNING OBJECTIVES

- To be able to clearly articulate the overall objectives on which this book is based.
- To explain how the changing nature of entrepreneurial theory has influenced our understanding of how entrepreneurs develop new opportunities.
- To explain how effective entrepreneurs are able to combine bootstrapping and bricolage to enhance the sustainability of any new business.

## 12.3 THEORY, PRACTICE AND LEARNING

In Chapter 2, we discussed changes to the nature of entrepreneurial theory over the last 15 years (Landström *et al.* 2012). The most significant issue for the would-be entrepreneur relates to ideas about the nature of business opportunities. The traditional, largely economic, view suggests that new opportunities have an objective reality, which means they are 'out there' awaiting entrepreneurial discovery (Shane 2000). This is linked to the idea that there is a small group of individuals who possess the necessary 'entrepreneurial alertness' to identify and exploit those opportunities (Kirzner 1973). The view expressed by the 'causal school' has been increasingly challenged by a number of competing theories including bricolage (Baker and Nelson 2005), effectuation (Sarasvathy 2001, 2008) and the narrative approach (Fletcher 2007). A common theme in these theories is that entrepreneurs create opportunities through a process of sensemaking. What this means is that the entrepreneur's own resources and interests provide the basis of a business opportunity (Baker and Nelson 2005). This approach is illustrated clearly by Ben and Sam Wilson's experience of establishing *Jazooli*, which began as a hobby and has grown into a company that has 10 employees with a turnover of £1.6 million (see Chapter 2).

**203**

There are many implications arising from an acceptance of the idea that entrepreneurs create rather than discover opportunities. In particular, starting at a relatively small-scale enables the entrepreneur to develop the appropriate skills and knowledge as they establish the business. As we outline in Chapter 4, the nature of skills and capabilities depends on the entrepreneur's education and previous experience. It is clear that the type of business/opportunity is also an important factor. Many start-ups established by young entrepreneurs replicate existing businesses and therefore do not require specialist knowledge, skills or capabilities. We accept that such businesses can still be extremely demanding for inexperienced entrepreneurs, as they have to develop the appropriate organizational routines by which to deliver their products/services. However, if they are introducing a product or service that redefines an existing market then, in addition to basic organizational skills, nascent entrepreneurs will need to be creative and innovatory. It is also likely that such ventures demand far higher levels of financial resources (see Chapter 7). Although there is little agreement on the exact nature of the appropriate skills and competencies, we suggest that functional skills including marketing, finance, sales, planning and customer relationship management are likely to be highly relevant whatever the type of start-up.

Researchers also increasingly recognize that social skills are important for successful entrepreneurs (Baron and Tang 2009, Cornelissen *et al.* 2012). We suggest that developing the appropriate social skills is central to the effective mobilization of entrepreneurial social capital (Anderson *et al.* 2010). This is particularly important in terms of accessing wider resources (finance, knowledge, information and business opportunities) by moving beyond the 'strong ties' that are important in the very early stages of start-up to 'weaker ties' associated with professional networks. Figure 5.5 illustrates this process of converting 'essential dyads' into socio-economic exchanges. We also suggest that there are three forms of social capital, structural, relational and cognitive, that enable entrepreneurs to access wider, more resource-rich social networks. Cognitive social capital illustrates the forms of communication used by nascent entrepreneurs to build relationships with resource-providers (Lee and Jones 2008).

Entrepreneurial learning underpins the process of accessing a wider range of social contacts. As is evident by the title of this book, building dynamic entrepreneurial learning capabilities is of central importance to young entrepreneurs wanting to establish successful businesses. As we have described in Chapters 3 and 6, we believe that 'learning-to-learn' is an important capacity for any potential entrepreneur studying in higher education. Furthermore, we see the Kolb cycle, which is based on two dialectical processes (prehension and transformation), as an essential tool for understanding learning activities. What this means in practice is that courses/modules designed to develop entrepreneurial skills and capabilities must have an experiential element in which students can gain experience of what it means to be an entrepreneur. Courses can promote such learning in a variety of ways including writing business plans, engaging in simulation games (*SimVenture*), actually starting a small-scale business, as well as engaging in clubs and societies. Our view is that the more 'real' such experiences then the more likely students are to develop the appropriate skills and competencies (Pittaway *et al.* 2011). In the previous Chapter (11), we describe how this approach fits with Ajzen's theory of planned behaviour (Figure 11.7), which suggests that behaviours are influenced by intentions that, in turn, are influenced by behavioural, normative and control beliefs (Ajzen 1991). Those students who perceive there are real benefits in learning about entrepreneurship are more likely to have intentions to exploit their learning (Lourenço *et al.* 2012). This view is based on the concept of self-efficacy; individuals are more likely to undertake particular tasks when they believe they have the appropriate knowledge and skills (Bandura 1997).

## 12.4 RESOURCES, BOOTSTRAPPING AND BRICOLAGE

Creating opportunities, and learning from experience, requires the application of human capital and other resources in order to establish and develop new ventures. While highly capitalized start-ups may have an abundance of resources, the reality is that most new entrepreneurs have a limited ability to attract funding from external sources and rely mainly on the creative energy of just one or two people. This means that, in new firms, resource capacity is generally limited. Financial and other tangible resources are clearly necessary to be able to start and maintain the venture. However, as Hitt *et al.* (2001a) argue, it is the intangible resources that distinguish firms from each other since these are more difficult to replicate. In addition, despite similar resource endowments, some firms will prosper while others diminish. Penrose (1959) attributes this to the unique capabilities and capacity of entrepreneurial individuals. At the start of any venture, Sarasvathy (2001, 2012) argues that nascent entrepreneurs have three categories of means – their own personal traits, tastes and abilities, their own knowledge gained through education and experience, and their social networks. In particular, as suggested by Sarasvathy, and discussed in Chapter 6, an entrepreneur's human capital is an important foundational capability. This resource provides access to social networks, and the purposeful capacity and capability to transform resources into rents (Penrose 1959). Human capital resources include the knowledge, experience, judgment, intelligence, relationships and insight of people working in the firm and in particular the entrepreneur. These are not static capacities, but an entrepreneur is continually developing them through experience and learning (see above in Section 12.3), and a new venture owner can appropriate, or borrow, them from others within their social network (Xiang-yang *et al.* 2010).

Teece (2011) recognizes that such human capital resources are not equally distributed, but he argues that they can be enhanced through education (generic human capital) and, more importantly, through experience, to create specific and unique capabilities. However, if new firms that are generally resource poor are to become established and self-sustaining, then 'a series of resource acquisitions and combinations might be necessary' (Lichtenstein and Brush 2001: 41). Here the concepts of bootstrapping and bricolage help us to explore resource development and enhancement through the dynamic capabilities that provide opportunities for new firms to learn to grow. Researchers have spent a great deal of time discussing how entrepreneurs successfully manage the complexities of establishing a venture to supplement their own human capital through resources, advice and knowledge available in their networks (West and Noel 2009). Since new venture owners do not hold all the resources they need to establish and grow the firm, the environment (and particularly the network) in which their firm operates is potentially a vital resource base. For example, while traditional collateral sources are available these are often difficult to access (see Chapter 7), and financial bootstrapping can provide a source of tangible resources at little or no cost (Harrison *et al.* 2004). As noted above, social skills and the ability to manage relationships to establish and extend networks is a particularly useful capability, since this gives access, potentially at least, to a broader array of resources (Baron and Tang 2009, Cornelissen *et al.* 2012).

While a number of routes and options exist to 'bootstrap', most rely on the availability and strength of network ties the entrepreneur is able to leverage in order to do so. This means that the extent to which entrepreneurs are dependent upon a given environment or social group can determine their capacity for resource acquisition. Therefore, the growth trajectory and opportunities that ventures can generate depend on the level and nature of relationships and dependencies they develop (Villanueva *et al.* 2012). These relationships will change as the firm grows, and there will inevitably be some alteration to the availability and desirability of bootstrapping techniques and opportunities. So, human capital, in the form of prior education and experience, is not only relevant because of the way in which new entrepreneurs might apply it to manage the business; it is also important because it can mediate access to wider capital resources available within internal and external networks. This also highlights how, in different social contexts and cultures, some social groups will have a significant advantage in terms of bootstrapping their business (see Chapter 8). It should not be a shock, therefore, that, in developing countries and deprived social contexts, most new enterprises arise out of necessity-based entrepreneurship and have limited capacity to grow. Moreover, this social dimension makes entrepreneurship a 'gendered profession' since societies can place limitations on women's ability to accrue necessary resources for their businesses (Gupta *et al.* 2009, Jayawarna *et al.* 2012).

Social networks can also provide access to knowledge, experience and capabilities not possessed by a new, young entrepreneur. This may be particularly useful when, in dynamic contexts, the entrepreneur has to respond to changes in the market in order to create opportunities. In large firms, the strategic ability to manage these volatile contexts has been termed dynamic capabilities (Teece *et al.* 1997), the ability to reconfigure and integrate both internal and external resources in response to environmental shifts. However, small firms, and particularly new ones, lack the resource capacity, or resource slack, to manage such situations. In this regard, the concept of bricolage is particularly useful. Bricolage is the art of making do with resources at hand or discarded by others (Baker and Nelson 2005) – see Chapter 9. Given the limited resources with which most new ventures operate, being able to scrounge and borrow resources discarded by others, or being able to access knowledge and capabilities available in their network of contacts, is a potential resource multiplier. In new firms, the application of these resources is likely be through improvisation and trial-and-error (or experiential) learning (Zahra *et al.* 2006). Thus, the effective evolution of the firm depends on the ability of new entrepreneurs to acquire the ability to problem-solve when responding to changing contexts (Breslin and Jones 2012) – see Chapter 10. Bricolage is thus intimately linked to the learning ability of the entrepreneur (developing their human capital), and the capability to bootstrap both tangible and intangible resources. Thus, bootstrapping, bricolage and the social skills to navigate network relationships may be the most important capabilities nascent entrepreneurs bring to their venture. If new ventures are to grow, certainly at the outset, they will need to overcome their resource constraints. In doing so, Baker *et al.* (2003) and Baker and Nelson (2005) argue that entrepreneurs are essentially refusing to accept the resource limitations imposed by their situation. Establishing a new firm, from this perspective, is a dynamic creative process, one that requires tenacity and the ability to learn (from others) while working (Zhang *et al.* 2006).

## 12.5 CONCLUSIONS

As discussed in Chapters 3 and 6, the idea that entrepreneurs are born remains an issue of some contention. The debate has largely moved on from the idea that entrepreneurs have specific psychological attributes, such as a tolerance of ambiguity and a high need for achievement (McClelland 1961), to a search for the 'entrepreneurial gene' (Nicolaou *et al.* 2008, Shane *et al.* 2010). Our view is that anyone attending college or university has the potential to start their own business. We acknowledge that there are a number of skills and competencies that students should acquire if they are intending to start their own business (Chapter 4). At least as important is that students should learn to learn, so that they can make sense of an environment that is rapidly changing. Anyone starting a business will be confronted with a large number of crises in the first 12 months of operation (Deverell 2009). Such crises will be particularly challenging for young people who are gaining their first exposure to the 'real world' of business and, therefore, have no previous experience on which to draw. According to a recent study of young entrepreneurs (Hickie 2011), those who are the most successful did initiate entrepreneurial ventures while still at school. The *Jazooli* case also illustrates the benefits of gaining early trading experience as well as having supportive parents with appropriate business expertise (Chapter 2). Aldrich and Yang (2012) suggest that family members are crucial influences on the 'substrate of individual habits' that help new entrepreneurs embed their learning as they build a set of routines, habits and heuristics. Such dispositions help new entrepreneurs use their rules of thumb to make decisions when they do not possess the time or resources required for optimal solutions.

However, the majority of those studying enterprise/entrepreneurship courses/ modules are unlikely to have had previous experience of operating a business or have family members willing to share their experience of self-employment or managing a small firm. Therefore, encouraging students to gain real benefits from their educational experiences is an important contribution to building dynamic learning companies. As outlined in Chapter 3, our view is that the delivery of conventional lectures has to be supplemented by more active approaches to learning (Pfeifer and Borozan 2011). We believe that entrepreneurship can be learned as long as modules, courses and programmes are designed in such a way that students are provided with the opportunities to engage in meaningful experiential learning (Corbett 2005, Higgins and Elliott 2011). At the same time, students of entrepreneurship should be prepared to continue their learning outside the classroom. That could involve trading goods on *eBay*, observing organizational routines in places of employment such as bars, restaurants and retail outlets, as well as learning vicariously from TV programmes (*Dragons' Den*) and experienced entrepreneurs. In Hickie's (2011) study, 14 of his 15 high-growth young entrepreneurs had acquired previous work experience before starting their businesses. In most cases, this experience was mundane involving the kind of retail activities familiar to most of those studying at school, college or university. The point of this experience was that it provided insight into key factors such as understanding the customer, working in teams and the nature of 'business'. In more formal terms, these experiences made a significant contribution to the development of their human capital (Unger *et al.* 2011), which, in turn, contributed to the creation of businesses with real growth potential (Zimmerman and Zeitz 2002, Chen *et al.* 2009). Our ultimate objective is that students should acquire the dynamic entrepreneurial learning capabilities that will enable them to establish businesses that have real potential for growth, and the creation of employment opportunities for others.

## 12.6 KEY LEARNING POINTS

■ If start-up businesses are to make a real contribution to economic development, they need to grow beyond sole-trader status. To do so, it is important that nascent entrepreneurs create 'dynamic learning companies'.

■ Effective entrepreneurial learning needs to have a strong experiential element if students are to develop the appropriate entrepreneurial skills and competencies.

■ It is important to understand the distinction between tangible and intangible resources and their relative contributions to the success of entrepreneurial businesses.

## 12.7 DISCUSSION QUESTIONS

■ What do you think are the main sources of learning for nascent entrepreneurs?

■ Why is the distinction between opportunity identification and opportunity creation/development so important?

■ To what extent do the entrepreneur's social skills contribute to the success of a new business venture?

■ Why are bootstrapping and bricolage described as dynamic capabilities?

# Notes

## 1 INTRODUCTION: DYNAMIC ENTREPRENEURIAL LEARNING CAPABILITIES

1   Our case study of Sam and Ben's start-up company, *Jazooli*, is discussed in Chapter 2.

## 2 THE CHANGING NATURE OF ENTREPRENEURIAL THEORY

1   Percentages refer to the amount of time taken-up by these activities and functions during the working day.

2   The case study companies were 37signals, Bloglines, del.icio.us, Six Apart, Flickr and Trip Advisor.

## 3 LEARNING TO BE AN ENTREPRENEUR

1   The big five personality attributes are described as: extraversion, openness to experience, agreeableness, conscientiousness and emotional stability (see Zhao, H. and Seibert, S. E. (2006) 'The Big Five Personality Dimensions and Entrepreneurial Status: A Meta-analytical Review', *Journal of Applied Psychology*, 91(2), 259–271.

2   See Chapter 1, 'The process of experiential learning', in Kolb, D. A. (1984) *Experiential Learning: Experience as the Source of Learning and Development*, Englewood Cliffs, NJ: Prentice-Hall.

3   In 2012 SIFE was rebranded as ENACTUS.

# 5 NETWORKS, SOCIAL CAPITAL AND ENTREPRENEURIAL RESOURCES

1   As discussed in Chapter 2, our view is that opportunities are created by entrepreneurs rather than being discovered. Even if they are adopting an effectual approach entrepreneurs still have to decide on an area of the market that they are intending to target (see the *Jazooli* case).

2   Larson and Starr (1993) include an additional stage – 'layering the exchanges' – which is concerned with the functional linkages as the firm grows. As we are dealing with the early stages of operation this phase does not apply here.

# References

Acs, Z. J. and Szerb, L. (2007) 'Entrepreneurship, Economic Growth and Public Policy', *Small Business Economics*, 28(2/3), 109–122.

Acs, Z. J., Audretsch, D. B. and Feldman, M. P. (1994) 'R&D Spillovers and Innovative Activity', *Managerial and Decision Economics*, 15(2), 131–138.

Ahn, J.-H. (2008) 'Application of the Experiential Learning Cycle in Learning from a Business Simulation Game', *E-Learning*, 5(2), 146–156.

Ajzen, I. (1991) 'The Theory of Planned Behaviour', *Organizational Behaviour and Human Decision Processes*, 50(2), 179–211.

Aldrich, H. (1999) *Organizations Evolving*, London: Sage.

Aldrich, H. E. and Auster, E. R. (1986) 'Even Dwarfs Started Small: Liabilities of Age and Size and their Strategic Implications', *Research in Organizational Behaviour*, 8, 165–199.

Aldrich, H. E. and Yang, T. (2012) 'Lost in Translation: Cultural Codes Are Not Blueprints', *Strategic Entrepreneurship Journal*, 6(1), 1–17.

Aldrich, H. E., Rosen, B. and Woodward, W. (1987) 'The Impact of Social Networks on Business Founding and Profit: A Longitudinal Study', in Churchill, N., Hornaday, J., Krasner, O. and Vesper, K., eds, *Frontiers of Entrepreneurship Research*, Wellesley, MA: Babson College, 154–168.

Alvarez, S. A. and Barney, J. B. (2007) 'Discovery and Creation: Alternative Theories of Entrepreneurial Action', *Strategic Entrepreneurship Journal*, 1(2), 11–26.

Alvarez, S. A. and Barney, J. B. (2013) 'Epistemology, Opportunities, and Entrepreneurship: Comments on Venkataraman *et al.* (2012) and Shane (2012)', *Academy of Management Review*, 38(1), 154–157.

Alvarez, S. A. and Busenitz, L. W. (2001) 'The Entrepreneurship of Resource-based Theory', *Journal of Management*, 27(6), 755–775.

Ambrosini, V. and Bowman, C. (2009) 'What Are Dynamic Capabilities and Are They a Useful Construct in Strategic Management?', *International Journal of Management Reviews*, 11(1), 29–49.

Anderson, A. (2005) 'Enacted Metaphor: The Theatricality of the Entrepreneurial Process', *International Small Business Journal*, 23(6), 587–603.

Anderson, A. R. and Jack, S. L. (2002) 'The Articulation of Social Capital in Entrepreneurial Networks: A Glue or a Lubricant?', *Entrepreneurship and Regional Development*, 14(3), 193–210.

Anderson, A. R., Drakopoulou-Dodd, S. and Jack, S. L. (2010) 'Network Practices and Entrepreneurial Growth', *Scandinavian Journal of Management*, 26, 121–133.

Anderson, A. R., Drakopoulou-Dodd, S. and Michael, G. S. (2000) 'Religion as an Environmental Influence on Enterprise Culture – The Case of Britain in the 1980s', *International Journal of Entrepreneurial Behaviour and Research*, 6(1), 5–21.

Anderson, A. R. and Miller, C. J. (2003) '"Class Matters": Human and Social Capital in the Entrepreneurial Process', *Journal of Socio-economics*, 32, 17–36.

Anyadike-Danes, M., Bonner, K. and Hart, M. (2011) *Job Creation and Destruction in the UK: 1998–2012*, Department for Business Innovation and Skills, London.

Arend, R. J. and Lévesque, M. (2010) 'Is the Resource-based View a Practical Organizational Theory?', *Organization Science*, (4), 913–930.

Arend, R. J. (2013) 'Promises, Premises . . . An Alternative View on the Effects of the Shane and Venkataraman 2000 AMR Note', *Journal of Management Inquiry – Online First*, published online 24 January 2013 (doi: 10.1177/105649261247 2731).

Argyris, C. (1992) *On Organizational Learning*, Oxford: Blackwell.

Atherton, A. (2012) 'Cases of Start-up Financing: An Analysis of New Venture Capitalisation Structures and Patterns', *International Journal of Entrepreneurial Behaviour and Research*, 18(1), 28–47.

Atkinson, J. and Storey, D. (1993) *Employment, the Small Firm and the Labour Market / Beschäftigung, Kleinbetriebe und Arbeitsmarkt*, London: Routledge & Kegan Paul.

Austin, J., Stevenson, H. and Wei-Skillern, J. (2006) 'Social and Commercial Entrepreneurship: Same, Different, or Both?', *Entrepreneurship: Theory and Practice*, 30(1), 1–22.

Baker, A. C., Jensen, P. J. and Kolb, D. A. (2005) 'Conversation as Experiential Learning', *Management Learning*, 36(4), 411–427.

Baker, T. and Nelson, R. E. (2005) 'Creating Something from Nothing: Resource Construction through Entrepreneurial Bricolage', *Administrative Science Quarterly*, 50, 329–366.

Baker, T., Miner, A. S. and Eesley, D. T. (2003) 'Improvising Firms: Bricolage, Account Giving and Improvisational Competencies in the Founding Process', *Research Policy*, 32(2), 255–276.

Baker, T., Pricer, R. and Nenide, B. (2000) *When Less is More: Undercapitalisation as a Predictor of Firm Success*, in Churchill, N., Hornaday, J., Krasner, O. and Vesper, K., eds, *Frontiers of Entrepreneurship Research*, Wellesley, MA: Babson College.

Bakhtin, M. M. (1981) *The Dialogical Imagination*, Austin, TX: University of Texas Press.

**213**

# REFERENCES

Bandura, A. (1997) *Self-efficacy: The Exercise of Control*, New York: W. H. Freeman.

Barney, J. (1991) 'Firm Resources and Sustained Competitive Advantage', *Journal of Management*, 17(1), 99–121.

Baron, J. N., Hannan, M. T. and Burton, M. D. (1999) 'Building the Iron Cage: Determinants of Managerial Intensity in the Early Years of Organizations', *American Sociological Review*, 64(4), 527–547.

Baron, R. A. (2008) 'The Role of Effect in the Entrepreneurial Process', *Academy of Management Review*, 33(2), 328–340.

Baron, R. A. (2012) *Entrepreneurship: An Evidence-based Guide*, Northampton, MA: Edward Elgar.

Baron, R. A. and Markman, G. D. (2000) 'Beyond Social Capital: How Social Skills Can Enhance Entrepreneurs' Success', *Academy of Management Executive*, 14(1), 106–116.

Baron, R. A. and Markman, G. D. (2003) 'Beyond Social Capital: The Role of Entrepreneurs' Social Competence in their Financial Success', *Journal of Business Venturing*, 18(1), 41–60.

Baron, R. A. and Tang, J. (2009) 'Entrepreneurs' Social Skills and New Venture Performance: Mediating Mechanisms and Cultural Generality', *Journal of Management*, 35(2), 282–306.

Basu, A. and Parker, S. C. (2008) 'Family Finance and New Business Start-ups', in Auerswald, P. and Bozkaya, A., eds, *Financing Entrepreneurship*, Elgar Reference Collection, International Library of Entrepreneurship: 12, Cheltenham, UK and Northampton, MA: Edward Elgar, 335–360.

Batjargal, B. (2006) 'The Dynamics of Entrepreneurs' Networks in a Transitioning Economy: The Case of Russia', *Entrepreneurship and Regional Development*, 18(4), 305–320.

Battisti, M. and McAdam, M. (2012) 'The Challenges of Social Capital Development within the University Science Incubator: The Case of the Graduate Entrepreneur', *International Journal of Entrepreneurship and Innovation*, 13(4), 261–276.

Bauernschuster, S., Falck, O. and Heblich, S. (2010) 'Social Capital Access and Entrepreneurship', *Journal of Economic Behaviour and Organization*, 76, 821–833.

Becker, G. S. (1964) *Human Capital: A Theoretical and Empirical Analysis, with Special Reference to Education*, New York: Columbia University Press.

Bennett, R. (2008) 'SME Policy Support in Britain since the 1990s: What Have We Learnt?', *Environment and Planning C: Government and Policy*, 26(2), 375–397.

Bercovitz, J. and Feldman, M. (2006) 'Entrepreneurial Universities and Technology Transfer: A Conceptual Framework for Understanding Knowledge-based Economic Development', *Journal of Technology Transfer*, 31(1), 175–188.

Beresford, R. and Saunders, M. N. K. (2005) 'Professionalization of the Business Start-up Process', *Strategic Change*, 14(6), 337–347.

Berger, P. L. and Luckmann, T. (1966) *The Social Construction of Reality: A Treatise in the Sociology of Knowledge*, New York: Doubleday.

Bessant, J., Phelps, B. and Adams, R. (2005) *External Knowledge: A Review of the Literature Addressing the Role of External Knowledge and Expertise at Key Stages of Business Growth and Development*, London: Advanced Institute of Management Research.

Bhide, A. (1992) 'Bootstrap Finance: The Art of Start-ups', *Harvard Business Review*, 70(6), 109–117.

Bhide, A. V. (2000) *The Origin and Evolution of New Businesses*, New York: Oxford University Press.

Birch, D. L. (1979) *The Job Generation Process: MIT Program on Neighborhood and Regional Change*, Cambridge, MA: MIT.

Birch, D. L. (1987) *Job Creation in America*, London: Free Press.

Birch, D., Haggerty, A. and Parsons, W. (1995) *Corporate Evolution*, Cambridge, MA: Cognetics.

Birkinshaw, J., Probst, G. and Tushman, M. (2009) 'Organizational Ambidexterity: Balancing Exploration and Exploitation for Sustained Corporate Performance', *Organization Science*, 20(4), 685–695.

Birley, S. (1985) 'The Role of Networks in the Entrepreneurial Process', *Journal of Business Venturing*, 1(1), 107–117.

BIS (2012) SME Access to External Finance, BIS Economics Paper No. 16, Department for Business, Innovation and Skills, London.

Black, S. E. and Strahan, P. E. (2002) 'Entrepreneurship and Bank Credit Availability', *The Journal of Finance*, 57(6), 2807–2833.

Block, J. and Sandner, P. (2009) 'Necessity and Opportunity Entrepreneurs and their Duration in Self-employment: Evidence from German Micro Data', *Journal of Industry, Competition and Trade*, 9(2), 117–137.

Block, J., Hoogerheide, L. and Thurik, R. (2013) 'Education and Entrepreneurial Choice: An Instrumental Variables Analysis', *International Small Business Journal*, 31(1), 23–33.

Blumberg, B. F. and Letterie, W. A. (2008) 'Business Starters and Credit Rationing', *Small Business Economics*, 30(2), 187–200.

Boeker, W. and Karichalil, R. (2002) 'Entrepreneurial Transitions: Factors Influencing Founder Departure', *The Academy of Management Journal*, 45(4), 818–826.

Bolton, J. E. (1971) Report of the Committee of Enquiry on Small Firms, London: HMSO.

Bood, R. (1998) 'Charting Organizational Learning: A Comparison of Multiple Mapping Techniques', in Eden, C. and Spender, J. C., eds, *Managerial and Organizational Cognition: Theory, Methods and Research*, London: Sage, 210–230.

Bottazzi, L. and Da Rin, M. (2002) 'Venture Capital in Europe and the Financing of Innovative Companies', *Economic Policy: A European Forum*, 17(34), 229–263.

Bourdieu, P. (1977) *Outline of a Theory of Practice*, translated by Richard Nice, Cambridge Studies in Social and Cultural Anthropology: 16, Cambridge: Cambridge University Press.

**215**

# REFERENCES

Bourdieu, P. (1986) *The Forms of Capital*, New York: Greenwood.

Bourdieu, P. (2002) 'Habitus', in Hillier, J. and Rooksby, E., eds, *Habitus: A Sense of Place*, Aldershot, UK: Ashgate.

Boussouara, M. and Deakins, D. (1999) 'Market-based Learning, Entrepreneurship and the High Technology Small Firm', *International Journal of Entrepreneurial Behaviour and Research*, 5(4), 204–223.

Boussouara, M. and Deakins, D. (2000) 'Trust and the Acquisition of Knowledge from Non-executive Directors by High Technology Entrepreneurs', *International Journal of Entrepreneurial Behaviour and Research*, 6(4), 204–226.

Bowman, C. and Ambrosini, V. (2003) 'How the Resource-based and the Dynamic Capability Views of the Firm Inform Corporate-level Strategy', *British Journal of Management*, 14, 289–303.

Bozkaya, A. and De La Potterie, B. (2008) 'Who Funds Technology-based Small Firms? Evidence from Belgium', *Economics of Innovation and New Technology*, 17(1–2), 97–122.

Breslin, D. (2008) 'A Review of the Evolutionary Approach to the Study of Entrepreneurship', *International Journal of Management Reviews*, 10(4), 399–423.

Breslin, D. and Jones, C. (2012) 'The Evolution of Entrepreneurial Learning', *International Journal of Organizational Analysis*, 20(3), 294–308.

Bretherton, P. and Chaston, I. (2005) 'Resource Dependency and SME Strategy: An Empirical Study', *Journal of Small Business and Enterprise Development*, 12(2), 274–289.

Bridge, S. (2010) *Rethinking Enterprise Policy: Can Failure Trigger New Understanding?* Basingstoke, UK: Palgrave Macmillan.

Brinckmann, J., Salomo, S. and Gemuenden, H. G. (2011) 'Financial Management Competence of Founding Teams and Growth of New Technology-based Firms', *Entrepreneurship: Theory and Practice*, 35(2), 217–243.

Brockhaus, S. R. H. (1980) 'Risk Taking Propensity of Entrepreneurs', *Academy of Management Journal*, 23(3), 509–520.

Bruni, D. S. and Verona, G. (2009) 'Dynamic Marketing Capabilities in Science-based Firms: An Exploratory Investigation of the Pharmaceutical Industry', *British Journal of Management*, 20(SI): S101–S117.

Brush, C. G. (2002) 'The Role of Social Capital and Gender in Linking Financial Suppliers and Entrepreneurial Firms: A Framework for Future Research', *Venture Capital*, 4(4), 305–323.

Brush, C. G. (2008) 'Pioneering Strategies for Entrepreneurial Success', *Business Horizons*, 51, 21–27.

Brush, C. G., Carter, N. M., Gatewood, E. J., Greene, P. G. and Hart, M. M. (2006) 'The Use of Bootstrapping by Women Entrepreneurs in Positioning for Growth', *Venture Capital*, 8(1), 15–31.

Brush, C. G., Carter, N. M., Greene, P. G., Hart, M. M. and Gatewood, E. (2002) 'The Role of Social Capital and Gender in Linking Financial Suppliers and

Entrepreneurial Firms: A Framework for Future Research', *Venture Capital*, 4(4), 305–323.

Brush, C. G., Ceru, D. J. and Blackburn, R. (2009) 'Pathways to Entrepreneurial Growth: The Influence of Management, Marketing, and Money', *Business Horizons*, 52(5), 481–491.

Brush, C. G., Greene, P. G. and Hart, M. M. (2001) 'From Initial Idea to Unique Advantage: The Entrepreneurial Challenge of Constructing a Resource Base', *Academy of Management Executive*, 15(1), 64–78.

Bruyat, C. and Julien, P. A. (2001) 'Defining the Field of Research in Entrepreneurship', *Journal of Business Venturing*, 16(2), 165–180.

Bryan, J. (2006) 'Training and Performance in Small Firms', *International Small Business Journal*, 24(6), 635–660.

Burchinal, M. R., Campbell, F. A., Bryant, D. M., Wasik, B. H. and Ramey, C. T. (1997) 'Early Intervention and Mediating Processes in Cognitive Performance of Children of Low-income African American Families', *Child Development*, 68(5), 935–954.

Burgoyne, J. G. (1995) 'Learning from Experience: From Individual Discovery to Meta-dialogue via the Evolution of Transitional Myths', *Personnel Review*, 24(6), 61–72.

Burke, A. E., FitzRoy, F. R. and Nolan, M. A. (2002) 'Self-employment Wealth and Job Creation: The Roles of Gender, Non-pecuniary Motivation and Entrepreneurial Ability', *Small Business Economics*, 19, 255–270.

Burke, P. J. (2006) 'Identity Change', *Social Psychology Quarterly*, 1, 81–96.

Burns, P. (1996) 'Growth', in Burns, P. and Dewhurst, J., eds, *Small Business and Entrepreneurship*, London: Macmillan, 40–72.

Burns, P. (2007) *Entrepreneurship and Small Business*, 2nd edn, Basingstoke, UK: Palgrave Macmillan.

Burt, R. S. (1992) *Structural Holes: The Social Structure of Competition*, Cambridge, MA: Harvard University Press.

Burt, R. S. (2005) *Brokerage and Closure: An Introduction to Social Capital*, Clarendon Lectures in Management Studies, Oxford: Oxford University Press.

Byrne, J., Fayolle, A. and Toutain, O. (2013) 'Entrepreneurship Education: What We Know and What We Need to Know', in Chell, E., ed., *Handbook of Research in Entrepreneurship and Small Business*.

Cantillon, R. (1732/1931) *Essai Sur La Nature Du Commerce General*, London: Macmillan.

Carter, N., Brush, C., Greene, P., Gatewood, E. and Hart, M. (2003) 'Women Entrepreneurs Who Break through to Equity Financing: The Influence of Human, Social and Financial Capital', *Venture Capital*, 5(1), 1–21.

Carter, N., Gartner, W. and Reynolds, P. (1996) 'Exploring Start-up Event Sequences', *Journal of Business Venturing*, 11(3), 151–166.

**217**

Carter, N., Williams, M. and Reynolds Paul, D. (1997) 'Discontinuance among New Firms in Retail: The Influence of Initial Resources, Strategy, and Gender', *Journal of Business Venturing*, 12, 125–145.

Carter, R. B. and Van Auken, H. (2005) 'Bootstrap Financing and Owners' Perceptions of their Business Constraints and Opportunities', *Entrepreneurship and Regional Development*, 17(2), 129–144.

Carter, S., Mason, C. and Tagg, S. (2004) *Lifting the Barriers to Growth in UK Small Businesses*, London: Federation of Small Businesses.

Cassar, G. (2004) 'The Financing of Business Start-ups', *Journal of Business Venturing*, 19, 261–283.

Cassar, G. (2006) 'Entrepreneur Opportunity Costs and Intended Venture Growth', *Journal of Business Venturing*, 21, 610–632.

Castells, M. (2000) *The Rise of the Network Society*, Information Age: 1, Oxford: Blackwell.

Chandler, A. (1977) *The Visible Hand: The Managerial Revolution in American Business*, Cambridge, MA: Harvard University Press.

Chell, E., Haworth, J. and Brearley, S. (1991) *The Entrepreneurial Personality: Concepts, Cases and Categories*, London and New York: Routledge.

Chen, X., Zou, H. and Wang, D. T. (2009) 'How Do New Ventures Grow? Firm Capabilities, Growth Strategies and Performance', *International Journal of Research in Marketing*, 26(4), 294–303.

Child, J. (1972) 'Organizational Structure, Environment and Performance: The Role of Strategic Choice', *Sociology*, 6, 1–22.

Chirico, F. and Nordqvist, M. (2010) 'Dynamic Capabilities and Trans-generational Value Creation in Family Firms: The Role of Organizational Culture', *International Small Business Journal*, 28(5), 487–504.

Chrisman, J. J. (1999) 'The Influence of Outsider-generated Knowledge Resources on Venture Creation', *Journal of Small Business Management*, 37(4), 42–58.

Churchill, N. C. and Lewis, V. L. (1983) 'The Five Stages of Small Business Growth', *Harvard Business Review*, 61(3), 30–50.

Clark, B. R. (1998) *Creating Entrepreneurial Universities: Organizational Pathways to Transformation*, Oxford: International Association of Universities and Elsevier Science.

Clarke, J. (2011) 'Revitalizing Entrepreneurship: How Visual Symbols Are Used in Entrepreneurial Performances', *Journal of Management Studies*, 48(6), 1365–1391.

Coen, C. A. and Maritan, C. A. (2011) 'Investing in Capabilities: The Dynamics of Resource Allocation', *Organization Science*, 22(1), 99–117.

Cohen, M. D. and Bacdayan, P. (1994) 'Organizational Routines Are Stored as Procedural Memory: Evidence from a Laboratory Study', *Organization Science*, 5(4), 554–568.

Cohen, W. M. and Levinthal, D. A. (1990) 'Absorptive Capacity: A New Perspective on Learning and Innovation', *Administrative Science Quarterly*, 35(1), 128–152.

Coleman, J. S. (1988) 'Social Capital in the Creation of Human Capital', *The American Journal of Sociology: Supplement, Organizations and Institutions: Sociological and Economic Approaches to the Analysis of Social Structure*, 94, S95–S120.

Colombo, M. G. and Grilli, L. (2010) 'On Growth Drivers of High-tech Start-ups: Exploring the Role of Founders' Human Capital and Venture Capital', *Journal of Business Venturing*, 25(6), 610–626.

Colombo, M. G., Grilli, L. and Verga, C. (2007) 'High-tech Start-up Access to Public Funds and Venture Capital: Evidence from Italy', *International Review of Applied Economics*, 21(3), 381–402.

Conway, S. and Jones, O. (2012) 'Networks and the Small Business', in Carter, S. and Jones-evans, D., eds, *Enterprise and Small Business: Principles, Practice and Policy*, 2nd edn, Harlow, UK: Pearson.

Cooper, A. C., Folta, T. B. and Woo, C. (1995) 'Entrepreneurial Information Search', *Journal of Business Venturing*, 10, 107–120.

Cooper, S. Y. and Park, J. S. (2008) 'The Impact of "Incubator" Organizations on Opportunity Recognition and Technology Innovation in New, Entrepreneurial High-Technology Ventures', *International Small Business Journal*, 26(1), 27–56.

Cope, J. (2003) 'Entrepreneurial Learning and Critical Reflection: Discontinuous Events as Triggers for "Higher-Level" Learning', *Management Learning*, 34(4), 429–450.

Cope, J. (2005) 'Toward a Dynamic Learning Perspective of Entrepreneurship', *Entrepreneurship: Theory and Practice*, 29(4), 373–397.

Cope, J. (2010) 'Entrepreneurial Learning from Failure: An Interpretive Phenomenological Analysis', *Entrepreneurship Theory and Practice*, 26, 604–623.

Cope, J. (2011) 'Entrepreneurial Learning from Failure: An Interpretative Phenomenological Analysis', *Journal of Business Venturing*, 26(6), 604–623.

Cope, J. and Down, S. (2010) 'I Think Therefore I Learn? Entrepreneurial Cognition, Learning and Knowledge and Knowing in Practice', conference proceedings, Babson College Entrepreneurship Research Conference, Lausanne, Switzerland.

Cope, J. and Watts, G. (2000) 'Learning by Doing – An Exploration of Experience, Critical Incidents and Reflection in Entrepreneurial Learning', *International Journal of Entrepreneurial Behaviour and Research*, 6(3), 104–125

Cope, J., Jack, S. and Rose, M. B. (2007) 'Social Capital and Entrepreneurship: An Introduction', *International Small Business Journal*, 25(3), 213–219.

Corbett, A. C. (2005) 'Experiential Learning within the Process of Opportunity Identification and Exploitation', *Entrepreneurship: Theory and Practice*, 29(4), 473–491.

Cornelissen, J. P. and Clarke, J. S. (2010) 'Imagining and Rationalizing Opportunities: Inductive Reasoning and the Creation and Justification of New Ventures', *The Academy of Management Review*, 35(4), 539–557.

Cornelissen, J. P., Clarke, J. S. and Cienki, A. (2012) 'Sensegiving in Entrepreneurial Contexts: The Use of Metaphors in Speech and Gesture to Gain and Sustain Support for Novel Business Ventures', *International Small Business Journal*, 30(4), 213–241.

**219**

# REFERENCES

Cornwall, J. R. (2010) *Bootstrapping*, Upper Saddle River, NJ: Prentice Hall.

Cressy, R. (2002) 'Funding Gaps: A Symposium', *The Economic Journal*, 112, F1–F16.

Crossan, M. M., Lane, H. W. and White, R. E. (1999) 'An Organizational Learning Framework: From Intuition to Institution', *Academy of Management Review*, 24(3), 522–537.

Cunliffe, A. L. (2002) 'Reflexive Dialogical Practice in Management Learning', *Management Learning*, 33(1), 35–61.

Curran, J. (1986) *Bolton 15 Years On: A Review and Analysis of Small Business Research in Britain 1971–1986*, London: Small Business Research Trust.

Curran, J. and Storey, D. (1993) *Small Firms in Urban and Rural Locations*, London and New York: Routledge Small Business Series.

Curtin, R. (1982) 'Indicators of Consumer Behaviour: The University of Michigan Survey of Public Consumers', *Public Opinion Quarterly*, 46, 340–362.

David, P. (1985) 'Clio and the Economics of Qwerty', *The American Economic Review*, 75(2), 332–337.

Davidsson, P. and Honig, B. (2003) 'The Role of Social and Human Capital among Nascent Entrepreneurs', *Journal of Business Venturing*, 18(3), 301–331.

Davidsson, P. and Klofsten, M. (2003) 'The Business Platform: Developing an Instrument to Gauge and to Assist the Development of Young Firms', *Journal of Small Business Management*, 41(1), 1–27.

Davidsson, P., Hunter, E. and Klofsten, M. (2006) 'Institutional Forces – the Invisible Hand that Shapes Venture Ideas?', *International Small Business Journal*, 24(2), 115–131.

De Carolis, D. M. and Saparito, P. (2006) 'Social Capital, Cognition, and Entrepreneurial Opportunities: A Theoretical Framework', *Entrepreneurship: Theory and Practice*, 30(1), 41–56.

De Clercq, D. and Honig, B. (2011) 'Entrepreneurship as an Integrating Mechanism for Disadvantaged Persons', *Entrepreneurship and Regional Development*, 23(5/6), 353–372.

De Clercq, D. and Voronov, M. (2009) 'Toward a Practice Perspective of Entrepreneurship: Entrepreneurial Legitimacy as Habitus', *International Small Business Journal*, 27(4), 395–419.

Deeds, D., De Carolis, D. and Coombs, J. (1999) 'Dynamic Capabilities and New Product Development in High-technology Ventures: An Empirical Analysis of New Biotechnology Firms', *Journal of Business Venturing*, 15, 211–229.

Desa, G. (2012) 'Resource Mobilization in International Social Entrepreneurship: Bricolage as a Mechanism of Institutional Transformation', *Entrepreneurship: Theory and Practice*, 36(4), 727–751.

Deverell, E. (2009) 'Crises as Learning Triggers: Exploring a Conceptual Framework of Crisis-induced Learning', *Journal of Contingencies and Crisis Management*, 17(3), 179–188.

Dewey, H. E. (1938) 'Teaching Social Problems Without Textbooks', *Education Digest*, 3(7), 56–57.

DfES (2003) The Future of Higher Education, CM 5735, Department for Education and Skills.

Di Domenico, M., Haugh, H. and Tracey, P. (2010) 'Social Bricolage: Theorizing Social Value Creation in Social Enterprises', *Entrepreneurship: Theory and Practice*, 34(4), 681–703.

Di Gregorio, D. and Shane, S. (2003) 'Why Do Some Universities Generate More Start-ups Than Others?', *Research Policy*, 32(2), 209–227.

Diaz-Garcia, C. and Jimenez-Moreno, J. (2010) 'The Impact of Legitimacy Building Signals on Access to Resources', in Smallbone, D., Leitao, J., Raposo, M. and Welter, F., eds, *The Theory and Practice of Entrepreneurship: Frontiers in European Entrepreneurship Research*, Cheltenham, UK and Northampton, MA: Edward Elgar, 215–235.

Dodge, H. R., Fullerton, S. and Robbins, J. E. (1994) 'Stage of the Organizational Lifecycle and Competition as Mediators of Problem Perception for Small Business', *Strategic Management Journal*, 15(2), 121–134.

Dohse, D. and Walter, S. (2012) 'Knowledge Context and Entrepreneurial Intentions among Students', *Small Business Economics*, 39(4), 877–895.

Douglas, E. J. and Shepherd, D. A. (2000) 'Entrepreneurship as a Utility Maximizing Response', *Journal of Business Venturing*, 15, 231–251.

Dowd, K. (2009) 'Moral Hazard and the Financial Crisis', *Cato Journal*, 29(1), 141–166.

Down, S. and Warren, L. (2008) 'Constructing Narratives of Enterprise: Cliches and Entrepreneurial Self-identity', *International Journal of Entrepreneurial Behaviour and Research*, 14(1), 4–23.

DTI (1998) *Our Competitive Future: Building the Knowledge Driven Economy*, London: HMSO.

DTI (2000) *Excellence and Opportunity: A Science and Innovation Policy for the 21st Century*, London: The Stationery Office.

Dutta, D. K. and Crossan, M. M. (2005) 'The Nature of Entrepreneurial Opportunities: Understanding the Process Using the 4I Organizational Learning Framework', *Entrepreneurship Theory and Practice*, 29(4), 425–449.

Dyer, J. and Singh, H. (1998) 'The Relational View: Cooperative Strategy and Sources of Interorganizational Competitive Advantage', *Academy of Management Review*, 23(4), 660–679.

Easterby-Smith, M. and Prieto, I. (2008) 'Dynamic Capabilities and Knowledge Management: An Integrative Role for Learning', *British Journal of Management*, 19(3), 235–249.

Easterby-Smith, M., Lyles, M. and Peteraf, M. (2009) 'Dynamic Capabilities: Current Debates and Future Directions', *British Journal of Management*, 20(SI), S1–S8.

Ebben, J. J. (2009) 'Bootstrapping and the Financial Condition of Small Firms', *International Journal of Entrepreneurial Behaviour and Research*, 15(3/4), 346–363.

Ebben, J. J. and Johnson, A. (2006) 'Bootstrapping in Small Firms: An Empirical Analysis of Change over Time', *Journal of Business Venturing*, 21, 851–865.

**221**

Edelman, L. and Yli-Renko, H. (2010) 'The Impact of Environment and Entrepreneurial Perceptions on Venture-creation Efforts: Bridging the Discovery and Creation Views of Entrepreneurship', *Entrepreneurship: Theory and Practice*, 34(5), 833–856.

Eisenhardt, K. and Martin, J. (2000) 'Dynamic Capabilities: What Are They?', *Strategic Management Journal*, 21(10&11), 1105–1121.

Eisenhardt, K. M. and Schoonhoven, C. B. (1990) 'Organizational Growth: Linking Founding Team, Strategy, Environment, and Growth among U.S. Semiconductor Ventures, 1978–1988', *Administrative Science Quarterly*, 35(3), 504–529.

Elfring, T. and Hulsink, W. (2003) 'Networks in Entrepreneurship: The Case of High-technology Firms', *Small Business Economics*, 21(4), 409–422.

Elfring, T. and Hulsink, W. (2008) 'Networking by Entrepreneurs: Patterns of Tie-formation in Emerging Organizations', *Organization Studies*, 28(12), 1849–1872.

Engeström, Y. (2001) 'Expansive Learning at Work: Toward an Activity Theoretical Reconceptualization', *Journal of Education and Work*, 14(1), 133–156.

Ensley, M. D. and Hmieleski, K. M. (2005) 'A Comparative Study of New Venture Top Management Team Composition, Dynamics and Performance Between University-based and Independent Start-ups', *Research Policy*, 34(7), 1091–1105.

Eraut, M. and Hirsh, W. (2007) *The Significance of Workplace Learning for Individuals, Groups and Organizations*, Oxford and Cardiff: ESRC Centre on Skills, Knowledge and Organizational Performance.

Esteve-Perez, S. and Manez-Castillejo, J. A. (2008) 'The Resource-based Theory of the Firm and Firm Survival', *Small Business Economics*, 30(3), 231–249.

Etzkowitz, H. (1998) 'The Norms of Entrepreneurial Science: Cognitive Effects of the New University–Industry Linkages', *Research Policy*, 27, 823–833.

Etzkowitz, H. (2003) 'Research Groups as "Quasi-Firms": The Invention of the Entrepreneurial University', *Research Policy*, 32(1), 109–121.

Etzkowitz, H. and Leydesdorff, L. (2000) 'The Dynamics of Innovation: From National Systems and "Mode 2" to a Triple Helix of University–Industry–Government Relations', *Research Policy*, 29(2), 109–123.

Etzkowitz, H., Webster, A., Gebhardt, C. and Terra, B. R. C. (2000) 'The Future of the University and the University of the Future: Evolution of Ivory Tower to Entrepreneurial Paradigm', *Research Policy*, 29, 313–330.

Evald, M. R., Klyver, K. I. M. and Svendsen, S. G. (2006) 'The Changing Importance of the Strength of Ties Throughout the Entrepreneurial Process', *Journal of Enterprising Culture*, 14(1), 1–26.

Fairweather, J. S. (1990) 'The University's Role in Economic Development: Lessons for Academic Leaders', *Journal of the Society of Research Administrators*, 22(3), 5–11.

Fernhaber, S. A., McDougall-Covin, P. P. and Shepherd, D. A. (2009) 'International Entrepreneurship: Leveraging Internal and External Knowledge Sources', *Strategic Entrepreneurship Journal*, 3(4), 297–320.

Ferrary, M. (2010) 'Syndication of Venture Capital Investment: The Art of Resource Pooling', *Entrepreneurship: Theory and Practice*, 34(5), 885–907.

Ferris, G., Davidson, S. and Perrewé, P. (2005) 'Developing Political Skill at Work', 42(40–45).

Fiol, C. M. (2001) 'Revisiting an Identity-based View of Sustainable Competitive Advantage', *Journal of Management*, 27(6), 691–699.

Fisher, G. (2012) 'Effectuation, Causation, and Bricolage: A Behavioural Comparison of Emerging Theories in Entrepreneurship Research', *Entrepreneurship: Theory and Practice*, 36(5), 1019–1051.

Fletcher, D. (2007) '"Toy Story": The Narrative World of Entrepreneurship and the Creation of Interpretive Communities', *Journal of Business Venturing*, 22, 649–672.

Florida, R. (2002) *The Rise of the Creative Class and How It's Transforming Work, Life, Leisure, Community and Everyday Life*, New York: Perseus Books.

Foss, N. J., Klein, P. G., Kor, Y. Y. and Mahoney, J. T. (2008) 'Entrepreneurship, Subjectivism, and the Resource-based View: Toward a New Synthesis', *Strategic Entrepreneurship Journal*, 2(1), 73–94.

Franck, T., Huyghebaert, N. and D'Espallier, B. (2010) 'How Debt Creates Pressure to Perform When Information Asymmetries Are Large: Empirical Evidence from Business Start-ups', *Journal of Economics and Management Strategy*, 19(4), 1043–1069.

Fraser, S. (2009) *How Have SME Finance Been Affected by the Credit Crisis?*, BERR/ESRC Seminar, March, London.

Freel, M. S. (2005) 'Patterns of Innovation and Skills in Small Firms', *Technovation*, 25(2), 123–134.

Freel, M. S. (2007) 'Are Small Innovators Credit Rationed?', *Small Business Economics*, 28(1), 23–35.

Fritsch, M. and Mueller, P. (2004) 'Effects of New Business Formation on Regional Development over Time', *Regional Studies*, 38(8), 961–975.

Fuller-Love, N. (2006) 'Management Development in Small Firms', *International Journal of Management Reviews*, 8(3), 175–190.

Gabrielsson, J., Tell, J. and Politis, D. (2010) 'Business Simulation Exercises in Small Business Management Education: Using Principles and Ideas from Action Learning', *Action Learning: Research and Practice*, 7(1), 3–16.

Gartner, W. B. (1985) 'A Conceptual Framework for Describing the Phenomenon of New Venture Creation', *The Academy of Management Review*, 5(4), 696–706.

Gartner, W. B. (2006) 'Entrepreneurial Narrative and a Science of the Imagination', *Journal of Business Venturing*, 22(5), 613–627.

Gartner, W. B. and Shaver, K. G. (2012) 'Nascent Entrepreneurship Panel Studies: Progress and Challenges', *Small Business Economics*, 39(3), 659–665.

Gartner, W. B., Bird, B. J. and Starr, J. A. (1992) 'Acting As If: Differentiating Entrepreneurial from Organizational Behaviour', *Entrepreneurship: Theory and Practice*, 16(3), 13–31.

**223**

Gartner, W. B., Frid, C. J. and Alexander, J. C. (2012) 'Financing the Emerging Firm', *Small Business Economics*, 39(3), 745–761.

Garud, R. and Giuliani, A. P. (2013) 'A Narrative Perspective on Entrepreneurial Opportunities', *Academy of Management Review*, 38(1), 157–160.

Garud, R. and Karnøe, P. (2003) 'Bricolage versus Breakthrough: Distributed and Embedded Agency in Technology Entrepreneurship', *Research Policy*, 32, 277–300.

Gates, B., Myhrvold, N. and Rinearson, P. (1996) *The Road Ahead*, New York: Penguin.

Gatewood, E., Shaver, K. and Gartner, W. (1995) 'A Longitudinal Study of Cognitive Factors Influencing Start-up Behaviours and Success at Venture Creation', *Journal of Business Venturing*, 10, 371–391.

GEM (2007) Global Entrepreneurship Monitor Financing Report, 2006, available at: www.gemconsortium.org/docs/download/274 [accessed 17 October 2012].

Gibb, A. (1987) 'Education for Enterprise: Training for Small Business Initiation – Some Contrasts', *Journal of Small Business and Entrepreneurship*, 4(3), 42–47.

Gibb, A. A. (1996) 'Entrepreneurship and Small Business Management: Can We Afford to Neglect Them in the Twenty-first Century Business School?', *British Journal of Management*, 7, 309–321.

Gibb, A. (1997) 'Small Firms' Training and Competitiveness: Building upon the Small Firm as a Learning Organization', *International Small Business Journal*, 15(3), 13–29.

Gibb, A. (2002) 'In Pursuit of a New "Enterprise" and "Entrepreneurship" Paradigm for Learning: Creative Destruction, New Values, New Ways of Doing Things and New Combinations of Knowledge', *International Journal of Management Reviews*, 4(3), 213–232.

Gibb, A. (2009) 'Meeting the Development Needs of Owner Managed Small Enterprise: A Discussion on the Centrality of Action Learning', *Action Learning: Research and Practice*, 6(3), 209–227.

Gibb, A. (2011) 'Concepts into Practice: Meeting the Challenge of Development of Entrepreneurship Educators Around an Innovative Paradigm: The Case of the International Entrepreneurship Educators' Programme (IEEP)', *International Journal of Entrepreneurial Behaviour and Research*, 17(2), 146–165.

Gibb, A. and Ritchie, J. (1982) 'Understanding the Process of Starting Small Businesses', *International Small Business Journal*, 1(1), 26–45.

Giddens, A. (1987) *Social Theory and Modern Sociology*, Cambridge: Polity Press.

Giurca-Vasilescu, L. (2009) 'Business Angels: Potential Financial Engines for Start-ups', *Economic Research*, 22(3), 86–97.

Goffee, R. and Scase, R. (1995) *Corporate Realities: The Dynamics of Large and Small Organizations*, London: Routledge.

Gold, J., Holman, D. and Thorpe, R. (2002) 'The Role of Argument Analysis and Story Telling in Facilitating Critical Thinking', *Management Learning*, 33(3), 371–389.

Gold, J., Holt, R. and Thorpe, R. (2008) 'A Good Place for a Chat: Activity Theory and MBA Education', in Reynolds, M. and Vincent, R., eds, *The Handbook of Experiential Learning and Management Education*, Oxford: University Press, 35–52.

Gordon, I., Hamilton, E. and Jack, S. (2011) 'A Study of a University-led Entrepreneurship Education Programme for Small Business Owner/Managers', *Entrepreneurship and Regional Development*, 24(9/10), 1–39.

Granovetter, M. S. (1973) 'The Strength of Weak Ties', *American Journal of Sociology*, 78(6), 1360–1380.

Grant, R. M. (1996) 'Toward a Knowledge-based Theory of the Firm', *Strategic Management Journal*, 17(SPI 2), 109–122.

Greenberger, D. B. and Sexton, D. L. (1988) 'An Interactive Model of New Venture Initiation', *Journal of Small Business Management*, 26(3), 1–7.

Greenburg, Z. O. (2011) *Empire State of Mind: J-Zay's Journey from Street Corner to Corner Office*, New York: Penguin.

Greene, P. G., Brush, C. G., Hart, M. M. and Saparito, P. (2001) 'Patterns of Venture Capital Funding: Is Gender a Factor?', *Venture Capital*, 3(1), 63–83.

Greiner, L. E. (1972) 'Evolution and Revolution as Organizations Grow', *Harvard Business Review*, 50(4), 37–46.

Greiner, L. E. (1998) 'Evolution and Revolution as Organizations Grow', *Harvard Business Review*, 76(3), 55–68.

Guo, C. and Acar, M. (2005) 'Understanding Collaboration among Nonprofit Organizations: Combining Resource Dependency, Institutional, and Network Perspectives', *Nonprofit and Voluntary Sector Quarterly*, 34(3), 340–361.

Gupta, V. K., Turban, D. B., Wasti, S. A. and Sikdar, A. (2009) 'The Role of Gender Stereotypes in Perceptions of Entrepreneurs and Intentions to Become an Entrepreneur', *Entrepreneurship: Theory and Practice*, 33(2), 397–417.

Hagen, R. (2002) 'Globalization, University Transformation and Economic Regeneration: A UK Case Study of Public/Private Sector Partnership', *The International Journal of Public Sector Management*, 15(3), 204–218.

Hamilton, E. (2006) 'Whose Story is it Anyway? Narrative Accounts of the Role of Women in Founding and Establishing Family Businesses', *International Small Business Journal*, 24(3), 253–271.

Han, L., Fraser, S. and Storey, D. J. (2009a) 'Are Good or Bad Borrowers Discouraged from Applying for Loans? Evidence from US Small Business Credit Markets', *Journal of Banking and Finance*, 33(2), 415–424.

Han, L., Fraser, S. and Storey, D. J. (2009b) 'The Role of Collateral in Entrepreneurial Finance', *Journal of Business Finance and Accounting*, 36(3/4), 424–455.

Handscombe, R. D. (2003) 'The Promotion of an Entrepreneurial Culture in Universities: Capturing Change in the Cultural Web', *Industry and Higher Education*, 17(3), 219–222.

Hanlon, D. and Saunders, C. (2007) 'Marshaling Resources to Form Small New Ventures: Toward a More Holistic Understanding of Entrepreneurial Support', *Entrepreneurship: Theory and Practice*, 31(4), 619–641.

**225**

Hannan, M. T. and Freeman, J. H. (1977) 'The Population Ecology of Organizations', *American Journal of Sociology*, 82(9), 29–84.

Harding, R. (2002) 'Plugging the Knowledge Gap: An International Comparison of the Role for Policy in the Venture Capital Market', *Venture Capital*, 4(1), 59–76.

Harris, K. J., Kacmar, K. M., Zivnuska, S. and Shaw, J. D. (2007) 'The Impact of Political Skill on Impression Management Effectiveness', *Journal of Applied Psychology*, 92(1), 278–285.

Harris, S., Forbes, T. and Fletcher, M. (2000) 'Taught and Enacted Strategic Approaches in Young Enterprises', *International Journal of Entrepreneurial Behaviour and Research*, 6(3), 125–146.

Harrison, R. T., Mason, C. M. and Girling, P. (2004) 'Financial Bootstrapping and Venture Development in the Software Industry', *Entrepreneurship and Regional Development*, 16(4), 307–333.

Hartas, D. (2011) 'Families' Social Backgrounds Matter: Socio-economic Factors, Home Learning and Young Children's Language, Literacy and Social Outcomes', *British Educational Research Journal*, 37(6), 893–914.

von Hayek, F. (1990) 'Economics and Knowledge', in Casson, M., ed., *Entrepreneurship*, Aldershot, UK: Edward Elgar, 33–80.

Heinz, W. R. (2002) 'Transition Discontinuities and the Biographical Shaping of Early Work Careers', *Journal of Vocational Behaviour*, 60(2), 220–240.

Henley, A. (2007) 'Entrepreneurial Aspiration and Transition into Self-employment: Evidence from British Longitudinal Data', *Entrepreneurship and Regional Development*, 19(3), 253–280.

Henry, E. (1998) 'The Norms of Entrepreneurial Science: Cognitive Effects of the New University–Industry Linkages', *Research Policy*, 27, 823–833.

Herbane, B. (2010) 'Small Business Research: Time for a Crisis-based View', *International Small Business Journal*, 28(1), 43–64.

Herrmann, K., Hannon, P., Cox, J., Ternouth, P. and Crowley, T. (2008) *Developing Entrepreneurial Graduates: Putting Entrepreneurship at the Centre of Higher Education*, London.

Hickie, J. (2011) 'The Development of Human Capital in Young Entrepreneurs', *Industry and Higher Education*, 25(6), 469–481.

Higgins, D. and Elliott, C. (2011) 'Learning to Make Sense: What Works in Entrepreneurial Education?', *Journal of European Industrial Training*, 35(4), 345–367.

Hite, J. M. (2005) 'Evolutionary Processes and Paths of Relationally Embedded Network Ties in Emerging Entrepreneurial Firms', *Entrepreneurship: Theory and Practice*, 29(1), 113–144.

Hite, J. M. and Hesterly, W. S. (2001) 'The Evolution of Firm Networks: From Emergence to Early Growth of the Firm', *Strategic Management Journal*, 22(3), 275–286.

Hitt, M. A., Biermant, L., Shimizu, K. and Kochhar, R. (2001a) 'Direct and Moderating Effects of Human Capital on Strategy and Performance in Professional Service

Firms: A Resource Based Perspective', *Academy of Management Journal*, 44(1), 13–28.

Hitt, M. A., Ireland, R. D., Camp, S. M. and Sexton, D. L. (2001b) 'Guest Editors' Introduction to the Special Issue Strategic Entrepreneurship: Entrepreneurial Strategies for Wealth Creation', *Strategic Management Journal*, 22(6), 479–491.

Hmieleski, K. M. and Corbett, A. C. (2006) 'Proclivity for Improvisation as a Predictor of Entrepreneurial Intentions', *Journal of Small Business Management*, 44(1), 45–63.

Hmieleski, K. M. and Ensley, M. D. (2007) 'A Contextual Examination of New Venture Performance: Entrepreneur Leadership Behaviour, Top Management Team Heterogeneity, and Environmental Dynamism', *Journal of Organizational Behaviour*, 28(7), 865–889.

HMT, DTI and DfES (2004) 'Science and Innovation Investment Framework 2004–2014', HM Treasury, Department for Education and Skills and Department of Trade and Industry, London: HMSO.

Hodgson, G. M. (2009) 'The Nature and Replication of Routines', in Becker, M. C. and Lazaric, N., eds, *Organizational Routines: Advancing Empirical Research*, Cheltenham, UK and Northampton, MA: Edward Elgar, 26–44.

Holman, D., Pavlica, K. and Thorpe, R. (1997) 'Rethinking Kolb's Theory of Experiential Learning in Management Education – The Contribution of Social Constructionism and Activity Theory', *Management Learning*, 28(2), 135–148.

Holt, R. and Macpherson, A. (2010) 'Sensemaking, Rhetoric and the Socially Competent Entrepreneur', *International Small Business Journal*, 28(1), 20–42.

Honey, P. and Mumford, A. (2001) *The Learning Styles Questionnaire*, London: Peter Honey Publications.

Huebscher, J. and Lendner, C. (2010) 'Effects of Entrepreneurship Simulation Game Seminars on Entrepreneurs' and Students' Learning', *Journal of Small Business and Entrepreneurship*, 23(4), 543–554.

Huggins, R. and Williams, N. (2009) 'Enterprise and Public Policy: A Review of Labour Government Intervention in the United Kingdom', *Environment and Planning C: Government and Policy*, 27(1), 19–41.

Hughes, A. and Storey, D. J. (1994) *Finance and the Small Firm*, London: Routledge.

Hughes, M., Ireland, R. D. and Morgan, R., E. (2007) 'Stimulating Dynamic Value: Social Capital and Business Incubation as a Pathway to Competitive Success', *Long Range Planning*, 40, 154–177.

Huyghebaert, N. and Van de Gucht, L. M. (2007) 'The Determinants of Financial Structure: New Insights from Business Start-ups', *European Financial Management*, 13(1), 101–133.

Huyghebaert, N., Van de Gucht, L. and Van Hulle, C. (2007) 'The Choice between Bank Debt and Trace Credit in Business Start-ups', *Small Business Economics*, 29(4), 435–452.

**227**

Jack, S., Dodd, S. D. and Anderson, A. R. (2008) 'Change and the Development of Entrepreneurial Networks over Time: A Processual Perspective', *Entrepreneurship and Regional Development*, 20(2), 125–159.

Jacobs, J. M. (1965) *The Death and Life of Great American Cities*, Harmondsworth: Penguin.

Jayawarna, D. and Jones, O. (2012) 'Social Enterprise: Bootstrapping as a Strategic Response to Recession', conference proceedings, Institute of Small Business and Entrepreneurship Conference (ISBE), Dublin, UK.

Jayawarna, D., Jones, O. and Macpherson, A. (2011) 'New Business Creation and Regional Development: Enhancing Resource Acquisition in Areas of Social Deprivation', *Entrepreneurship and Regional Development*, 23(9–10), 735–761.

Jayawarna, D., Macpherson, A. and Wilson, A. (2007a) 'Training Commitment and Performance in Manufacturing SMEs: Incidence, Intensity and Approaches', *Journal of Small Business and Enterprise Development*, 14(2), 321–328.

Jayawarna, D., Rouse, J. and Kitching, J. (2013) 'Entrepreneur Motivations and Life Course', *International Small Business Journal*, 31(1), 34–56.

Jayawarna, D., Rouse, J. and Macpherson, A. (2007b) 'Pathways to Entrepreneurship across the Lifecourse: An Innovative Model Utilizing Longitudinal Data from the British Household Panel Survey', conference proceedings, in Institute of Small Business and Entrepreneurship Conference (ISBE), Glasgow, UK.

Jayawarna, D., Woodhams, C. and Jones, O. (2012) 'Gender and Alternative Start-up Business Funding', *Competition and Change*, 16(4), 303–322.

Jenssen, J. I. and Koenig, H. F. (2002) 'The Effect of Social Networks on Resource Access and Business Start-ups', *European Planning Studies*, 10(8), 1039–1046.

Jiangyong, L. and Zhigang, T. (2010) 'Determinants of Entrepreneurial Activities in China', *Journal of Business Venturing*, 25, 261–273.

Jing, Z., Pek-Hooi, S. and Poh-kam, W. (2011) 'Direct Ties, Prior Knowledge, and Entrepreneurial Resource Acquisitions in China and Singapore', *International Small Business Journal*, 29(2), 170–189.

Johannisson, B. (2011) 'Towards a Practice Theory of Entrepreneuring', *Small Business Economics*, 36(2), 135–150.

Jones, O. (2006) 'Developing Absorptive Capacity in Mature Organizations: The Change Agent's Role', *Management Learning*, 37(3), 355–376.

Jones, O. and Craven, M. (2001a) 'Beyond the Routine: Innovation Management and the Teaching Company Scheme', *Technovation*, 21(5), 267–280.

Jones, O. and Craven, M. (2001b) 'Expanding Capabilities in a Mature Manufacturing Firm: Absorptive Capacity and the TCS', *International Small Business Journal*, 19(3), 39–56.

Jones, O. and Holt, R. (2008) 'The Creation and Evolution of New Business Ventures: An Activity Theory Perspective', *Journal of Small Business and Enterprise Development*, 15(1), 51–73.

Jones, O. and Jayawarna, D. (2010) 'Resourcing New Businesses: Social Networks, Bootstrapping and Firm Performance', *Venture Capital*, 12(2), 127–152.

Jones, O. and Jayawarna, D. (2011) 'Entrepreneurial Potential: The Role of Human Capital', conference proceedings, Institute of Small Business and Entrepreneurship (ISBE) Conference, Sheffield, UK.

Jones, O. and Macpherson, A. (2006) 'Inter-organizational Learning and Strategic Renewal in SMEs: Extending the 4I Network', *Long Range Planning*, 39(2), 155–175.

Jones, O. and Macpherson, A. (2013) 'Research Perspectives on Learning in Small Firms', in Chell, E., ed., *Handbook of Research in Entrepreneurship and Small Business*.

Jones, O. and Tang, N. (1998) 'Mature Firms in the Mid-corporate Sector: Strategies for Innovation and Employment', in Delbridge, R. and Lowe, J., eds, *Manufacturing in Transition*, London: Macmillan, 112–129.

Jones, O., Ghobadian, A., O'Regan, N. and Antcliffe, V. (2013) 'Dynamic Capabilities in a Sixth Generation Family Firm: Entrepreneurship and the Bibby Line', *Business History*, 55(2).

Jones, O., Macpherson, A. and Jayawarna, D. (2010a) 'Bootstrapping as a Dynamic Capability: Innovation in TBSFs (Technology-based Start-up Firms)', conference proceedings, Institute of Small Business and Entrepreneurship Conference (ISBE), London, UK.

Jones, O., Macpherson, A. and Thorpe, R. (2010b) 'Learning in Owner-managed Small Firms: Mediating Artefacts and Strategic Space', *Entrepreneurship and Regional Development*, 22(7/8), 649–673.

Jones, O., Macpherson, A. and Woollard, D. (2008) 'Entrepreneurial Ventures in Higher Education: Analysing Organizational Growth', *International Small Business Journal*, 26(6), 683–708.

de Jong, J. P. J. and Freel, M. (2010) 'Absorptive Capacity and the Reach of Collaboration in High Technology Small Firms', *Research Policy*, 39(1), 47–54.

Kakati, M. (2003) 'Success Criteria in High-tech New Ventures', *Technovation*, 23(5), 447–457.

Kanter, R. M. (1983) *The Change Masters: Innovation for Productivity in the American Corporation*, New York: Simon & Schuster.

Karatas-Ozkan, M. (2011) 'Understanding Relational Qualities of Entrepreneurial Learning: Towards a Multi-layered Approach', *Entrepreneurship and Regional Development*, 23(9–10), 877–906.

Karatas-Ozkan, M. and Chell, E. (2010) *Nascent Entrepreneurship and Learning*, Cheltenham, UK and Northampton, MA: Edward Elgar.

Katila, R. and Shane, S. (2005) 'When Does Lack of Resources Make New Firms Innovative?', *Academy of Management Journal*, 48(5), 814–829.

Katz, J. A. (2003) 'The Chronology and Intellectual Trajectory of American Entrepreneurship Education, 1876–1999', *Journal of Business Venturing*, 18, 283–300.

Katz, J. A. (2008) 'Fully Mature But Not Fully Legitimate: A Different Perspective on the State of Entrepreneurship Education', *Journal of Small Business Management*, 46(4), 550–566.

Katz, J. and Gartner, W. B. (1988) 'Properties of Emerging Organizations', *Academy of Management Review*, 13(3), 429–441.

Kaulio, M. A. (2003) 'Initial Conditions or Process of Development? Critical Incidents in the Early Stages of New Ventures', *R&D Management*, 33(2), 165–176.

Kayes, D. C. (2002) 'Experiential Learning and Its Critics: Preserving the Role of Experience in Management Learning and Education', *Academy of Management Learning and Education*, 1(2), 137–149.

Kelley, D., Bosma, N. and Amoros, J. E. (2011) *Global Entrepreneurship Monitor: 2010 Global Report*, Babson Park, MA: Babson College.

Kelly, D. J., Singer, S. and Herrington, M. (2012) Global Entrepreneurship Monitor: 2011 Global Report, Global Entrepreneurship Research Association.

Khaire, M. (2010) 'Young and No Money? Never Mind: The Material Impact of Social Resources on New Venture Growth', *Organization Science*, 21(1), 168–185.

Kim, P. H., Aldrich, H. E. and Keister, L. A. (2006) 'Access (Not) Denied: The Impact of Financial, Human, and Cultural Capital on Entrepreneurial Entry in the United States', *Small Business Economics*, 27(1), 5–22.

Kirzner, I. M. (1973) *Competition and Entrepreneurship*, Chicago, IL: University of Chicago.

Kirzner, I. M. (2009) 'The Alert and Creative Entrepreneur: A Clarification', *Small Business Economics*, 32(2), 145–152.

Kitila, R. and Shane, S. (2005) 'When Does Lack of Resources Make New Firms Innovate?', *Academy of Management Journal*, 48(5), 814–829.

Klapper, L. and Love, I. (2010) *The Impact of the Financial Crisis on New Firm Registration*, Washington, DC: The World Bank.

Klapper, L., Laeven, L. and Rajan, R. (2009) 'Entry Regulation as a Barrier to Entrepreneurship', in Beck, T., ed., *Entrepreneurship in Developing Countries*, Elgar Reference Collection, International Library of Entrepreneurship: 15, Cheltenham, UK and Northampton, MA: Edward Elgar, 340–378.

Knight, F. (1921) *Risk, Uncertainty and Profit*, New York: Houghton Mifflin.

Kohler, W. (1925) *The Mentality of Apes*, Norwood, NJ: Ablex.

Kolb, D. A. (1984) 'Experiential Learning: Experience as the Source of Learning and Development, Englewood Cliffs, NJ: Prentice-Hall.

Kothari, S. and Handscombe, R. D. (2007) 'Sweep or Seep? Structure, Culture, Enterprise and Universities', *Management Decision*, 45(1), 43–61.

Krugman, P. (2009) *The Return of Depression Economics and the Crisis of 2008*, New York: Norton Company Limited.

Lam, W. (2010) 'Funding Gap, What Funding Gap? Financial Bootstrapping; Supply, Demand and Creation of Entrepreneurial Finance', *International Journal of Entrepreneurial Behaviour and Research*, 16(4), 268–295.

Lambert, R. (2003) *Lambert Review of Business–University Collaboration*, London: The Stationery Office.

Landström, H., Harirchi, G. and Åström, F. (2012) 'Entrepreneurship: Exploring the Knowledge Base', *Research Policy*, 41, 1154–1181.

Lans, T., Biemans, H., Verstegen, J. and Mulder, M. (2008) 'The Influence of the Work Environment on Entrepreneurial Learning of Small Business Owners', *Management Learning*, 39(5), 597–614.

Large, D. and Muegge, S. (2008) 'Venture Capitalists' Non-financial Value-added: An Evaluation of the Evidence and Implications for Research', *Venture Capital*, 10(1), 21–53.

Larson, A. and Starr, J. A. (1993) 'A Network Model of Organization Formation', *Entrepreneurship: Theory and Practice*, 17(2), 5–15.

Latour, B. (1986) 'The Powers of Association', in Law, J., ed., *Power, Action and Belief*, London: Routledge & Kegan Paul, 264–280.

Lave, J. and Wenger, E. (1991) *Situated Learning: Legitimate Peripheral Participation*, New York: Cambridge University Press.

Lechner, C. and Dowling, M. (2003) 'Firm Networks: External Relationships as Sources for the Growth and Competitiveness of Entrepreneurial Firms', *Entrepreneurship and Regional Development*, 15(1), 1–27.

Lee, R. and Jones, O. (2008) 'Networks, Communication and Learning During Business Start-up', *International Small Business Journal*, 26(5), 559–594.

Lee, R., Tüselmann, H., Jayawarna, D. and Rouse, J. (2011) 'Investigating the Social Capital and Resource Acquisition of Entrepreneurs Residing in Deprived Areas of England', *Environment and Planning C: Government and Policy*, 29(6), 1054–1072.

Lengnick-Hall, C. A. and Beck, T. E. (2005) 'Adaptive Fit versus Robust Transformation: How Organizations Respond to Environmental Change', *Journal of Management*, 31, 738–757.

Leonard-Barton, D. (1995) *Wellsprings of Knowledge: Building and Sustaining the Sources of Innovation*, Boston, MA: Harvard Business School Press.

Levie, J. and Lichtenstein, B. B. (2010) 'A Terminal Assessment of Stages Theory: Introducing a Dynamic States Approach to Entrepreneurship', *Entrepreneurship: Theory and Practice*, 34(2), 317–350.

Lévi-Strauss, C. (1967) *The Savage Mind*, Chicago, IL: University of Chicago Press.

Lewin, K. (1951) *Field Theory in Social Science*, Harper Row, London.

Lichtenstein, B. B. (2000) 'Self Organized Transitions: A Pattern amid the Chaos of Transformative Change', *Academy of Management Executive*, 14(4), 128–141.

Lichtenstein, B. B., Dooley, K. J. and Lumpkin, G. T. (2006) 'Measuring Emergence in the Dynamics of New Venture Creation', *Journal of Business Venturing*, 21, 153–175.

Lichtenstein, B. M. and Brush, C. G. (2001) 'How Do "Resource Bundles" Develop and Change in New Ventures? A Dynamic Model and Longitudinal Exploration', *Entrepreneurship: Theory and Practice*, 25(3), 37–59.

Littunen, H. and Tohmo, T. (2003) 'The High Growth in New Metal-based Manufacturing and Business Service Firms in Finland', *Small Business Economics*, (2), 187–200.

**231**

Liu, S. L. and Dubinsky, A. J. (2000) 'Institutional Entrepreneurship – A Panacea for Universities-in-transition', *European Journal of Marketing*, 34(11/12), 1315–1337.

Lockett, A., Thompson, S. and Morgenstern, U. (2009) 'The Development of the Resource-based View of the Firm: A Critical Appraisal', *International Journal of Management Reviews*, 11(1), 9–28.

Lounsbury, M. and Glynn, M. (2001) 'Cultural Entrepreneurship: Stories, Legitimacy and the Acquisition of Resources', *Strategic Management Journal*, 22, 545–564.

Lourenço, F. and Jones, O. (2006) *Learning Paradigms in Entrepreneurship Education: Comparing the Traditional and Enterprise Modes*, London: NCGE.

Lourenço, F., Jones, O. and Jayawarna, D. (2012) 'Promoting Sustainable Development: The Role of Entrepreneurship Education', *International Small Business Journal*, published online 24 April 2012 (doi: 10.1177/0266242611435825).

Low, M. B. and MacMillan, I. C. (1988) 'Entrepreneurship: Past Research and Future Challenges', *Journal of Management*, 14(2), 139–161.

Lumpkin, G. T. and Lichtenstein, B. B. (2005) 'The Role of Organizational Learning in the Opportunity–Recognition Process', *Entrepreneurship Theory and Practice*, 29(4), 451–472.

McAdam, M. and Marlow, S. (2008) 'A Preliminary Investigation into Networking Activities within the University Incubator', *International Journal of Entrepreneurial Behaviour and Research*, 14(4), 219–241.

McAdam, R., McAdam, M. and Brown, V. (2009) 'Proof of Concept Processes in UK University Technology Transfer: An Absorptive Capacity Perspective', *R&D Management*, 39(2), 192–210.

McCann, J. E. (1991) 'Patterns of Growth, Competitive Technology, and Financial Strategies in Young Ventures', *Journal of Business Venturing*, 6(3), 189–208.

McClelland, D. C. (1961) *The Achieving Society*, New York: Free Press.

McClelland, D. C. (1962) 'Business Drive and National Achievement', *Harvard Business Review*, 40(4), 99–113.

Macpherson, A. (2005) 'Learning to Grow: Resolving the Crisis of Knowing', *Technovation*, 25 (10), 1129–1140.

Macpherson, A. and Holt, R. (2007) 'Knowledge, Learning and Small Firm Growth: A Systematic Review of the Evidence', *Research Policy*, 36(2), 172–192.

Macpherson, A. and Jones, O. (2008) 'Object-mediated Learning and Strategic Renewal in a Mature Organization', *Management Learning*, 39(2), 177–201.

Macpherson, A., Jones, O. and Zhang, M. (2004) 'Evolution or Revolution? Dynamic Capabilities in a Knowledge-dependent Firm', *R&D Management*, 34(2), 161–177.

Madill, J. J., Haines Jr, G. H. and Riding, A. L. (2005) 'The Role of Angels in Technology SMEs: A Link to Venture Capital', *Venture Capital*, 7(2), 107–129.

Maine, E. M., Shapiro, D. M. and Vining, A. R. (2010) 'The Role of Clustering in the Growth of New Technology-based Firms', *Small Business Economics*, 34(2), 127–146.

Man, T. W. Y., Lau, T. and Chan, K. F. (2002) 'The Competitiveness of Small and Medium Enterprises a Conceptualization with Focus on Entrepreneurial Competencies', *Journal of Business Venturing*, 17(2), 123–142.

Mangham, I. (1985) 'In Search of Competence', *Journal of General Management*, 12(2), 5–12.

Manolis, C., Burns, D. J., Assudani, R. and Chinta, R. (2013) 'Assessing Experiential Learning Styles: A Methodological Reconstruction and Validation of the Kolb Learning Style Inventory', *Learning and Individual Differences*, 23(1), 44–52.

Manolova, T. S., Manev, I. M., Carter, N. M. and Gyoshev, B. S. (2006) 'Breaking the Family and Friends' Circle: Predictors of External Financing Usage among Men and Women Entrepreneurs in a Transitional Economy', *Venture Capital*, 8(2), 109–132.

March, J. G. (1991) 'Exploration and Exploitation in Organizational Learning', *Organization Science*, 2(1), 71–87.

March, J. G. and Simon, H. A. (1958) *Organizations*, Oxford: Wiley.

Marshall, N. (2008) 'Cognitive and Practice-based Theories of Organizational Knowledge and Learning: Incompatible or Complementary?', *Management Learning*, 39(4), 413–435.

Martin, G. and Staines, H. (1994) 'Managerial Competencies in Small Firms', *Journal of Management Development*, 13(7), 23–34.

Mason, C. and Stark, M. (2004) 'What Do Investors Look for in a Business Plan? A Comparison of the Investment Criteria of Bankers, Venture Capitalists and Business Angels', *International Small Business Journal*, 22(3), 227–248.

Mason, C. M. (2009) 'Public Policy Support for the Informal Venture Capital Market in Europe: A Critical Review', *International Small Business Journal*, 27(5), 536–556.

Mason, C. M. and Harrison, R. T. (1995) 'Closing the Regional Equity Capital Gap: The Role of Informal Venture Capital', *Small Business Economics*, 7(2), 153–172.

Mason, C. M. and Harrison, R. T. (1999) '"Venture Capital": Rationale, Aims and Scope: Editorial', *Venture Capital*, 1(1), 1–46.

Mason, C. M. and Harrison, R. T. (2010) *Annual Report on the Business Angel Market in the United Kingdom: 2008/09*, URN 10/994, available at: www.ukbusiness angelsassociation.org.uk/sites/default/files/media/files/bbaa_annual_market_report_ 2008-2009.pdf [accessed 19 April 2013].

Matlay, H. and Hyland, T. (1997) 'NVQs in the Small Business Sector: A Critical Overview', *Education + Training*, 39(9), 325–332.

Maxwell, A. L., Jeffrey, S. A. and Lévesque, M. (2011) 'Business Angel Early Stage Decision Making', *Journal of Business Venturing*, 26(2), 212–225.

Mazzarol, T., Volery, T., Doss, N. and Thein, V. (1999) 'Factors Influencing Small Business Start-ups: A Comparison with Previous Research', *International Journal of Entrepreneurial Behaviour and Research*, 5(2), 48–63.

Meyskens, M., Carsrud, A. L. and Cardozo, R. N. (2010a) 'The Symbiosis of Entities in the Social Engagement Network: The Role of Social Ventures', *Entrepreneurship and Regional Development*, 22(5), 425–455.

Meyskens, M., Robb-Post, C., Stamp, J. A., Carsrud, A. L. and Reynolds, P. D. (2010b) 'Social Ventures from a Resource-based Perspective: An Exploratory Study Assessing Global Ashoka Fellows', *Entrepreneurship: Theory and Practice*, 34(4), 661–680.

Miner, A. S., Bassoff, P. and Moorman, C. (2001) 'Organizational Improvisation and Learning: A Field Study', *Administrative Science Quarterly*, 46(2), 304–337.

Mintzberg, H. (1973) *The Nature of Managerial Work*, New York: Harper & Row.

von Mises, L.(1949) *Human Actions: A Treatise on Economics*, New Haven, CT: Yale University Press.

Mitchelmore, S. and Rowley, J. (2010) 'Entrepreneurial Competencies: A Literature Review and Development Agenda', *International Journal of Entrepreneurial Behaviour and Research*, 16(2), 92–111.

Moizer, J. and Tracey, P. (2010) 'Strategy Making in Social Enterprise: The Role of Resource Allocation and Its Effects on Organizational Sustainability', *Systems Research and Behavioural Science*, 27(3), 252–266.

Mole, K. F. and Keogh, W. (2009) 'The Implications of Public Sector Small Business Advisers Becoming Strategic Sounding Boards: England and Scotland Compared', *Entrepreneurship and Regional Development*, 21(1), 77–97.

Moroz, P. W. and Hindle, K. (2012) 'Entrepreneurship as a Process: Toward Harmonizing Multiple Perspectives', *Entrepreneurship: Theory and Practice*, 36(4), 781–818.

Moynihan, D. (2008) 'Learning under Uncertainty: Networks in Crisis Management', *Public Administration Review*, 68(2), 350–365.

Mueller, S. L. and Thomas, A. S. (2001) 'Culture and Entrepreneurial Potential: A Nine Country Study of Locus of Control and Innovativeness', *Journal of Business Venturing*, 16(1), 51–75.

Mueller, S., Volery, T. and von Siemens, B. (2012) 'What Do Entrepreneurs Actually Do? An Observational Study of Entrepreneurs' Everyday Behaviour in the Start-up and Growth Stages', *Entrepreneurship: Theory and Practice*, 36(5), 995–1017.

Myers, S. C. (1984) 'The Capital Structure Puzzle', *Journal of Finance*, 39(3), 575–592.

Nahapiet, J. and Ghoshal, S. (1998) 'Social Capital, Intellectual Capital, and the Organizational Advantage', *Academy of Management Review*, 23(2), 242–266.

Naudé, W. (2011) 'Entrepreneurship is Not a Binding Constraint on Growth and Development in the Poorest Countries', *World Development*, 39, 33–44.

Nelson, R. R. and Winter, S. G. (1982) *An Evolutionary Theory of Economic Change*, Cambridge, MA: Belknap Press of Harvard University Press.

Newbert, S. (2005) 'New Firm Formation: A Dynamic Capability Perspective', *Journal of Small Business Management*, 43(1), 55–77.

Newey, L. R. and Zahra, S. A. (2009) 'The Evolving Firm: How Dynamic and Operating Capabilities Interact to Enable Entrepreneurship', *British Journal of Management,* 20, S81–S100.

Nicholls-Nixon, C. L. (2005) 'Rapid Growth and High Performance: The Entrepreneur's "Impossible Dream?"', *Academy of Management Executive,* 19(1), 77–89.

Nicolaou, N., Shane, S., Cherkas, L., Hunkin, J. and Spector, T. D. (2008) 'Is the Tendency to Engage in Entrepreneurship Genetic?', *Management Science,* (1), 167–179.

Nofsinger, J. R. and Wang, W. (2011) 'Determinants of Start-up Firm External Financing Worldwide', *Journal of Banking and Finance,* 35(9), 2282–2294.

O'Connor, E. (2002) 'Storied Business: Typology, Intertextuality, and Traffic in Entrepreneurial Narrative', *Journal of Business Communication,* 39(1), 36–54.

OECD (2006) *The SME Financing Gap: Theory and Evidence, Volume 1,* Paris: OECD Publishing.

OECD (2009) *The Impact of the Global Crisis on SME and Entrepreneurship Financing and Policy Responses,* Paris: OECD Centre for Entrepreneurship, SMEs and Local Development.

Orlikowski, W. (2002) 'Knowing in Practice: Enacting a Collective Capability in Distributed Organizing', *Organization Science,* 13(3), 249–273.

Ostgaard, T. A. and Birley, S. (1996) 'New Venture Growth and Personal Networks', *Journal of Business Research,* 36(1), 37–50.

Ou, C. and Haynes, G. W. (2006) 'Acquisition of Additional Equity Capital by Small Firms – Findings from the National Survey of Small Business Finances', *Small Business Economics,* 27(2–3), 157–168.

Painter, M. A. (2010) 'Get a Job and Keep It! High School Employment and Adult Wealth Accumulation', *Research in Social Stratification and Mobility,* 28, 233–249.

Patton, D. and Marlow, S. (2011) 'University Technology Business Incubators: Helping New Entrepreneurial Firms to Learn to Grow', *Environment and Planning C: Government and Policy,* 29(5), 911–926.

Pavlov, I. P. (1927) *Conditioned Reflexes: An Investigation of the Physiological Activity of the Cerebral Cortex,* translated and edited by Anrep, G. V., London: Oxford University Press.

Penrose, E. T. (1959) *The Theory of the Growth of the Firm,* Oxford: Basil Blackwell.

Pentland, B. T. and Feldman, M. S. (2005) 'Organizational Routines as a Unit of Analysis', *Industrial and Corporate Change,* 14(5), 793–815.

Pentland, B. T., Feldman, M. S., Becker, M. C. and Liu, P. (2012) 'Dynamics of Organizational Routines: A Generative Model', *Journal of Management Studies,* 49(8), 1484–1508.

Perks, K. (2006) 'Influences on Strategic Management Styles among Fast Growth Medium-sized Firms in France and Germany', *Strategic Change,* 15(3), 153–164.

Perry, J. T., Chandler, G. N. and Markova, G. (2012) 'Entrepreneurial Effectuation: A Review and Suggestions for Future Research', *Entrepreneurship: Theory and Practice*, 36(4), 837–861.

Pfeffer, J. and Salancik, G. (1978) *The External Control of Organizations*, New York: Harper & Row.

Pfeifer, S. and Borozan, D. (2011) 'Fitting Kolb's Learning Style Theory to Entrepreneurship Learning Aims and Contents', *International Journal of Business Research*, 11(2), 216–223.

Phelps, R., Adams, R. and Bessant, J. (2007) 'Life Cycles of Growing Organizations: A Review with Implications for Knowledge and Learning', *International Journal of Management Reviews*, 9(1), 1–30.

Piaget, J. (1926) *The Language and Thought of the Child*, Oxford: Harcourt, Brace & Co.

Piaget, J. (1951) *Play, Dreams and Imitation in Childhood*, London: Routledge.

Pintado, T. R., de Lema, D. G. P. and Van Auken, H. (2007) 'Venture Capital in Spain by Stage of Development', *Journal of Small Business Management*, 45(1), 68–88.

Pitelis, C. (2012) 'Clusters, Entrepreneurial Ecosystem Co-creation, and Appropriability: A Conceptual Framework', *Industrial and Corporate Change*, 21(6), 1359–1388.

Pitelis, C., ed., (2002) *The Growth of the Firm: The Legacy of Edith Penrose*, Oxford: Oxford University Press.

Pittaway, L. (2012) 'The Evolution of Entrepreneurship Theory', in Carter, S. and Jones-Evans, D., eds, *Entrepreneurship and Small Business: Principles, Practice and Policy*, Harlow, UK: Pearson, 9–26.

Pittaway, L. and Cope, J. (2007) 'Simulating Entrepreneurial Learning', *Management Learning*, 38(2), 211–233.

Pittaway, L. and Thorpe, R. (2012) 'A Framework for Entrepreneurial Learning: A Tribute to Jason Cope', *Entrepreneurship and Regional Development*, 24(9/10), 837–859.

Pittaway, L., Robertson, M., Munir, K., Denyer, D. and Neely, A. (2004) 'Networking and Innovation: A Systematic Review of the Evidence', *International Journal of Management Reviews*, 5/6(3/4), 137–168.

Pittaway, L., Rodriguez-Falcon, E., Aiyegbayo, O. and King, A. (2011) 'The Role of Entrepreneurship Clubs and Societies in Entrepreneurial Learning', *International Small Business Journal*, 29(1), 37–57.

Politis, D. (2005) 'The Process of Entrepreneurial Learning: A Conceptual Framework', *Entrepreneurship: Theory and Practice*, 29(4), 399–424.

Politis, D., Winborg, J. and Dahlstrand, Å. L. (2012) 'Exploring the Resource Logic of Student Entrepreneurs', *International Small Business Journal*, 30(6), 659–683.

Popper, M. and Lipshitz, R. (2000) 'Organizational Learning: Mechanisms, Culture and Feasibility', *Management Learning*, 31(2), 181–196.

Porter, M. (1998) *The Competitive Advantage of Nations*, Basingstoke, UK: Macmillan.

Porter, M., Takeuchi, H. and Sakaibara, M. (2000) *Can Japan Compete?* New York: Basic Books.

Putnam, R. D. (1995) 'Bowling Alone: America's Declining Social Capital', *Current*, (373), 3–10.

Qian, H., Haynes, K. E. and Riggle, J. D. (2011) 'Incubation Push or Business Pull? Investigating the Geography of U.S. Business Incubators', *Economic Development Quarterly*, 25(1), 79–90.

Rae, D. (2004) 'Practical Theories from Entrepreneurs Stories: Discursive Approaches to Entrepreneurial Learning', *Journal of Small Business and Enterprise Development*, 11(2), 195–202.

Rae, D. (2005) 'Entrepreneurial Learning: A Narrative-based Conceptual Model', *Journal of Small Business and Enterprise Development*, 12(3), 323–335.

Rae, D. (2012) 'Action Learning in New Creative Ventures', *International Journal of Entrepreneurial Behaviour and Research*, 18(5), 603–623.

Rae, D. and Carswell, M. (2001) 'Towards a Conceptual Understanding of Entrepreneurial Learning', *Journal of Small Business and Enterprise Development*, 8(2), 150–158.

Raelin, J. A. (2007) 'Toward an Epistemology of Practice', *Academy of Management Learning and Education*, 6(4), 495–519.

Rahman, M. W. and Jianchao, L. (2011) 'The Development Perspective of Finance and Microfinance Sector in China: How Far is Microfinance Regulations?', *International Journal of Economics and Finance*, 3(1), 160–170.

Raspe, O. and Oort, F. (2011) 'Growth of New Firms and Spatially Bounded Knowledge Externalities', *Annals of Regional Science*, 46(3), 495–518.

Read, S. and Sarasvathy, S (2005) 'Knowing What To Do and Doing What You Know: Effectuation as a Form of Entrepreneurial Expertise', *Journal of Private Equity*, 9(1), 46–62.

Read, S., Sarasvathy, S., Nick, D., Wiltbank, R. and Ohisson, A.-V. (2011) *Effectual Entrepreneurship*, London and New York: Routledge.

Renko, M., Shrader, R. C. and Simon, M. (2012) 'Perception of Entrepreneurial Opportunity: A General Framework', *Management Decision*, 50(7), 1233–1251.

Renski, H. (2009) 'New Firm Entry, Survival, and Growth in the United States: A Comparison of Urban, Suburban, and Rural Areas', *Journal of the American Planning Association*, 75(1), 60–77.

Revans, R. W. (1980) *Action Learning: New Techniques for Management*, London: Blond & Briggs.

Reynolds, P. and Miller, B. (1992) 'New Firm Gestation: Conception, Birth, and Implications for Research', *Journal of Business Venturing*, 7, 405–417.

Reynolds, P. D. (2011) 'Informal and Early Formal Financial Support in the Business Creation Process: Exploration with PSED II Data Set', *Journal of Small Business Management*, 49(1), 27–54.

# REFERENCES

Reynolds, P. D. and White, S. B. (1997) *The Entrepreneurial Process. Economic Growth, Men, Women, and Minorities*, Westport, CT: Quorum Books.

Rindova, V., Barry, D. and Ketchen, J. D. J. (2009) 'Entrepreneuring as Emancipation', *Academy of Management Review*, 34(3), 477–491.

Roberts, J. (2001) *Class in Modern Britain*, Oxford: Open University Press.

Rogers, N. (2006) 'Social Networks and the Emergence of the New Entrepreneurial Ventures in Russia: 1987–2000', *American Journal of Economics and Sociology*, 65(2), 295–312.

Romano, C. A., Tanewski, G. A. and Smyrnios, K. X. (2001) 'Capital Structure Decision Making: A Model for Family Business', *Journal of Business Venturing*, 16(3), 285–310.

Rostow, W. W. (1960) *The Stages of Economic Growth: A Non-communist Manifesto*, Cambridge: Cambridge University Press.

Rothaermel, F. T. and Thursby, M. (2005) 'Incubator Firm Failure or Graduation? The Role of University Linkages', *Research Policy*, 34(7), 1076–1090.

Rotter, J. (1966) 'Generalized Expectancies for Internal versus External Control of Reinforcements', *Psychological Monographs*, 80 Whole No. 609.

Rouse, J. and Jayawarna, D. (2011) 'Structures of Exclusion from Enterprise Finance', *Environment and Planning C: Government and Policy*, 29(4), 659–676.

Sadler-Smith, E., Hampson, Y., Chaston, I. and Badger, B. (2003) 'Managerial Behaviour, Entrepreneurial Style and Small Firm Performance', *Journal of Small Business Management*, 41(1), 47–67.

Sadler-Smith, E., Spicer, D. P. and Chaston, I. (2001) 'Learning Orientations and Growth in Smaller Firms', *Long Range Planning*, 34, 139–158.

Samra-Fredericks, D. (2003) 'A Proposal for Developing a Critical Pedagogy in Management from Researching Organizational Members' Everyday Practice', *Management Learning*, 34(3), 291–312.

Sanz-Velasco, S. (2006) 'Opportunity Development as a Learning Process for Entrepreneurs', *International Journal of Entrepreneurial Behaviour and Research*, 12(5), 251–271.

Sarason, Y., Dean, T. and Dillard, J. F. (2006) 'Entrepreneurship as the Nexus of Individual and Opportunity: A Structuration View', *Journal of Business Venturing*, 21(3), 286–305.

Sarasvathy, S. D. (2001) 'Causation and Effectuation: Toward a Theoretical Shift from Economic Inevitability to Entrepreneurial Contingency', *The Academy of Management Review*, (2), 243–263.

Sarasvathy, S. D. (2004) 'Making it Happen: Beyond Theories of the Firm to Theories of Firm Design', *Entrepreneurship: Theory and Practice*, 28(6), 519–531.

Sarasvathy, S. D. (2008) *Effectuation: Elements of Entrepreneurial Expertise* Cheltenham, UK: Edward Elgar.

Sarasvathy, S. D. (2012) 'Effectuation and Entrepreneurship', in Carter, S. and Jones-Evans, D., eds, *Enterprise and Small Business: Principles, Practice and Policy*, 3rd edn, Harlow, UK: Pearson, 135–151.

Saxenian, A. (1996) *Regional Advantages: Culture and Competition in Silicon Valley and Route 128*, Cambridge, MA: Harvard University Press.

Say, J.-B. (1880) *A Treatise on Political Economy*, Philadelphia, PA: Claxton, Remsen & Haffelfinger.

Schumpeter, J. (1934) *The Theory of Economic Development*, Cambridge, MA: Harvard University Press.

Scott, M. and Bruce, R. (1987) 'Five Stages of Growth in Small Business', *Long Range Planning*, 20(3), 45–52.

Scott, R. H. (2009) 'The Use of Credit Card Debt by New Firms', Ewing Marion Kauffman Foundation, available at: www.kauffman.org/uploadedFiles/kfs_credit_card_debt_report.pdf [accessed 27 June 2013].

SFEDI (2012) 'SFEDI Standards for Business Enterprise', Small Firms Enterprise Development Initiative, available at: www.sfedi.co.uk/standards/enterpriseoverview.pdf [accessed 17 April 2013].

Shah, S. K. and Tripsas, M. (2007) 'The Accidental Entrepreneur: The Emergent and Collective Process of User Entrepreneurship', *Strategic Entrepreneurship Journal*, 1(2), 123–140.

Shane, S. (2000) 'Prior Knowledge and the Discovery of Entrepreneurial Opportunities', *Organization Science*, 11(4), 448–469.

Shane, S. (2003) *A General Theory of Entrepreneurship: The Individual–Opportunity Nexus*, Cheltenham, UK: Edward Elgar.

Shane, S. (2009) 'Why Encouraging More People to Become Entrepreneurs is Bad Public Policy', *Small Business Economics*, 33(2), 141–149.

Shane, S. (2012) 'Reflections on the 2010 Amr Decade Award: Delivering on the Promise of Entrepreneurship as Field of Research', *Academy of Management Review*, 37(1), 10–20.

Shane, S. and Cable, D. (2002) 'Network Ties, Reputation, and the Financing of New Ventures', *Management Science*, 48(3), 364–381.

Shane, S. and Stuart, T. (2002) 'Organizational Endowments and the Performance of University Start-ups', *Management Science*, 48(1), 154–170.

Shane, S. and Venkataraman, S. (2000) 'The Promise of Entrepreneurship as a Field of Research', *Academy of Management Review*, 25(1), 217–226.

Shane, S., Nicolaou, N., Cherkas, L. and Spector, T. D. (2010) 'Genetics, the Big Five, and the Tendency to Be Self-employed', *Journal of Applied Psychology*, 95(6), 1154–1162.

Sharifi, S. and Zhang, M. (2009) 'Sense-making and Recipes: Examples from Selected Small Firms', *International Journal of Entrepreneurial Behaviour and Research*, 15(6), 555–571.

Simon, H. A. (1959) 'Theories of Decision Making in Economics and Behavioural Science', *American Economic Review*, 49, 253–283.

Sirmon, D. G. and Hitt, M. A. (2003) 'Managing Resources: Linking Unique Resources, Management, and Wealth Creation in Family Firms', *Entrepreneurship: Theory and Practice*, 27(4), 339–358.

**239**

Skinner, B. F. (1938) *The Behaviour of Organisms*, New York: Appleton-Century-Crofts.

Smith, A. (1925/1776) *The Wealth of Nations*, Cannan, E., ed., 4th edn, London: Methuen.

Smith, D. A. and Lohrke, F. T. (2008) 'Entrepreneurial Network Development: Trusting in the Process', *Journal of Business Research*, 61(4), 315–322.

Smith, I. H. and Woodworth, W. P. (2012) 'Developing Social Entrepreneurs and Social Innovators: A Social Identity and Self-efficacy Approach', *Academy of Management Learning and Education*, 11(3), 390–407.

Smith, K. G., Collins, C. J. and Clark, K. D. (2005) 'Existing Knowledge, Knowledge Creation Capability, and the Rate of New Product Introduction in High-technology Firms', *The Academy of Management Journal*, 48(2), 346–357.

Smith, N. R. and Miner, J. B. (1983) 'Type of Entrepreneur, Type of Firm, and Managerial Motivation: Implications for Organizational Life Cycle Theory', *Strategic Management Journal*, 4(4), 325–340.

Smith, R. L. and Smith, J. K. (2000) *Entrepreneurial Finance*, New York: John Wiley & Sons.

Sohl, J. E. (2009) *The Angel Investor Market in 2008: A Down Year in Investment Dollars But Not in Deals*, Center for Venture Research, available at: http://wsbe.unh.edu/files/2008_Analysis_Report_Final.pdf [accessed 19 September 2012].

Sørensen, J. F. L. (2012) 'Testing the Hypothesis of Higher Social Capital in Rural Areas: The Case of Denmark', *Regional Studies*, 46(7), 873–891.

Spence, L. and Schmidpeter (2003) 'SMEs, Social Capital and the Common Good', *Journal of Business Ethics*, 45(1), 93–108.

Spender, J. C. (1989) *Industry Recipes: The Nature and Source of Management Judgement*, Oxford: Basil Blackwell.

Spender, J.-C. (2005) 'An Essay on the State of Knowledge Management', *Prometheus*, 23(1), 101–116.

Spicer, D. P. and Sadler-Smith, E. (2006) 'Organizational Learning in Smaller Manufacturing Firms', *International Small Business Journal*, 24(2), 133–158.

Stanworth, J. and Curran, G. (1991) *Bolton 20 Years On: The Small Firm in the 1990s*, London: Paul Chapman.

Starr, J. A. and Fondas, N. (1992) 'A Model of Entrepreneurial Socialization and Organization Formation', *Entrepreneurship: Theory and Practice*, 17(1), 67–76.

Stel, A., Storey, D. J. and Thurik, A. R. (2007) 'The Effect of Business Regulations on Nascent and Young Business Entrepreneurship', *Small Business Economics*, (2/3), 171–186.

Sterling, S. (2001) *Sustainable Education: Re-visioning Learning and Change*, Schumacher Briefings No. 6, Totnes, UK: Green Books.

Steyaert, C. (2004) 'The Prosaics of Entrepreneurship', in Hjorth, D. and Steyaert, C., eds, *Narrative and Discursive Approaches in Entrepreneurship*, Cheltenham, UK: Edward Elgar, 8–21.

Steyaert, C. (2007) '"Entrepreneuring" as a Conceptual Attractor? a Review of Process Theories in 20 Years of Entrepreneurship Studies', *Entrepreneurship and Regional Development*, 19(6), 453–477.

Steyaert, C. and Katz, J. (2004) 'Reclaiming the Space of Entrepreneurship in Society: Geographical, Discursive and Social Dimensions', *Entrepreneurship and Regional Development*, 16(3), 179–196.

Stiglitz, J. E. and Weiss, A. (1981) 'Credit Rationing in Markets with Imperfect Information', *American Economic Review*, 71(3), 393–410.

Stinchcombe, A., L. (1965) 'Organizations as Social Structures', in March, J., ed., *Handbook of Organizations*, Chicago, IL: Rand McNally.

Stokes, D. and Wilson, N. (2010) *Small Business Management and Entrepreneurship*, Andover: Cengage.

Storey, D. J. (1994) *Understanding the Small Business Sector*, London: Routledge.

Storey, D. J. (2004) 'Exploring the Link, among Small Firms, between Management Training and Firm Performance: A Comparison Between the UK and Other OECD Countries', *International Journal of Human Resource Management*, 15(1), 112–130.

Storey, D. J. (2011) 'Optimism and Chance: The Elephants in the Entrepreneurship Room', *International Small Business Journal*, 29(4), 303–321.

Storey, D. J. and Greene, F. J. (2010) *Small Business and Entrepreneurship*, Harlow, UK: Pearson Education.

Storey, D. J., Greene, F. and Mole, K. (2007) *Three Decades of Enterprise Culture? Entrepreneurship, Economic Regeneration and Public Policy*, Basingstoke, UK: Palgrave Macmillan.

Stringfellow, L. and Shaw, E. (2009) 'Conceptualising Entrepreneurial Capital for a Study of Performance in Small Professional Service Firms', *International Journal of Entrepreneurial Behaviour and Research*, 15(2), 137–161.

Stritar, R. (2012) 'Resource Hijacking as a Bricolage Technique', *Economic and Business Review*, 14(1), 5–15.

Sullivan-Taylor, B. and Branicki, L. (2011) 'Creating Resilient SMEs: Why One Size Might Not Fit All', *International Journal of Production Research*, 49(18), 5565–5579.

Taylor, D. and Pandza, K. (2003) 'Networking Capability: The Competitive Advantage of Small Firms', in Jones, O. and Tilley, F., eds, *Competitive Advantage in SMEs. Organising for Innovation and Change*, Chichester: John Wiley & Sons, 156–173.

Teasdale, S. (2010) 'How Can Social Enterprise Address Disadvantage? Evidence from an Inner City Community', *Journal of Nonprofit and Public Sector Marketing*, 22(2), 89–107.

Teece, D. (2007) 'Explicating Dynamic Capabilities: The Nature and Microfoundations of (Sustainable) Enterprise Performance', *Strategic Management Journal*, 28(13), 1319–1350.

Teece, D. J., ed., (2011) *Human Capital, Capabilities, and the Firm: Literati, Numerati, and Entrepreneurs in the Twenty-first Century Enterprise,* Oxford: Oxford University Press.

Teece, D., Pisano, G. and Shuen, A. (1997) 'Dynamic Capabilities and Strategic Management', *Strategic Management Journal,* 18(7), 509–533.

Thorndike, E. L. (1913) *Educational Psychology,* New York: Teachers College.

Timmons, J. A. (1999) *New Venture Creation: Entrepreneurship for the 21st Century,* 5th edn, New York: McGraw Hill.

Timmons, J. and Spinelli, S. (2004) *New Venture Creation,* 6th edn, Boston, MA: Irwin McGraw-Hill.

Tocher, N., Oswald, S. L., Shook, C. L. and Adams, G. (2012) 'Entrepreneur Political Skill and New Venture Performance: Extending the Social Competence Perspective', *Entrepreneurship and Regional Development,* 24(5–6), 283–305.

Tomory, E. M. (2011) 'Bootstrap Financing: Four Case Studies of Technology Companies', *International Journal of Management Cases,* 13(3), 531–538.

Tushman, M. L., Newman, W.H and Romanelli, E. (1986) 'Convergence and Upheaval: Managing the Unsteady Pace of Change', *California Management Review,* 19(1), 29–44.

Unger, J. M., Rauch, A., Frese, M. and Rosenbusch, N. (2011) 'Human Capital and Entrepreneurial Success: A Meta-analytical Review', *Journal of Business Venturing,* 26, 341–358.

Valliere, D. and Peterson, R. (2009) 'Entrepreneurship and Economic Growth: Evidence from Emerging and Developed Countries', *Entrepreneurship and Regional Development,* 21(5–6), 459–480.

Van Auken, H. (2002) 'A Model of Community-based Venture Capital Formation to Fund Early-stage Technology-based Firms', *Journal of Small Business Management,* 40(4), 287–301.

Van Vught, F. (1999) 'Innovative Universities', *Tertiary Education and Management,* 5(4), 347–355.

Vanacker, T. R. and Manigart, S. (2010) 'Pecking Order and Debt Capacity Considerations for High-growth Companies Seeking Financing', *Small Business Economics,* 35(1), 53–69.

Vanacker, T., Manigart, S., Meuleman, M. and Sels, L. (2011) 'A Longitudinal Study on the Relationship Between Financial Bootstrapping and New Venture Growth', *Entrepreneurship and Regional Development,* 23(9/10), 681–705.

Venkataraman, S. (2004) 'Entrepreneurial Opportunity', in Hitt, M. and Ireland D., eds, *Encyclopedic Dictionary of Entrepreneurship,* Malden, MA: Blackwell Press,100–103.

Venkataraman, S., ed., (1997) *The Distinctive Domain of Entrepreneurship Research: An Editor's Perspective,* Greenwich, CT: JAI Press.

Venkataraman, S., Sarasvathy, S. D., Dew, N. and Forster, W. R. (2012) 'Reflections on the 2010 Amr Decade Award: Whither the Promise? Moving Forward with

Entrepreneurship as a Science of the Artificial', *Academy of Management Review*, 37(1), 21–33.

Vesper, K. (1990) *New Venture Strategies*, Englewood Cliffs, NJ: Prentice-Hall.

Villanueva, J., Van de Ven, A. H. and Sapienza, H. J. (2012) 'Resource Mobilization in Entrepreneurial Firms', *Journal of Business Venturing*, 27(1), 19–30.

Vygotsky, L. S. (1978) *Mind in Society: The Development of Higher Psychological Processes*, Cambridge: Cambridge University Press.

Weick, K. (1979) *The Social Psychology of Organizing*, 2nd edn, Reading, MA: Addison-Wesley.

Weick, K. (1995) *Sensemaking in Organizations*, Thousand Oaks, CA: Sage.

Weick, K. E., Sutcliffe, K. M. and Obstfeld, D. (2002) 'High Reliability: The Power of Mindfulness', in Hesselbein, F. and Johnson, R., eds, *On High Performance Organizations*, San Francisco, CA: Jossey Bass.

Weiskopf, R. and Steyaert, C. (2009) 'Metamorphoses in Entrepreneurship Studies: Towards an Affirmative Politics of Entrepreneuring', in Hjorth, D. and Steyaert, C., eds, *The Politics and Aesthetics of Entrepreneurship: A Fourth Movement in Entrepreneurship*, Cheltenham, UK: Edward Elgar, 183–201.

Welter, F. (2011) 'Entrepreneurship: Conceptual Challenges and Ways Forward', *Entrepreneurship Theory and Practice*, 35(1), 165–184.

Wennekers, S., van Stel, A., Thurik, R. and Reynolds, P. (2005) 'Nascent Entrepreneurship and the Level of Economic Development', *Small Business Economics*, 24(3), 293–309.

West, G. P. and Noel, T. W. (2009) 'The Impact of Knowledge Resources on New Venture Performance', *Journal of Small Business Management*, 47(1), 1–22.

Whittington, R. (1996) 'Strategy as Practice', *Long Range Planning*, 29(5), 731–735.

Wiklund, J. and Shepherd, D. (2003a) 'Aspiring For, and Achieving Growth: The Moderating Role of Resources and Opportunities', *Journal of Management Studies*, 40(8), 1919–1941.

Wiklund, J. and Shepherd, D. (2003b) 'Knowledge-based Resources, Entrepreneurial Orientation, and the Performance of Small and Medium-sized Businesses', *Strategic Management Journal*, 24(13), 1307–1314.

Williams, D. R. (2004) 'Effects of Childcare Activities on the Duration of Self-employment in Europe', *Entrepreneurship: Theory and Practice*, 28(5), 467–485.

Winborg, J. (2009) 'Use of Financial Bootstrapping in New Businesses: A Question of Last Resort?', *Venture Capital*, 11(1), 71–83.

Winborg, J. and Landström, H. (2001) 'Financial Bootstrapping in Small Businesses. Examining Small Business Managers' Resource Acquisition Behaviours', *Journal of Business Venturing*, 16, 235–254.

Witt, P. (2004) 'Entrepreneurs' Networks and the Success of Start-ups', *Entrepreneurship and Regional Development*, 16(5), 391–412.

Witt, P., Schroeter, A. and Merz, C. (2008) 'Entrepreneurial Resource Acquisition via Personal Networks: An Empirical Study of German Start-ups', *Service Industries Journal*, 28(7/8), 953–971.

**243**

Woollard, D., Zhang, M. and Jones, O. (2007) 'Academic Enterprise and Regional Economic Growth: Towards an Enterprising University', *Industry and Higher Education*, 21(6), 387–403.

The World Bank (2012) *Doing Business in a More Transparent World*, Washington, DC.

Wu, L. (2007) 'Entrepreneurial Resources, Dynamic Capabilities and Start-up Performance of Taiwan's High-tech Firms', *Journal of Business Research*, 60, 549–555.

Xiang-yang, Z., Frese, M. and Giardini, A. (2010) 'Business Owners' Network Size and Business Growth in China: The role of Comprehensive Social Competency', *Entrepreneurship and Regional Development*, 22(7/8), 675–705.

Zahra, S. A. and Dess, G. G. (2001) 'Entrepreneurship as a Field of Research: Encouraging Dialogue and Debate', the *Academy of Management Review*, 26(1), 8–10

Zahra, S. A., Sapienza, H. and Davidsson, P. (2006) 'Enterpreneurship and Dynamic Capabilities: A Review, Model and Research Agenda', *Journal of Management Studies*, 43(4), 917–955.

Zellweger, T. M., Nason, R. S. and Nordqvist, M. (2012) 'From Longevity of Firms to Transgenerational Entrepreneurship of Families: Introducing Family Entrepreneurial Orientation', *Family Business Review*, 25(2), 136–155.

Zellweger, T., Sieger, P. and Halter, F. (2011) 'Should I Stay or Should I Go? Career Choice Intentions of Students with Family Business Background', *Journal of Business Venturing*, 26, 521–536.

Zhang, M., Macpherson, A. and Jones, O. (2006) 'Conceptualizing the Learning Process in SMEs: Improving Innovation through External Orientation', *International Small Business Journal*, 24(3), 299–323.

Zhao, H. and Seibert, S. E. (2006) 'The Big Five Personality Dimensions and Entrepreneurial Status: A Meta-analytical Review', *Journal of Applied Psychology*, 91(2), 259–271.

Zimmerman, M. A. and Zeitz, G. J. (2002) 'Beyond Survival: Achieving New Venture Growth by Building Legitimacy', *Academy of Management Review*, 27(3), 414–431.

Zollo, M. and Winter, S. G. (2002) 'Deliberate Learning and the Evolution of Dynamic Capabilities', *Organization Science*, 13, 339–351.

Zott, C. and Huy, Q. N. (2007) 'How Entrepreneurs Use Symbolic Management to Acquire Resources', *Administrative Science Quarterly*, 52(1), 70–105.

# Index

Page numbers in *italic* refers to figures/tables

absorptive capacity 2, 40, 96, 102, 167, 171
Acs, Z. J. 192
action learning 33, 44, 65
active learning 44–47
activity theory 9, 36
age 16, 31, 74, 97, 102, 150, 188
Ajzen, I. 198, 199, 205, 206
Aldrich, H. E. 3, 4, 5, 22, 31, 71, 165, 172, 202, 208
alertness 16
Allen, Paul 136
Anyadike-Danes, M. 194, 195
Apple 136
apprehension-comprehension 36–37
apprenticeship programmes 98
Atherton, A. 107–108
Austrian school 28–29

Baker, T. 24, 25, 29, 39, 60, 149–150, 152, 153 171
bank loans 104, 109, 114–115
Baron, J. N. 3, 100, 141
Baron, R. A. 4, 67, 84, 85
behavioural theory 6, 23
Birch, David 14, 15, 177, 178, 194, 195, 197, 199
Blair, Tony 3
Bolton Report (1971) 14, 178
bootstrapping 5, 87, 94, 104–105, 107, 114, 122–140, 206; benefits 135; and bricolage 135; and community leadership 138; customer-related 125, 127, 132; definition

and theoretical perspectives 123–124, *124*; and dynamic capabilities 148, 152–153, 155–156; entrepreneurs financial motives and use of 127–128; gendered nature of 128–130; as a growth strategy 132–137; joint-utilization 127, 129; lifestyle approach to 130–132, *131*; methods and techniques 125–128; and networking 137; owner-financed 125, 129; payment-related 125, 130; in social ventures 137–138, *138*; variations in the use of 128–132; and volunteerism 137–138; and women 128–130, 134
Bourdieu, Pierre 7, 40
Brazil 3, 41, 176, 184, 185, 187, 188, 191
bricolage 5, 23, 24–25, *26*, 29, 58, 135, 153–154, 155–156, 171, 203, 206, 207; and bootstrapping 135; definition 153; parallel and selective 58, 153–154, 155, 156
BRICS 184, 185, 191, 197, 202
Bridge, S. 179, 197–198
Brown, Gordon 3
Bruce, R. *162*, 164
Brush, C. G. 89, 96, 129, 142, 168, 169
Burns, P. 160, 174
business angels 19, 90, 104, 111–112
business entry, barriers to 190
business lifecycle: and finance 114–115
business plan 4, 20, 37, 45, 147, 168, 179, 205

Business Schools 33
Business Structure Database (BSD) 195

Cameron, David 3
Cantillon, Richard 13
capabilities 51–69, 180–181, 204; and
   managing early stage growth 55–65;
   substantive 145, see also dynamic
   capabilities; skills
capital: types of 7–8; see also human capital;
   social capital
capital structure theory 114
causal approach 21–22, 23, 29, 203
childhood 97–98
China 164, 165; growth of 185–186
Churchill, N. C. 162
Clarke, J. 67
clubs and societies, entrepreneurship 47–49
cognitive learning 2, 6, 36, 37, 38–40, 39
cognitive social capital 78–79, 80, 204
Coleman, James 75
community leadership, and bootstrapping
   138
competencies, generic 56–59
competitive advantage 15, 87, 88, 91–92,
   95–96, 101, 105, 124, 144
contextual learning 80
conversational learning 36
Cope, Jason 2, 38, 42, 62, 81
core competencies 144
Cornwall, J. R. 134
creation perspective 23, 29
creative class 192
creative destruction 92
creativity 58–59
credit cards 108–109
crisis: making sense of in context 165–166,
   166
crowd financing 107, 108
cultural capital 7
cultural entrepreneurship 66–68, 68

de Clercq, D. 7
debt finance 108–110, 110
decision theory 26
Dell Computer Corporation 135, 136
Dewey, John 6–7
Dodge, H. R 165, 167
double-loop learning 46

Dragon's Den (TV show) 113
dynamic capabilities 89, 141–157; and
   bootstrapping 148, 152–153, 155–156;
   and bricolage 153–154, 155–156;
   distinction between substantive capabilities
   and 145; and learning processes 146,
   149–151; main processes 145; in new
   ventures 147–149; routines that support
   change 145–147; types of 145–146
dynamic learning business creation 202–209

ease-of-use 199
Ebben, J. 133, 136–137
economic capital 7
economic development 40, 176–201; and
   efficiency-driven economies 185–187, 191,
   201; and factor-driven countries 184–185,
   187, 191, 191, 193, 197, 201; impact of
   policy initiatives 177–179; and innovation-
   driven economies 186–187, 188, 191,
   191, 192, 197, 200; and new businesses
   176–201; stages of growth 178
Economic and Social Research Council (ESRC)
   178
economics 10
education 63–65, 180, 199, 208
effectuation 10, 17–18, 23, 25–26, 26, 29, 54,
   55, 62, 152, 203
efficiency-driven economies 3, 185–187, 191,
   201, 202
Eisenhardt, K. M. 145
Elliott, C. 9
employment growth 195–196
employment models 3
enactment 20
enterprise education 32, 33, 42–43, 47, 180
entrepreneur, definition 1, 15–16, 53, 180
entrepreneurial bricolage see bricolage
entrepreneurial life course 33; process 15,
   22–23, 39, 73, 87, 88, 183, 196; quality
   62; theory 13–30; university 42
entrepreneuring 10, 23, 24
entrepreneurship: definition 15, 18; growing
   importance of 2–6; OECD determinants
   of 180–182, 181; phases of research 14
Entrepreneurship Indicators Programme (EIP)
   179–180
equity finance 104, 110–114, 110; business
   angels 111–112; external 111; internal

(personal investment) 110–111; venture capital 112–114
Eurostat 180
experience: as human capital 94–95; role of 61–63
experience equity 111
experiential learning theory (ELT) 6–7, 9
expressiveness 85

factor-driven economies 3, 184–185, 187, 191, *191*, 193, 197, *201*, 202
factoring 119
failure rates 3
family business finance 116
family and friends 2, 19, 33, 39, 43, 70, 71, 73, 82–83, 84, *84*, 86, 90, 97–98, 110–111, 198, 208
finance: and business lifecycle 114–115
financial crisis (2008) 191
financial resources 90, 104, 106–121, 182, 206; debt finance 108–110, *110*; equity finance 104, 110–114, *110*; factors influencing choice of 107–108; and family business finance 117; funding gap for entrepreneurs 118–120; high-tech firms 117–118; and moral hazard problem 106–107; reasons for difficulty in obtaining 106–107; and social entrepreneurs 116–117; *see also* bootstrapping
Fisher, G. 22, 23, 25
*Fit Co.* xx
Flickr 23
foreign direct investment 193
forfeiting 119
*Fume Co.* xix
funding gap 118–120

Gartner, W. B. 15, 17, 18, 20, 22, 30
Gates, Bill 136
GDP growth 194
GEM (Global Entrepreneurship Monitor) studies 15, 177, 183–188, 197
gender 188; and bootstrapping 128–130
generic competence maps 64
generic human capital 92
generic skills and competencies 56–59
genetics 31
Gibb, Allan 2, 33, 44, 65, 178
Global Entrepreneurship Monitor *see* GEM

government policies 176, 177–179, 193–194
Greiner, L.E. 160–161, *161*, 162
growth 158–175; crisis-based view of 158; critical reflections on stage models 163–165; dealing with crises during 168–170, *169*; Greiner's model 160–161, *161*, 162; making sense of crisis in context 165–166, *166*; and management competencies 159; managing of dynamically 167–170; managing of through resilience 170–173; routines/practices influencing 167; traditional stage models of 159–163, 168
*Guanxi* 164

habits 2, 4, 5, 11, 31, 202, 208
habitus 7, 8
Herbane, B. 165
heterogeneity 82
heuristics 3, 4, 5, 9, 16, 174, 202, 208
Heyes, Anna 129
Higgins, D. 9
high-tech firms: and financial resources 117–118
higher education 8, 198 *see also* universities
Hitt, M. A. 205
Holt, R. 9
human capital 81, 91, 101–102, 205, 206; accumulation of over the life course 96–99, *98*; effects of on entrepreneurial success 99–100; and entrepreneurship 92–96; experience as 94–95; generic 92; knowledge as 95–96; specific 92–93

ideas, business 9, 16, 39, 51, 87, 111
identity, entrepreneurial 39–40, 80
improvisation 149–150, 151, 154, 155, 171
informal training, role of 61–63
ingratiation 85
*Innospace* xvi, 44
innovation 23, 33, 42, 54, 58–59, 60–61, 73, 93, 117, 147, 151, 162, 171, 182
innovation-driven economies 186–187, 188, 191, *191*, 192, 197, *200*, 202
intangible resources 11, 70, 82, 86, 87, 89, 90–91, 104, 205
International Entrepreneurship Educators Programme (IEEP) 33

James, William 7
Jayawarna, D. 97, 129, 137, 138, 176
*Jazooli* xviii, 27, 28, 133, 203, 208
job creation: and entrepreneurship 194–196, *195*, *196*
Job, Steve 136
Jones, O. 9, 60, 78, 135, 137, 149
Jones, Phil 44, 76, 84
Kanter, R. M. 19
Karatas-Ozkan, M. 7–8, 40
Katz, J. 18, 20, 24, 33
Kauffman Foundation 33
Klapper, L. 191
knowledge 3–4, 39, 170; creation and diffusion of 182; as human capital 95–96; and managing early stage growth 55–65; necessary for start-up 52
Kolb, David 6–7, 34–35
Kolb's learning cycle 34–38, *35*, *37*, 204

labour market 97, 101, 185, 194
Landström, H. 13, 14
Lans, T. 149
Latour 4
LEAD 64–65
Learn-to-learn 204, 207
learning 1–2, 10, 11, 31–50, 145, 146, 158–159, 204–205; clubs and societies 47–49; cognitive and practice perspectives 2, 6, 36, 38–40, *39*; contextual 80; conversational 36; double-loop and single-loop 46; and dynamic capabilities 146, 149–151; improvisational 149–150; key areas of 38, *38*; and Kolb' experiential learning cycle 34–38, *35*, *37*, 204; learning style inventories 35–36; micro, meso and macro levels 40–41, *41*; models of 33–41; role of active learning and simulation 44–47; sources 202–203; trial-and-error 149, 150, 151, 154, 155; universities and graduate incubation 41–44
learning processes, and dynamic capabilities 146, 149–151
learning style inventories 35–36
learning-by-doing 81
letters of credit 119
leveraging 145
Levie, J. 159, 160, 163, 164, 168–169
Lewin, Kurt 6

Lewis, V.L. *162*
Lichtenstein, B. B. 142, 159, 160, 163, 164, 168–169
life course studies 97
lifestyle approach: and bootstrapping 130–132, *131*
Liverpool Enterprise Network Society (LENS) 49, 198
Lourenço F. 198
Love, I. 191

McCann, J. E. 163–164
McClelland, David 14
*Machine Co.* xix
Macpherson, A. 60, 147, 149, 169
Malaysia 187
Management Charter Initiative standard 56–57
management development programmes 64
market conditions 181–182
Martin, J. 145
Microsoft 136
moral hazard problem 106–107

narrative approach 17, 203
narrative sensemaking 66–67
natural entrepreneurs 10
Naudé, W. 197
necessity-based entrepreneurship 3, 97, 187, 188, 193, 194, 202
negotiated enterprise 80–81
Nelson, R. E. 3–4, 22, 24–25, 29, 152, 153–154, 171, 207
neo-classical theory 28
network success hypothesis 82
networks/networking 70–75, 143–144, 147–148; and bootstrapping 137 *see also* social networks
New Entrepreneur Scholarship (NES) 41, 176
new venture creation: factors influencing 188–192; processes 18–21

OECD (Organization for Economic Co-operation and Development) 177, 179–180; Entrepreneurship Indicators Programme (EIP) 179–180
opportunities 15–18, 22–23, 29; creation process of 23–28; developing the 53–55; recognition of 53–54, *53*

opportunity-based entrepreneurship 3, 97, 187, 193, 194, 199, 202
Organization for Economic Co-operation and Development *see* OECD
organizational assets 105–106
organizational resources 90
organizational routines 4, 5, 19, 22, 152, 158–159, 204, 208
overdrafts 108–109

*Packaging Co.* xx
Panel Study of Entrepreneurial Dynamics (PSED) 15
pecking order theory 124
Penrose, Edith 16–17, 25, 30, 56, 82, 141, 143, 159, 162, 205
personal investment/finance 110–111, 114
philanthropic funding 116–117
physical resources 105 *see also* tangible resources
Piaget, Jean 6
Pierce, Charles Sanders 7
Pittaway, L. 42, 47–48
planned behaviour, theory of 198–199, *199*, 206
policy initiatives: impact on economic performance 177–179
Porter, Michael 178, 183
*PPE Co.* xviii–xix
practice-based approach 6–10
pragmatism 7
process perspective 16
psychological attributes 8, 14, 15, 16, 36, 202, 207

R&D 180
Raelin, J. A. 8, 9
reciprocity 70; and social capital 75
reconfiguration 145
reflection-action 37
regulation 182; and business start-up 194, 197
resilience: managing of growth through 170–173; organizational 152
resilience capacity 171, *172*
resource hijacking 154
resource-based view (RBV) 15, 16–17, 52, 82, 87, 88–89, 101, 141, 142, 143, 170
resource-constraint theory 124

resource-dependency model 124, 131–132, 137
resources 87–103, and human capital 92–96 *see also* human capital; intangible 11, 70, 82, 86, 87, 89, 90–91, 104, 205; and social capital *see* social capital; and social networks 91; tangible *see* tangible resources; types of 89–92
Rostow, Walt 178
routines 3–6; developing new 5–6, *6*; and entrepreneurial practices *8*; organizational 4, 5, 19, 152, 158–159, 204, 208
RSL 5
Russia 186–187
Rwanda 190

salient resources 89, 142, 168
Sarasvathy, S. D. 17–18, 25–27, 29, 54, 87, 152, 205
Saxenian, A. 15
Say, Jean-Baptiste 13
SBA (Small Business Administration) 64, 65
Schumpeter, Joseph 13, 14, 28, 53, 92, 186
Science Enterprise Challenge (SEC) 43
Scott, M. *162*, 164
self-employment 27, 31, 100, 181, 192, 202
self-promotion 85
sensemaking 62, 66, 203
Shane, S. 14, 15, 16, 22, 26, 27, 28–29, 30, 31
simulation games 45–46, 49
*SimVenture* 45, 46, 47, 49
single-loop learning 46
skills 51–69, 204; generic 56–59; innovative and creative 58–59; and managing early stage growth 55–65; micro-level 67; necessary for start-up 52–55; social 51, 67–68, 70, 77, 83–85, *85*, 204, 206
SKYPE 154
Small Business Administration *see* SBA
Small Business Enterprise Centres (Australia) 64
Smith, Adam 13
social adaptability 85
social capital 8, 10, 70–71, 75–80, 86, 90–91, 204; bonding and bridging linkages 76–77, *77*, 79; cognitive 78–79, 80, 204; entrepreneurial 80–82; and reciprocity 75; relational 78, 80; and resourcing new

ventures 82–85; and social networks 75, 76, 78, 79–80, 79; structural 77–78, 79–80
social constructionism 8
social constructivist learning theory 36
social enterprises 154
social factors, and entrepreneurship 198
social learning 31, 65–66
social networks 10, 71–75, 87, 91, 153, 206; bonding and bridging ties 73–74, 74, 82; closed and open 73–74, 73, 76; development patterns 73; and professional periphery 75; and resources 82–83, 91; and social capital 75, 76, 78, 79–80, 79; weak and strong ties 71–73, 83; and women 75
social perception 84, 85
social skills 51, 67–68, 70, 77, 83–85, 85, 204, 206
social ventures: and bootstrapping 137–138, 138
socialization, organizational 19
societies, entrepreneurial 47–49, 50
South Africa 187
South Korea 187
Spark Revolutions Ltd xvii, 5
Stel, A. 193
Steyaert, C. 10, 24
Storey, David 15, 58, 62, 178
structural hole theory 76
Students in Free Enterprise (SIFE) 47, 48
symbolic capital 8
Szerb, L. 192

tacit knowledge 9–10, 92, 93, 95, 169
Tang, J. 67
tangible resources 11, 70, 82, 89–90, 91, 92, 102, 104–121, 205 see also financial resources

technological innovation 192
Teece, D. J. 92, 144, 145, 205
Thailand 187
training 61, 69, 92, 97, 180, 185, 194; formal 63–65; informal 61–63
trial-and-error learning 149, 150, 151, 154, 155
Trip Advisor 23
triple helix 192
Triple Helix III model 42

universities 33, 41–44, 47, 65, 180; and graduate incubation 42–43, 50, 70, 83
user entrepreneurship 23

Vanacker, T. R. 133
Venkataraman, S. 14, 15, 28–29
venture capital 104, 105, 107, 110, 112–114, 119, 120
Virgin Group 54
volunteerism: and bootstrapping 137–138
Voronov, M. 7

Wennekers, S. 192, 193, 197
White Rose Centre for Enterprise (WRCE) 43
Wigan Recycling xviii, 126
Wilson, Ben and Sam xviii, 4, 10, 28, 49, 133, 203
Women 188, 206; and bootstrapping 128–130, 134; and social networks 75
World Bank 177, 188–189, 188–191; Doing Business Project 188–189
Wozniak, Steve 136

Yang, T. 3, 202, 208
Young Enterprise 47, 48

Zahra, S. A. 141, 149, 150, 155
Zhang, M. 162